Dr Tim Hawkes, OAM, is the author of several books, including *Ten Conversations You Must Have with Your Son*, *Boy Oh Boy: How to Raise and Educate a Son*, the *Learning Leadership* series, and *Blizzard Lines*. He has taught in England and Australia for over 35 years and been a headmaster for much of that time.

A highly regarded educator, author and social commentator, Dr Hawkes is in demand as a conference speaker around the world.

Dr Hawkes is married and has three adult children.

For more details, go to Hawkes Eye: timhawkes.com

ten

leadership lessons you must teach your teenager

DR TIM HAWKES

hachette
AUSTRALIA

hachette
AUSTRALIA

Published in Australia and New Zealand in 2016
by Hachette Australia
(an imprint of Hachette Australia Pty Limited)
Level 17, 207 Kent Street, Sydney NSW 2000
www.hachette.com.au

10 9 8 7 6 5 4 3 2 1

National Library of Australia
Cataloguing-in-Publication data:

Hawkes, Tim, author.

Ten leadership lessons you must teach your teenager/Dr Tim Hawkes.

ISBN: 978 0 7336 3 5175 (paperback)

Leadership in adolescents.
Decision making in adolescence.
Parenting.

303.34083

Cover design by Luke Causby
Cover image courtesy of Getty Images
Author photograph by Ben McCloghry
Text design by Liz Seymour
Typeset in 12/16pt Bembo by Kirby Jones
Printed in Australia by Griffin Press, Adelaide, an Accredited ISO AS/NZS
4001:2004 Environmental Management Systems printer

To my grandsons,
Harrison and Hamish

Contents

Introduction

The urge to write this book has been growing for forty years. During this period, I've had the privilege of teaching many thousands of students in both hemispheres of the world. I've also met with many hundreds of parents, particularly in my role as a head of co-ed and single-sex schools. Both students and parents taught me a great deal, not least that although the mandated curriculum is useful, it is not as useful as timeless wisdom taught in the home.

I was further motivated to write this book when I became a father. A protective spirit rises deep within you when you are blessed with children. Then I became a grandfather and wanted my grandchildren to flourish. Would they enjoy and survive in this fast, exciting and dangerous world? Would they live kind and generous lives? Would they be happy?

What I did know was that too many children seemed to be living grey lives devoid of purpose or challenge. Sometimes, this was due to indulgence. Sometimes, this was due to neglect. Either way, I was meeting too many directionless and undiscovered teens. This was tragic when so many of them had a latent talent, a hidden strength that, if developed, would have proved a blessing to themselves and the broader community.

Furthermore, many had formed a dependency on others that rendered them invisible as people in their own right. They had developed a chameleon conformity.

Examples of good leadership, servant-hearted leadership and brave and principled leadership were becoming ominously rare. However, they can be found and used to inspire our children with what is possible.

Ten Leadership Lessons You Must Teach Your Teenager is a resource for the parent who wants their teenager to thrive, to be resilient and to realise their potential.

At a time when too many teens are becoming victims, too many are becoming discouraged and too many are frittering their lives away on the trivial and self-serving, we need an antidote that challenges them to fulfil a destiny worthy of them. That antidote is the caring parent – someone who loves their child enough to want them to flourish.

However, the generation gap can frustrate the passing of wisdom from parent to child. *Ten Leadership Lessons You Must Teach Your Teenager* gives ideas on how to enrich a teenager with the skills necessary to take the initiative, to be creative and to realise their destiny.

We cannot have our sons and daughters remain in a state of perpetual childhood. There are countless ways they can contribute to society and enrich it in a way that causes them, and those about them, to not only be the best they can be, but to take pride and pleasure in achievement. Taking the initiative, accepting responsibility, exercising a generous heart – these are skills that can be taught at an early age.

As parents, we need to be able to share stories with our children. A good story has the happy knack of capturing the imagination and interest of children. Furthermore, a story can smuggle into the lives of our young those values and virtues that no amount of parental sermonising will ever achieve. For this reason, a good number of stories are shared within this book. These stories could profitably be shared with teenage children.

In addition to these stories, there are a number of pages that can be photographed and sent as a text or email. Each is labelled 'A photo to take'. (Any other replication of material in this book will only be allowed with the permission of the author.) These photos can serve as a stimulus for further discussion about leadership. Throughout the book, several opportunities for photographing a page are offered. Not all should be accepted – only those thought to be helpful and appropriate. It might be wise not to pepper one's offspring with more than one of these photos a day. If nothing else happens, your children will know you are doing some reading about leadership, which may spark useful conversation.

Each of our children is a miracle of creation. Each has unique abilities. Each is called to be a leader – if not of others, then of themselves. They must understand that there are times when they must follow and times when they must lead. Wisdom comes from knowing when it is good to do either.

Ten Leadership Lessons You Must Teach Your Teenager is a compendium of accumulated wisdom, story and advice parents can share to get their teenage children to take command of their lives and impact positively on others.

This is a book on how to raise leaders.

Leaders? I hear you say. Why leaders? There is quite enough hubris and grandstanding going on in society. The world has little use for advice that is going to assist precocious children to nurture ideas well above their station. What about the virtues of being a follower? Little is served by refining the hopes of those hell-bent on securing a life of privilege and power for their offspring.

I agree! But this is not a book to satiate the spoiled. It is a book on how to raise the servant-hearted leader, someone who can take the initiative, who has the courage to get involved.

Talking about leadership

Talking about leadership is a lot more attractive to a teenager than sharing a treatise on morality and meaning. As a topic, leadership is enormously useful because it enables a parent to offer guidance without the censure normally found in intergenerational improvement initiatives.

Further reason to talk about leadership is given because, as a topic, it is intriguing. Leadership is written, tweeted and blogged about a great deal. It is a compelling topic to discuss in its own right. Several dinner conversations could be enriched by considering whether leadership is an inherited skill, or whether it can be taught. Debate can even be had as to whether it can be taught to the young. Failing all else, the usual exasperation at the repeated failure of our leaders can fuel some happily indignant conversations on the topic. These triggers for discussion about leadership should not be wasted. What follows is some fuel for such discussions.

THE NEED FOR AUTHENTIC LEADERSHIP

Our elected leaders are often unpopular, with sentiments such as *'Make your politicians work – don't re-elect them'* being common. The nations of the world hunger for authentic leadership. There is weariness with self-serving leaders whose vision fails to extend beyond short-term expediency.

However, although endangered, leadership is not yet extinct. Effective leadership can still be found. It's just that those who are leading are not necessarily found in leadership positions, and those found in leadership positions are not necessarily leading.

Just when we warm to this finger-pointing, we need to remember that the most common source of leadership failure is the home. Absentee parents, broken homes, domestic violence, teenage pregnancy, drug abuse and alcohol-fuelled violence are a feature in too many families.

Good parenting does not happen in bad homes. Even in average homes, too much training is left to peers, social-networking sites and the internet, and to a variety of electronic sources. These sources can introduce a morality that neutralises parental example. We must do more than look on impotently as our children absorb contradictory morals. As parents, we must take control of what is going on in our homes. We must not surrender our role as the major influence in the lives of our sons and daughters.

THE NEED TO REALISE POTENTIAL

Most parents want to unlock the potential in their children. This is not to say they wish the fruit of their loins to rule the world and live pampered lives adored by minions. It is to say they love their children and recognise that they have unique strengths that should be developed.

Some parents pursue strengths in their children that don't exist. This exhausts their children and threatens to alienate them from their parents. Others adopt a laissez-faire approach to parenting and leave their children to find their own destiny.

There needs to be a balance. Giftedness needs to be identified, developed and celebrated. However, excellence cannot be expected in all areas of a child's life. Each child has a fingerprint that is unique and a strength that is special. If any child needs to be encouraged in this regard, then some gentle affirmation by parents might be appropriate – as might the passing on of this book for them to read.

THE IMPORTANCE OF UNDERSTANDING MODERN LEADERSHIP

Contemporary leadership is not necessarily about heroics. Modern leadership is often covert and unassuming. It is to be found in the gentle word of encouragement, the helping of another, the steering of a conversation, a suggestion, or some small service. These are tasks all can fulfil.

The traditional view of leadership is that it is autocratic. The contemporary view of leadership is more collegial. This represents a more accessible model of leadership for our sons and daughters.

A leader is not necessarily someone with an impressive badge, significant responsibilities and an invitation to dine with the gods. A leader need not even be someone with rank, power or position. Quite simply, a leader is someone who is followed by others. This means that any of our children can be leaders. If their words direct and their actions inspire, they are leading. If they cause another to follow their example, they are leading.

Therefore, leadership is a science for everyone, not just for the chosen few. Not all will be privileged to lead to the same extent as others, but all will lead in small ways if not in big ways. These small expressions of leadership should never be underestimated. Collectively they determine the character of a person and the health of a nation.

THE REQUIREMENT TO BUILD RESILIENCE

It is vital that our sons and daughters learn to cope with setback, opposition and disappointment.

Depression is the fastest-growing medical problem among young people today. Too many are not coping. They hide themselves. They cut themselves. They kill themselves. This appalling tragedy is no respecter of social class. Something must be done about this evil – and done quickly.

We live in an age of curious contradictions. There is a massive under-protection of children throughout the world. For example, the sex-trafficking of children remains rife in many countries. On the other hand, there is a massive over-protection of children throughout the world. The bubble-wrapping of children has reached such a stage that it imperils resilience. Both are damaging.

Resilience is not improved by inactivity and non-involvement. *Watching* is toxic to self-worth. *Doing* is generative: it involves purpose and creation, and brings a sense of achievement.

You cannot be a leader of others if you're not resilient. Leadership can be hard. Many of our leaders are stoned with ridicule, bruised by the challenge and accusation of those who, out of envy, spite or a love of mischief, enjoy making a leader's life difficult. If you can topple a leader you demonstrate power, and there are many who want to demonstrate that power. If you become a leader, you become a target; therefore, you need to learn skills to deal with this pressure.

THE NEED FOR INDEPENDENCE

Many of our sons and daughters are dependent on their parents for too long. It is quite right and proper for there to be significant dependency during the infant and pre-teen years, but the years beyond should see a gradual transference of responsibility from parent to child. In many cases, this is not happening. The privileges of adulthood are accepted with great appetite – the wider selection of drinks, the later bed-times, the freedom to leap into a car – but the responsibility is not. They enter the adult years as teenagers and live in perpetual 'middlescence'.

A further problem is that rather too many are entering adult life without the life skills necessary to live independently. They are domestic dyslexics. They want to drive the car, but they don't want to look after it.

This perpetual dependency on others can even extend to thinking. Some teens never get around to thinking things through, or forming their own opinion on politics, religion and ethics. They echo the opinions of others. In their early years, children will get most of their attitudes and values from their parents. This will gradually be modified by peers, the media and the internet. However, somewhere along this migration of life, our children need to 'own' their opinion. Too many don't do this and merely mimic the opinions of others. They go missing in their own lives.

THE IMPORTANCE OF A GENERATIVE LIFE

Every person must be able to contribute something to society. Failure to do so means they are at risk of sleeping through their life and limiting themselves to the drowsy role of spectator. Too many like to escape the challenges of leadership, with its hard edges, in order to live a pillowed existence.

We need to encourage our sons and daughters to develop a calling, a creed and a cause. There should be something in their lives that takes them away from a preoccupation with self. The prevalence of egocentricity in some teens has been described as narcissism. This feeling of inflated self-importance and entitlement leads to teenagers who are often insensitive to others yet are deeply sensitive to criticism about themselves.

Having noted the above, it is important not to overstate the case. There are many teens who model empathy, compassion, justice, service and kindness. They have what Hindus call *dharma*, which means duty. For Buddhists the word also means truth. Although both concepts are at risk of extinction, there are many families in which *dharma* can be found. Look at their fridge door. Is it littered with photos of a sponsored child, memos about blood donation and adorned with a spidery note of thanks from a neighbour's child for their birthday present?

How do parents encourage *dharma*? The social commentator Thomas Lickona suggests there are three steps. The first is to *tell* our sons and daughters what it is good to do. However, knowing the good is not enough. Thereafter, they must be encouraged to *desire* the good. This can be helped by becoming emotionally engaged with the issue and by appealing to a sense of justice. Finally, they must *do* the good. This should not be presented as an option.[1]

It might be that our sons and daughters don't particularly want to do the good. Tough tortillas. If they don't want to be nice, require them to be nice. Ask them to 'fake it' and pretend to be nice. This usually has the happy effect of making them nice. As Aristotle wrote:

> . . . *it is by doing just acts that the just man is produced* . . .
> **Aristotle,** *The Nicomachean Ethics*

Many parents can feel powerless when a child says they don't want to do something. If this should be the case, explain that much of your life involves doing things you don't want to do – the washing up, the shopping, going to work – but this has not prevented you from doing these things. Not wanting to do some things is understandable, but it should never be allowed to stop us doing something that should be done.

I can understand your feelings. But you will do it anyway.
Why?
Because it is the right thing to do.

DISCUSSIONS ABOUT LEADERSHIP

Meaningful conversation between many teenagers and their parents is occurring for only a few minutes a day. This can result in the marginalisation of parents. Our teens need to talk with someone. If they don't talk with their parents, they will talk to others whose influence may not be quite so positive.

More than once, as a headmaster, I've had to deal with the angry glare of an accusing parent and listen to them saying something like: *'I don't know where my son got this appalling habit from. He certainly didn't get it from us!'*

True – sadly true. The boy was getting nothing from his parents by way of mentoring. He was being reared by his mobile phone.

This is not a new problem; in fact, Plato raged against this sort of parenting thousands of years ago:

> *You know that the beginning is the most important part of any work, especially in the case of a young and tender thing; for that is the time at which the character is being formed and the desired impression is more readily taken . . . Shall we just carelessly allow children to hear any casual tale which may be devised by casual persons, and to receive into their minds ideas for the most part the very opposite of those which we should wish them to have when they are grown up?*
>
> *We cannot . . . Anything received into the mind at that age is likely to become indelible and unalterable; and therefore it is most important that the tales which the young first hear should be models of virtuous thoughts . . .*
>
> *Then will our youth dwell in a land of health, amid fair sights and sounds, and receive the good in everything . . .*
>
> *There can be no nobler training than that.*
>
> **Plato,** *The Republic*

It is often in the teen years that our sons and daughters are exposed to alternative values. Therefore it is tragic if the parental voice is not heard at this time.

The conversation problem is compounded when a family does not share meals together, when one or both parents are away from home for long periods, and when private spaces are permitted with only the cat allowed to ignore the 'Keep Out' signs.

Even when the family is together, there can be an absence of something to talk about. That is why fingers start massaging mobile phones and eyes start to focus on the television.

If conversation is in short supply, why not initiate talk about leadership? Tell your sons and daughters you're doing a spot of reading on the topic. Make no secret of it.

Much of what is written in *Ten Leadership Lessons You Must Teach Your Teenager* is designed to be talked about. There are many ideas to share and many stories to recount.

The use of story is a great way to engage with teens. They like stories. They also need stories. This is because stories teach us our cultural inheritance. All people, be they young or old, benefit from being reminded of their great tribal tales. Be they fictional or real, these stories need to be told. Doing so can help ensure that the value of good example is not lost.

In the western world, we sometimes shrink from the task of storytelling and leave it to others. This is not always wise. The stories others tell can be inappropriate and harmful. As parents, we need to be able to tell stories. For those feeling ill-equipped in this regard, *Ten Leadership Lessons You Must Teach Your Teenager* is full of stories you can share.

CAN LEADERSHIP BE TAUGHT?

It is entirely reasonable to ask whether leadership can be taught. Some would suggest not. *'Either you have got it or you haven't. You can't put in what God's left out.'*

There is both truth and error in these comments. The influence of nature (inherited traits) is powerful, but so too is the influence of nurture (subsequent impact of the environment in which a child is raised).

Studies on twins carried out in America have suggested that many of the qualities associated with leadership, such as authoritarianism, are inherited from parents. One of the major players in the positive psychology movement, Martin Seligman, states that between one-quarter and half of a person's main personality traits are inherited from their parents.[2]

This also suggests that between half and three-quarters of these traits are *not* inherited from parents. These traits are acquired, are learned throughout life – particularly in the early years of life.

There is no question that genetics plays a great role in determining leadership skills. Enough powerful dynasties exist to bear testimony to some families having rich leadership blood flowing through their veins. Think of the Kennedys, Mountbattens and Churchills of yesterday and the Packers and Murdochs of today.

However, failure to recognise the capacity to learn leadership skills, to acknowledge the power of the influence of nurture, is to risk lapsing into the stupor of fatalism. It suggests that nothing can be done.

Leadership skills can be taught, can be acquired and can be realised.

CAN TEENAGERS LEAD?

Is it realistic to expect teenagers to lead? Being of young and tender years, their capacity to lead must surely be limited. True. However, leadership – even on the world stage – is not impossible for the teenager. Consider the following two stories.

TWO STORIES TO SHARE

BOYAN SLAT (1994–)

When on holiday in Greece in 2010, sixteen-year-old Boyan Slat was alarmed to see the amount of plastic rubbish in the sea. It looked disgusting and threatened the viability of the local tourist trade. Not only that, Boyan recognised that it would probably damage ecosystems and endanger a variety of food chains.

Boyan started to research ways the problem of waste plastic might be solved. He studied a number of engineering reports that indicated solutions to this issue were problematic. However, Boyan continued on his quest.

Boyan designed a giant arm that would float on the sea to catch and process floating plastic waste. He calculated that because most sea currents rotated in local gyres, it was feasible to capture much of the waste without moving the arm. It was also a technique that lent itself to catching floating plastic close to its source rather than having to chase it across the world's oceans.

Some years later, Boyan became the CEO of 'The Ocean Cleanup'. By 2015, he had raised over $2 million to build a two-kilometre arm designed to catch floating plastic. Through the use of these great tethered arms, much of the floating plastic could be hugged into a recycling program. Self-supporting in terms of power, it has been estimated that our aquatic garbage fields might be cleaned up in a few decades using this method.

Boyan has met with Al Gore, Ban Ki-moon and Prince Albert of Monaco. He jets around the world speaking and raising money, and in 2015 had twelve employees and hundreds of volunteers working for him.

MALALA YOUSAFZAI (1997–)

Malala is the daughter of educators. Her parents owned and ran several schools in Pakistan. These schools catered for girls as well as boys, therefore it was not good news for the family when the Taliban decreed that girls were no longer permitted to attend school.

The Yousafzai family did not agree with the Taliban, and this made them a target. Further displeasure was caused in 2009 when twelve-year-old Malala started to blog for the BBC and participated in a *New York Times* documentary a year or two later about what it was like to live in the Swat Valley as it was ravaged by the Taliban.

On 9 October 2012, fifteen-year-old Malala was travelling by bus with her friends to school. Gunmen boarded the bus and asked for Malala by name. On identifying her, a gunman shot at Malala three times. One shot struck her in the forehead; the bullet travelled through her head and finally lodged in her shoulder.

Miraculously, Malala did not die. However, she was seriously injured and was rushed to a number of hospitals before ending up at the Queen Elizabeth Hospital in Birmingham, England. After months of painful rehabilitation, Malala recovered.

Malala resolved not to waste the gift of life. She wrote her story and engaged in extensive media work as an activist for female education. The 'voice' created by the Taliban bullets was so significant that in 2013 *Time* magazine named Malala one of the 100 most influential people in the world.

Malala is accredited with having played a very significant role in the passing of Pakistan's 'Right to Education' bill in 2012, which reaffirmed the right of girls to be educated.

At the age of seventeen, Malala shared the 2014 Nobel Peace Prize with Indian children's rights activist Kailash Satyarthi. Malala is the youngest person to have received a Nobel Prize.[4]

Although not necessarily destined to influence the world in quite the same way as Malala and Boyan, our sons and daughters can have an impact on their home, their school and their community. Leadership can be expressed on the world stage with YouTube speeches and TED talks bouncing around the ionosphere. It can also be expressed by inviting a lonely child into a friendship group. We must not limit what is possible for our children to achieve.

> *'Borders? I have never seen one.*
> *But I have heard they exist in the minds of some people.'*

The great Norwegian explorer Thor Heyerdahl said this about political borders. The saying would be just as relevant if borders were changed to boundaries – the sort of limits that simply should not be imposed on our children.

It is entirely reasonable to expect our sons and daughters to exercise leadership of themselves. It is also reasonable to expect them to exercise leadership of others. These leadership opportunities will ebb and flow. Sometimes our children will be awash with opportunities to lead and other times these opportunities will have dried up. This is normal.

It is also normal to be a follower. It is normal to be one of the team. It is normal for a child to be directed by their parents until they can operate independently as a mature individual.

The following chapters are designed to help parents equip their children to operate independently and be strong contributors to society. A course of instruction is suggested that, if followed, could do much to ensure the next generation are strong and effective in their leadership of self, as well as in their leadership of others.

A choice to make

The world offers myriad choices. Furthermore, it does so with a presumption that choice is a good thing.

Ordering sausage and eggs used to be easy. Now you have to navigate your way around hard-boiled, soft-boiled, fried, poached, sunny-side up, over easy, scrambled, omelette or coddled. Thereafter comes the beef sausage, pork sausage, chicken sausage, bratwurst, frankfurter, liverwurst, haggis, black-pudding decision, concluded by an enquiry as to whether buckwheat, cornbread, bagel, baguette, waffle, ryebread, sourdough, brown bread, crumpet, muffin, pumpernickel, raisin toast or white bread takes your fancy.

Freedom to choose can paralyse a teenager with indecision: *If I choose that, will I regret it because I miss out on this?*

One of the best meals I've ever had was with Venetian boatmen in Europe. Only one dish was served. It was pasta – and the restaurant hummed with noisy contentment.[1]

I CAN'T DECIDE IF I'M NO GOOD AT MAKING CHOICES OR NOT!

WHO SHOULD CHOOSE?

Should we let our sons and daughters choose whether or not to lead, or do we make that choice for them?

In Lewis Carroll's *Alice's Adventures in Wonderland*, Alice asks the Cat which way she should go. Not unreasonably, the Cat asks where she wants to get to. Alice confesses that she doesn't much care where she goes, to which the Cat responds that it therefore doesn't matter which way Alice goes.

Alice was protected from the consequences of not choosing by fiction. However, our children live in the real world – a world that insists that choices be made. So who should choose: the parents or the child?

Parental enthusiasm for allowing children to make choices should generally be in proportion to the capacity of the child to make good choices. This is often a function of the child having had enough learning experiences, both positive and negative, to make wise decisions.

For pre-teens, most choices are usually made by the parent. This is right and proper. However, the subsequent years are muddy and characteristically witness a growing challenge by our sons and daughters to decide for themselves. These are transition years. The rules are unclear, as the value of learning by trial and error grinds against child-protection imperatives.

The generally accepted formula of greater responsibility given with greater maturity is not always helpful. A teen can be mature and responsible in some areas but not in others. A teen can be creative at one moment but destructive the next.

Small wonder some parents are accused of making too many decisions for their teen and others too few.

The term 'helicopter parenting' is currently in vogue. It describes those parents who are up in the air, constantly hovering about their children and affording them little independence in the area of choice. These parents will speak for their child, will act for their child, will think for their child. The result can be a frightening dependency, a lack of resilience and a loss of identity. By protecting their children, these parents hurt them.

> *You will apply for prefect.*
> *You will get into the A stream.*
> *You will not make friends with . . .*

Other parents are all at sea. They disappear over the horizon to earn doubloons for the family. After months at work, the parental mariner returns to deal with such problems that have accumulated in their long absence.

> *I had no idea.*
> *He didn't learn this from me.*
> *She's a mystery to me.*

Mercifully, there are also the parents who have their feet on the ground. They are neither up in the air nor at sea. They are sufficiently engaged with their child's life to sense whose decision it is right to run with. They transfer responsibility with an understanding of the increased capacity of their sons and daughters to deal with it.

As parents, it's important to know the capacity of our sons and daughters and for there to be a commensurate shift of responsibility with growing maturity. This responsibility should not necessarily be a gift given with increasing age. Being sixteen years of age entitles a child to nothing other than sixteen candles on the birthday cake. Choice is a gift that should only be given when there is evidence of the maturity necessary to choose wisely.

But – be ready for a battle! For millennia, the young have wanted the privileges of adulthood. The pressure to give teenagers autonomy at ever younger ages can be significant. If the capacity to choose is not given, they complain.

It's just so unfair!

If this is the case, it can be an interesting exercise to take them through the choices they made in the past hour.

You ignored the alarm and switched off the snooze button. This was entirely understandable; it was the wrong side of midnight before you chose to stop texting and Facebooking. Then you spent too long in the shower and this made you run even later. Of the options available, you chose to squirt on the lemon-scented deodorant and you spent some time crafting your hair into the Cassowary look. You left your bed unmade, left your mess and left your washing on the floor. At breakfast, you chose the full-cream milk and finished off the Coco Pops. Then you texted Charlie, probably to find out whether you're going to hang out here or somewhere else tonight. After this, you pestered me to drive you to school using the toll road because it was too late for the normal route. In the car, you insisted on Foo Fighters before I could tune in to my station. We arrived just in time for your elective History class.

Our sons and daughters make more choices than they're aware of. They might be reminded that how they deal with these small choices hints at their readiness to deal with the big choices.

That said, not all our sons and daughters relish the freedom of making choices. Some are reluctant to choose and delay deciding what they will do until their herd has developed an indicative momentum. Unfortunately, this habit can stay with them and, as adults, they can become paralysed with indecision. They prevaricate about commitments. They protest they're not ready when pressed for an answer.

The problem with moving with the herd is that it is difficult to stand out. This is not necessarily a bad thing: those who stand out have the nasty habit of being eaten by predators, whereas those who blend in survive.

So – why choose to stand out? Why choose to lead?

MOTIVATION TO LEAD

The motivation that prompts a person to stand out and lead can vary. There can be good reasons and there can be bad reasons. For example, a politician can be driven by ego or they can be driven to advance the wellbeing of their constituency. Pandering to the ego is usually seen as a bad thing, whereas advancing the wellbeing of others is usually seen as a good thing. The two can overlap, not just in the lives of our politicians but in our own lives.

Leadership that is exercised exclusively for the betterment of others is rare. This is one of the reasons leadership suffers a rather ordinary reputation. It is difficult for people to break out from the jail of self-interest, resulting in a battle between the public purpose and the private purpose as to why a person wants to be a leader. It is unlikely that a leader will make public their understanding of why they want to be a leader because there are very few leaders who are exclusively committed to reasons that are admirable.

Therefore, we should not be surprised if our sons and daughters have good and bad reasons for seeking leadership. The battle between good and evil is found in literature, religion and philosophy – and in the lives of most leaders. Within us all there is to be found the good, the bad and the ugly. Inspirational leaders have been found to lie, to be unfaithful, to be hypocritical and to be plagued by all manner of vices.

A STORY TO SHARE

POL POT (1925–1998)

CAMBODIAN DICTATOR

Pol Pot was a strong leader. However, he used his strength to do horrendous things to his people. One Cambodian in five lost their lives during Pol Pot's period as the nation's leader.

Pol Pot was the nom de guerre of Saloth Sar, who was born into a well-to-do family in the French colony of Cambodia. Sar won a scholarship to study in France, where he was diverted from his studies by a desire to learn more about communism. This led to the removal of his scholarship.

On returning to Cambodia in 1953, Sar joined the Communist Party. He rose through its ranks and within ten years was the party's leader. They were turbulent years for the country.

Cambodia gained its independence from France in 1954 but was soon embroiled in a growing conflict between left-wing and right-wing political forces, both within Cambodia and in several surrounding countries. Civil war broke out.

Assisted by Vietnam and China, Saloth Sar and his Khmer Rouge army won the civil war. The Khmer Rouge entered the capital city of Phnom Penh in 1975 and took control of the country. By now, Saloth Sar was calling himself 'Pol Pot'.

Relief that the civil war was over did not last long. The Cambodians soon realised that they faced a new horror. Pol Pot drove his people out of the cities to create an ideal rural society run along communist lines. Such was his power that Pol Pot declared 'Year Zero', the start of a whole new era with a new system of numbering the years. Intellectuals were killed. Those not meeting food quotas were killed. Banks were closed and torture centres were opened. Schools were emptied and turned into extermination centres.

The Pol Pot reign of terror ended when the Vietnamese invaded Cambodia in 1979. Pol Pot went into hiding in the jungles of Thailand. After many years in the jungle, his former allies turned against him and imprisoned him. Pol Pot died on 15 April 1998. His body was cremated under a pile of rubbish and old tyres.

Pol Pot never acknowledged the pain his leadership caused. He dismissed the millions of dead as the sort of justifiable mistake a child might make when learning to walk.[2]

Pol Pot was driven by a political ideology. He wanted to create a perfect communist regime untainted by western decadence. Others choose to lead for different reasons, including the following:

- Religious convictions, such as the need to obey God.
- Humanist convictions, such as wanting to effect the greatest good for the greatest number.
- Evolutionist convictions, such as wanting to maintain a strong and healthy species.
- Hedonistic convictions, such as wanting to provide the greatest amount of pleasure for people.

To these worthy motives need to be added a range of rather less impressive reasons for wanting to lead, such as a lust for power, privilege and prestige.

The reason, why our sons and daughters may decide to pursue a leadership position will also vary. Some will want to be thought well of by their peers, some will want to be thought well of by their teachers, and some will want to be well thought of by their parents.

The desire to please parents can be a powerful force. Many children want to win the admiration of their parents. This can be particularly true of sons, who often feel a constant need to prove themselves. The desire to please is not helped by father hunger, a sense of loss caused by fathers having to work away from home for long periods. Neither is it helped by a critical spirit some fathers have, or by a habit of wanting to improve their sons. The same can be said about some mothers and their daughters. In short, many teens seek leadership positions to please their parents rather than because they want the responsibility themselves.

Another reason some teens want to lead is because they don't want to be led. They don't want to be told what to do by idiot prefects, stupid teachers or interfering parents. So, they take over.

WHY LEADERS ARE NEEDED

The reasons why we need leaders can be different from the reasons people lead. They shouldn't be different – but they often are.

We need leaders to:

- Give direction.
- Achieve a goal.
- Be an example.
- Inspire.
- Cultivate unity.
- Encourage productivity.
- Create synergy.
- Promote creativity.
- Solve problems.

Given the frenetic world of today, leadership in the twenty-first century is also required to cope with change and to manage complexity.

Leadership is needed to build on strengths, eliminate weakness, neutralise threats and to seize opportunities.

All this is worthy stuff, but there can be a tragic disconnect between what we want leaders to do and what leaders are prepared to do.

History gives very few examples of a leader who was not spoiled by some element of greed masquerading as need.

SOME QUESTIONS TO ASK

It can be useful to ask our sons and daughters whether they want to be a leader. If they do, then ask them why.

Their responses are likely to vary. Some might say they want to exercise the leadership gifts they have. Others might want to test themselves to see if they are up to the task of leadership. There might be other reasons, such as wanting to make Mum and Dad proud, or wanting to beef up their CV.

If responses run along these lines, a parent might gently remind their aspirant leaders that, *It's not about you!*

Leaders need to meet the needs of those they are leading, not their own needs. If this news comes as something of a shock, then further discussion can be had on leadership projects that they could engage in - for example:

- What needs to be changed at school?
- What needs to be changed in the neighbourhood?
- What needs to be changed at home?

THE MORALITY OF LEADERSHIP

A thin line exists between service and avarice. As previously mentioned, leadership that benefits most people most of the time is usually seen as good and will be supported, whereas leadership that only benefits the leader is usually seen as bad and will not be supported.

'What's in it for me?' is a frequently asked question for those considering whether to follow a leader. It is a question the leader must be able to answer.

A leader needs to be able to demonstrate that they are able to meet the needs of their followers.

We must remember that the benefits for followers need not be tangible. Doing something worthwhile can lead to less-tangible benefits, such as a sense of satisfaction and the 'feel-good' factor.

The famous benefactor and steel producer Andrew Carnegie would often say there were people in his organisation far more able than he was. However, what Carnegie was able to do was to make others feel good about themselves. He involved them in decision making, and encouraged them.

A DISCUSSION TO HAVE

Consider whether it is possible for a leader to be good all the time. If they are, will the more unscrupulous take advantage of them? Machiavelli thought so:

> *Anyone who tries to be good all the time is bound to come to ruin among the great number who are not good. Hence a prince who wants to keep his authority must learn how not to be good, and use that knowledge, or refrain from using it as necessity requires.*
>
> The Prince, Niccolò Machiavelli

A STORY TO SHARE

NICCOLÒ MACHIAVELLI

ITALIAN POLITICAL PHILOSOPHER (1469-1527)

Niccolò Machiavelli was an Italian political theorist who was thought to be so unprincipled that his first name became synonymous with that of the devil, otherwise known as 'Old Nick'.

This condemnation of Machiavelli was largely as a result of his book, *The Prince*, which was written in 1512-1513. These were turbulent years for Machiavelli. His city of Florence had been taken over by the Medici family and Machiavelli found himself in exile. With time on his hands, Machiavelli reflected on political power and the initiatives needed to secure it. He collected his thoughts in a book, *The Prince*.

Within *The Prince* is advice to the aspiring leader on how to survive. It is not always noble advice, nor does it always advocate worthy ideals. It suggests falsehood and immorality as justifiable means to gain required political ends. It was hardly surprising that this thinking should be thought devilish.

Machiavelli reasoned that any leader needed the strength, skill and boldness to apply *virtù* (the ability to adapt to the unexpected) to *fortuna* (the unexpected). He also argued that unprincipled means should be used if they allowed leaders to satisfy the desires of their followers. Put simply, if the majority of people were happy then it did not matter how the result was obtained. The leader stayed as a leader, and those being led would be comfortable to remain so.

It is worth noting that in *The Prince*, Machiavelli warned leaders that their power would inevitably decline, and that a new leader would ultimately emerge. The suggested response by Machiavelli was to stave off that day for as long as possible through the use of trickery, alliances and all manner of manipulation.

LEADERSHIP IS NOT ALWAYS PLANNED

It is appropriate to acknowledge that leadership can be thrust on a person by unforeseen circumstances. Our sons and daughters need to be alert to the fact that fate can offer a chance to lead when they least expect it.

Some years ago, one of my students was at Parramatta railway station in Sydney when a man at the station had a heart attack and fell down unconscious. People scattered. However, the boy didn't. He administered CPR and started the man's heart and then his breathing. Later, paramedics arrived and took over – but not before they acknowledged it was the sixteen-year-old boy who had saved the man's life. The boy had not shown any leadership tendencies until that day, and neither had he anticipated undertaking any leadership responsibilities.

Another story of accidental leadership is that of Gladys Aylward.

A STORY TO SHARE

In 1932, Gladys Aylward felt herself called to go to China. Two missionaries, Eleanor Harrison and Edith Nettleton, had been murdered by Chinese bandits and Aylward was moved to take their place.

On arrival in China, Aylward travelled to Shanxi Province and then to the town of Yangcheng to help a missionary named Jeannie

Lawson. To gain acceptance among the people, they changed the name of their Christian mission. It became a hostel for muleteers called The Inn of the Sixth Happiness. When Jeannie Lawson died, Aylward found herself in the unexpected position as leader of the mission.

Aylward took in orphans and engaged in prison reform. This led a local Mandarin to appoint Aylward to the position of 'Inspector of Feet'. It was an attempt to stop the ancient custom of binding the feet of baby girls. (Some thought small feet added to a woman's beauty; unfortunately, foot binding also led to deformity and a great deal of pain.) Aylward accepted the invitation and was so faithful in her duties that she became known as 'The Virtuous One' or 'Ai Weh Deh'.

In 1937, Japan invaded China. Opposing the Japanese was the Nationalist leader, Chiang Kai-shek, and a growing band of communists led by Mao Tse-tung. By this time Aylward had taken Chinese nationality and was therefore completely unprotected from the Japanese. The fighting was horrific and many atrocities were committed. Aylward's mission was bombed, but she did not stop caring for the wounded and orphaned. The Chinese intelligence officer of the district, Colonel Lin, became a close friend and, as a result, Aylward became an enemy of the Japanese. A reward was offered for her capture.

As the dangers increased, Aylward decided to lead her children to a safer area in China. This long and dangerous trek with 100 children became immortalised in the film *The Inn of the Sixth Happiness* starring Ingrid Bergman. The refugees sheltered behind rocks and in Buddhist temples, and eventually made their way to safety. Once her children were safe, Aylward collapsed with pneumonia and typhus, but her life was saved thanks to the intervention of American medical help.

Aylward returned to England in 1949. Her family and friends hardly recognised her, and in turn she barely recognised the land of her birth, for it was now so foreign to her. Aylward returned to work in the Far East once again and spent most of her time in Taiwan and Hong Kong. She died of pleurisy in January 1970 and was buried near Taipei.[3]

GETTING INVOLVED

Not only must our sons and daughters be awake to the possibility of leadership opportunities arising in a most unexpected way, they must also understand that they can create leadership opportunities – and one of the best ways to do this is to get involved.

This need not always be heroic leadership that involves rescuing a dying man at a railway station or saving hundreds of lives. It can be as simple as befriending someone who is lonely. Informal leadership opportunities present themselves each day.

Formal leadership roles also present themselves from time to time. It is not always easy to convince people to serve on a student representative council or help out at the local sports club or to assist at a holiday camp. Rather too often, the young ignore the leadership opportunities that exist, which is unfortunate because both the individual and society are weakened.

As parents, we need to encourage our sons and daughters to accept leadership opportunities when they arise. One of the best ways of doing this is for parents to model the behaviour wanted in their children. We must also accept opportunities to serve and get involved in our local communities. Failure to do so can result in too many young people standing back and watching as life, with all its leadership opportunities, slips by.

A PHOTO TO TAKE

IT IS NOT THE CRITIC WHO COUNTS

It is not the critic who counts, nor the person who points out where the strong have stumbled or whether the doer of deeds could have done better.

The credit belongs to those who are actually in the arena, whose faces are marred with dust and sweat and blood ... at best they know the thrill of battle and the triumph of high achievements.

If they fail, at least they failed while doing well.

They shall never be with those cold and timid souls who know neither victory nor defeat.

Theodore Roosevelt (adapted)

LEADERSHIP OF SELF

Whether our sons and daughters decide to lead others will ultimately be their choice. However, taking command and control of their lives should be non-negotiable. It is entirely reasonable to expect a teen to:

- Be well mannered.
- Be thoughtful and kind.
- Have at least eight hours' sleep a night.
- Keep to the law in relation to alcohol and other recreational drugs.
- Do their fair share of chores within the home.
- Make the most of their learning opportunities.
- Eat healthily.
- Exercise an appropriate amount.
- Responsibly manage their cyber experiences.
- Look after their possessions well.
- Manage their finances properly.
- Be honest.

LEADERSHIP OF OTHERS

Good leadership of self prepares a person to be a good leader of others. However, the option of leading others should not be forced upon our children. We have to be careful not to visit upon them expectations that have their genesis in our desire rather than theirs.

That said, there are some skills that can be encouraged that will give our sons and daughters the option to lead, should they choose to do so. These skills include:

- An ability to inspire others.
- A capacity to attract followers.
- Creativity.

- Problem-solving techniques.
- An acknowledged area of excellence.
- Good communication skills.
- Courage.
- Resilience.
- Stamina.
- An ability to shoulder responsibility.
- Tactical thinking skills.
- Interest in and support of a cause or a calling.

It is worth remembering that it is the leadership skills that need to be developed, not the leadership positions. Nonetheless, having these skills will increase the chances of leadership positions being obtained. Subsequent chapters will discuss how these skills might be developed.[5]

FINALLY

Apathy is a malaise of the post-modern era. This has not been helped by information overload. Nor is it aided by a rise in learned helplessness.

Our children's grandparents were a frugal generation that often used their spare time to create. They would knit, mend and make. Today's teens are different. They often use their spare time to consume and connect. They shop and engage in social networking, often with the aim of boosting their image. Often, it doesn't work.

A more effective antidote is to develop leadership skills. Start by taking command and control of oneself. Then work on acquiring the skills that leave open the option of leading others. The former should be made non-negotiable. The latter must be left conditional on whether our sons and daughters want to lead.

SUMMARY

- It's not always good to have choices. Being given a choice can paralyse a young person with indecision.
- The ability to choose should be commensurate with maturity, not age.
- Parents mustn't fall into the trap of making too many or too few choices for their children.
- Children make more choices than they think. Whether they make good choices is another matter.
- Some children leave a lot of decision making to their peers.
- Motives for leadership are not always neat and tidy.
- The decision to lead can be motivated by good and bad reasons. Very few leaders are motivated by pure motives.
- It is important to distinguish between leadership choices designed to satisfy public need and leadership choices designed to satisfy personal greed.
- Making choices about small things prepares a person for making decisions about big things.
- Initial choices can begin with decisions that impact on oneself.
- Training in choice making can begin in the home.
- Sometimes, leadership opportunities are planned. At other times, they come unexpectedly.
- Responsible leadership of oneself should be non-negotiable. However, the leadership of others is a choice our sons and daughters should make for themselves.

A discipline to learn

No self-respecting hero has ever acquired strength without hours of training. This training can be with footballs in ghettos, with intellectual books in universities or with swords in monastic fortresses.

Effective training involves operating at the edges of what can't already be done. This can be exhausting, and it can hurt. Small wonder many cannot cope with acquiring strength. Developing a musical ability, learning to spell or getting fit won't happen unless there is pain, inconvenience and an element of drudgery. A white belt in martial arts will only become black after many hours of practice. It's the same with leadership. Strength in leadership won't happen without perseverance.

Speaking of martial arts, there is a saying in China that all martial arts – and there are many martial-art styles, including plum-blossom style, flood style, explosive style and emperor's long-range style, to name but a few – arose out of the Shaolin martial arts style found on Songshan Mountain in China.

As legend has it, a beautiful woman called Ng Muia watched a crane do battle with a snake. Inspired by the movements of the bird, Ng Muia designed a form of martial art, which she taught her young disciple, Yim Wing Chung, to help her defend herself against a local bandit. To this day the martial arts style is called Wing Chung.

What makes the Shaolin martial arts remarkable is that they were practised by nuns as well as monks. Ng Muia was a Shaolin nun. These Shaolin warriors engaged in hours of disciplined training every day. (A search on YouTube will provide examples of their remarkable prowess.) Stories include improbable acts such as running over the surface of water and throwing needles through glass. Rather more factual was that, in the sixteenth century, the Shaolin were a powerful force that battled a variety of foes, including Japanese pirates.

However, power brings enemies. The Shaolin Buddhist temple was destroyed more than once and their warriors were scattered to become itinerant masters of their arts. This had the effect of ensuring their prowess became known beyond the mountains. There still exist a number of Shaolin warrior monks who amaze the world with their skills.

Discipline and skill often go together. This is an important lesson for those whose aspirations are not matched by effort.

The Shaolin warrior monks would rise at 5 a.m. and practise meditation. Thereafter, basic skills related to balance and flexibility would be honed. Three hours later, breakfast would be served. The rest of the day was taken up with domestic chores, Buddhist lessons and combat drill. After dinner there would be two hours spent reviewing the exercises and skills learned during the day. Bedtime was around 11 p.m. Small wonder the Shaolin monks developed extraordinary skills. They had a routine whose rigour was designed to crush mediocrity.[1]

Our teens can develop extraordinary skills, but it will take discipline. Rather too many feel that they already have extraordinary skills – and that it is the responsibility of others to recognise they have them!

A PHOTO TO TAKE

Life is not about finding yourself.

Life is about creating yourself.

(Source unknown)

Renowned martial artists such as Bruce Lee and Jackie Chan did not achieve what they did by tapping on mobile phones all day. Michelle Yeoh, who played Yu Shu Lien in the film *Crouching Tiger, Hidden Dragon,* was sublime in her handling of two swords. Likewise, Lucy Liu was pretty handy with a lethal fan as Madame Blossom in the film *The Man with the Iron Fists.* These skills are not developed easily. They are obtained by drills and discipline.

It's not always easy to develop discipline in a teenager. Yet, without it, they are unlikely to develop the skills necessary to become a leader. If they cannot take control of themselves, they cannot be expected to control others. If they cannot discipline themselves, they will not be able to discipline others.

Do our budding heroes and heroines have the Shaolin toughness? Have they the capacity to train? Are they able to challenge mediocrity?

In more than one culture, a teenager's acceptance into adult life requires them to demonstrate grit, an ability to survive and a capacity to handle pain. The Indigenous Australian boy is often required to 'go walkabout' and fend for himself for a few months in the wild in order to show he has become a man. Not much exists by way of comparable ritual in the western world, which is why exercises that encourage self-leadership in our young are so important.

Can our children fend for themselves? Have they learned the disciplines necessary to survive?

A TRIAL TO UNDERTAKE

Ancient Greek legend has it that Hercules was driven mad by the Greek goddess Hera. In his madness, Hercules slew his wife and children. On realising what he had done, Hercules sought forgiveness for his terrible crime. An Oracle at Delphi told Hercules to work twelve years for a weasel of a King called Eurystheus.

King Eurystheus set Hercules ten seemingly impossible tasks, and when Hercules completed them, Eurystheus refused to recognise two of them and set two more tasks. Therefore, Hercules ended up completing the following twelve tasks.

1. Kill a huge lion in a cave near Nemea. This lion had the nasty habit of turning itself into a damsel in distress and then rewarding gallant rescuers by eating them.
2. Kill the nine-headed Hydra whose snake heads, if chopped off, would grow two more in their place. The resourceful Hercules cauterised the stumps as he chopped off the heads and pinched some of the Hydra's venomous blood to put on his arrows.
3. Capture the Golden Hind belonging to Artemis. When this was done, the beast was given to the snivelling Eurystheus. However, things ended happily because the Hind ran away and went back to its mistress, Artemis.
4. Capture the Erymanthian Boar.
5. Clean the Augean Stables in a single day. So unlikely was it that the thirty years of horse manure could be shifted in twenty-four hours, Augeas promised to give Hercules one-tenth of the horses if he did it. Hercules completed the task by diverting a couple of rivers to run through the stables. Augeas went back on his word, which was not wise: Hercules killed him.

6. Slay the Stymphalian birds. These were no ordinary birds. With beaks of bronze and feathers that converted into deadly darts, it took a bit of doing. Hercules scared them into the air and used his poisoned arrows to kill them.

7. Capture a rampaging bull in Crete. King Minos of Crete gave a helping hand - he was glad to be rid of it.

8. Steal some feisty, man-eating mares. The horses were owned by an unpleasant fellow called Diomedes, who was fed to his own horses by Hercules.

9. Obtain the girdle of Hippolyta, the Queen of the Amazons. Unfortunately, through some more treachery by Hera, this task required Hercules to slay Hippolyta - which was a shame because they got on quite well.

10. Steal some cattle. Easy enough, but not when they belonged to a monster called Geryon. However, Geryon also fell to Hercules' poisoned arrows.

11. Continuing the larceny theme, Hercules had to steal some apples from Hesperides. He got Atlas to pinch the apples while he took over the task of holding up the world for a while.

12. Bring back a three-headed hell-hound with lion's claws called Cerberus. The beast guarded the gates of the underworld. Hades, the god of the underworld, said Hercules could take Cerberus if he could capture the beast without using weapons.[2]

A rather more contemporary example of trials is found in the film *The Trials of Cate McCall*. The main character, lawyer Cate McCall, played by Kate Beckinsale, is battling a chaotic work-life balance and alcohol addiction. She is estranged from her family and is placed on probation. In order to secure her career and the custody of her daughter, Augie, she has to prove herself competent, both professionally and personally. Cate has to undertake several tasks that, although not quite up there with cleaning out the Augean Stables, are difficult. They include having to win some important court cases and gain control of her various addictions.

If our teens want to be considered leaders, they need to show they are up to the task. Like Hercules, a few tests might need to be undertaken to show that they have what it takes.

Given that there are not many man-eating Stymphalian birds or hydra-headed monsters to slay, other tasks might need to be considered to test the mettle of our neophyte leaders.

Let them undertake ten life-skill challenges.

The idea of undertaking ten labours like Hercules is unlikely to go down well with our sons and daughters, so stand by for some mega whinges. Respond by explaining that those who want to lead others must first show that they can lead themselves. Those who want to tidy up the world's carbon-dioxide emissions can start with switching off the lights when not in their bedroom.

TEN LABOURS TO PERFORM
TASK 1

Cleaning up thirty years of horse manure in the Augean Stables is not quite as necessary as it was in Greek legend. However, requiring a teen to clean their room is entirely realistic. Taking care of their own environment gives greater integrity to campaigns to clear up the broader environment.

Associated tasks could include:

- Vacuuming the room and/or sweeping it. Bonus points can be awarded for emptying the filled vacuum.
- Dusting – not with the feather duster (which merely redistributes the dust) but with a damp cloth.
- Stripping and re-making the bed once a week.
- Tidying the room each day.
- Taking dirty linen and clothes to the laundry and separating them into machine wash and hand wash, then separating them into dark wash and light wash.

- Ensuring things are stored on hangers, in cupboards and in drawers.

TASK 2

Learn to cook at least seven wholesome meals. Taking responsibility for cooking one meal a fortnight could be a reasonable starting point. However, lest our heroes and heroines think it's all about cooking – and collapse with a glow of self-satisfaction after they have cooked a dinner – let them be reminded that cooking is only part of a trilogy of tasks associated with preparing a meal. There is the shopping, there is the cooking and there is the post-meal clean-up.

The menu will depend upon family culture and family circumstances. Here are some general options: sausage casserole, beef stir-fry, baked dinner, curry, pasta, barbecue and one or two junk-food options. Families will make up their own list of meals, which could be expanded to include a yummy dessert or two. Go online for the recipes. There are many delicious options to choose from.

TASK 3

Rather than steal golden hinds, our teens could be asked to show they have the mettle to accumulate other riches. That which is stowed away in the bank vault is not likely to amount to much in their early years but some saving should be possible. Pocket money and/or the wages accumulated working part time can be saved. Having saved it, the hard-earned wealth then needs to be managed. Therefore, instruction in handling such things as credit cards is necessary, as is an understanding of budgeting and the wisdom of not exceeding the cap on the mobile phone.

The goal might be to raise $100. It may be more – particularly if it is to help pay for something like the first car. Whatever the reason, our teens need to be able to manage their money wisely and not run pleading to parents whenever their wallets are empty.

TASK 4

Although not quite up there with grabbing the girdle of an Amazonian princess, grabbing their school shirt and learning how to wash it is a useful skill. The science of washing includes knowing which fabrics can be washed together and the damage a stray tissue and a pink pair of socks can do.

Then there is the ironing. What temperature to use? When is steam and starch a good idea? Perhaps our teen could be asked to iron all their clothes for a week to demonstrate they have the skill.

TASK 5

When of an age, the older teen needs to know how to drive and look after a car. Obtaining a driver's licence represents a rite of passage many pass through.

Learning to drive needs to happen under different conditions to be useful training. City driving and country driving. Rush hour and empty-road driving. Day and night driving. Short- and long-distance driving. Wet and dry conditions – all these situations need to be experienced with a skilled instructor before tackling them alone.

To these skills should be added parallel parking, reversing and a host of other manoeuvres. There is also a need to have a thorough knowledge of the road rules and of what to do if involved with, or witnessing, an accident.

Other items can be placed in the 'car curriculum'. For example, what to look for when buying a car. What is legal and illegal in terms of 'L' plates, wheel tread, window tinting, road clearance and a host of other things that can greatly excite the police if not done properly.

Learning common maintenance tasks is also useful, even if it is limited to:

- Refilling the tank (knowing which side the petrol tank is on and the difference between a petrol hose and a diesel hose).
- Topping up with the right kind of oil and knowing where to pour it in.

- Topping up the window wash.
- Checking oil and coolant levels and knowing not to open the top of a radiator when the water inside is hot.
- Knowing how to start a car with jump-leads.
- Rotating the tyres and knowing what pressure they should be kept up to.
- Being able to replace windshield wipers.
- Changing a tyre. Details on how to do this can easily be found online.

TASK 6

Time now for a totally different sort of task – sewing on a button and repairing a gaping seam. Advice on this can be found from a host of sources, both in the real world and virtual.[3]

In terms of usefulness, sewing skills are a tad more relevant than rounding up Erymanthian boars and Geryon's cattle. If your son should think it a touch wussy, get him to discuss his problem with a crusty old sail-maker.

TASK 7

This task is simple: look after something. Properly. The number of children who pester a parent for a pet, then leave all maintenance of said animal, bird or fish to others, is significant. Let's do something about it.

If the Body Corporate takes a dim view of pets, or someone breaks out in hives when a feather comes near them, other options exist, such as taking full responsibility for the veggie patch or the cactus collection. The key features are that the required care is constant and includes holidays as well as school days. Another feature is that the consequences of good and bad care are fully known and followed through.

Too many of our offspring cannot cope with long-term commitment. That's what good pet-care requires – a commitment that continues well after the Christmas bow around the neck has been removed.

TASK 8

This task is, in every sense of the word, a life skill: do a first-aid course. Failing that, do a swim-rescue course. This is not just a line that looks good on a CV – it can save a life.

Yes, the qualifications will need to be updated every now and again and there is time and expense involved in getting, as well as maintaining, the qualification, but it equips our young leader with the skills needed to be a hero. It enables them to be something other than hopeless and helpless when a medical emergency presents itself.

As a minimum, the technique of cardiopulmonary resuscitation (CPR) could be learned. It's not difficult but proper training is still required. For further information, contact organisations such as the National Safety Council, the Red Cross and St John's Ambulance.

TASK 9

Sponsoring a child can be enormously rewarding. There are children in desperate need all around the world. Their lives can be transformed for as little as $12 a week. This money can be used to educate a child who might otherwise remain illiterate. It can also be used to clothe, feed or house a child.

It is worth checking exactly what the sponsorship money is going to be used for before making a commitment. It is also wise to sponsor a child through a reputable organisation such as World Vision, Save The Children, Compassion International, The Smith Family, SOS Children's Villages, Children International or Barnardos.

Check out the organisation to find how much of every dollar actually makes it to the child you are supporting. Anything less than 60 per cent needs to be questioned.

If sponsoring a child is too problematic, then there are many more local initiatives that can be taken, including collecting pre-loved clothes and delivering them to a charity collection point.

The sponsorship of a child may not be within the financial reach of every son or daughter, but they can still take the initiative to get their family, their class or their school to sponsor a child. Supervising the sponsorship of a child is just as valuable as paying for the sponsorship of a child.

TASK 10

The final quest for our leader is perhaps the most difficult. It is similar to Hercules' last task, which was to capture the three-headed hell-hound, Cerberus ... and to do so without weapons. In the case of our sons and daughters, their final task could be to capture and tame the three-headed 'Cyber Cerberus'. The Cyber Cerberus is no less dangerous and will require Herculean strength.

The three heads of the Cyber Cerberus are made up of: cyber harm, cyber trivia and cyber addiction.

1. Cyber harm

Be warned. The Cyber Cerberus has teeth and it has claws. Our heroes need to know how to handle the cyber world so they don't get hurt. Social networking sites such as Facebook, Instagram, Twitter and YouTube can overpower our children. They need to learn how to use these sites properly.

For example, they need to be very careful about apps such as Snapchat and Telegram. Even though these posts are supposed to vanish after they have been seen, someone can take a screenshot and cause it to reappear in later life.

An increasing number of apps allow you to say anything you like to someone else without being identified. Apps including Yik Yak and Secret may provide anonymity, but they also give opportunities to bully and be bullied. They are best avoided.

Harm can also come from other forms of cyber activity: bullying, scams, rip-offs, access to porn and violence, gambling and a host of other dangers exist. The task for our teens is to demonstrate that they can deal with these risks.

2. Cyber trivia

The second challenge for our sons and daughters is to deal with cyber trivia. So much of what people post about themselves is worse than bad – it is boring and bad. Therefore, the challenge is to make comments, post photos and maintain a cyber-presence that is compelling to read.

Get them to evaluate their cyber presence. Encourage them to make their comments in the cyber world more thoughtful, arresting or amusing. Encourage them to make their photos more striking, interesting and engaging. Encourage them to make their reputation more attractive, positive and engaging.

When it comes to collecting 'friends' and 'followers' on social-networking sites, more is not necessarily better. Selectivity and proper categorisation – the difference between 'friends' and 'acquaintances' – is needed. Our teens shouldn't be afraid to make posts visible to 'friends excluding acquaintances'. Likewise, they shouldn't be afraid to 'de-friend' and declutter their friends list.

AN EXERCISE TO PERFORM

'De-friending' is not easy. We all want to be liked and we usually do not want to offend. Therefore, it can be a challenge for our sons and daughters to write an 'I am going to de-friend you' notification that is going to leave them smelling of roses – but encourage them to have a crack at it and, if necessary, help them to compose a de-friending letter.

Here's an attempt to show the sort of thing that could be written:

I like having Facebook friends because I learn a lot from them. But I've so many I'm not able to stay in touch properly with most. So I've decided to prune my friends list. This will mean I'm de-friending you. However, I want to say thank you for being my friend and hope you have great memories of our friendship.

Okay, now it's your turn. It should not be difficult to do better.

3. Cyber addiction

The third head of the Cyber Cerberus that needs to be managed is that of cyber addiction. Is our teen in control of technology, or is technology in charge of them?

Can our sons and daughters cope with:

- Online activity being limited to a few specified hours a day?
- Meals being a 'phone-free' time?
- Social networking being off-limits after bedtime and during study time?

Beware: the third head has hypnotic powers. It can lull the unwary into zombie-like compliance – a state where their mind is filled with trivia and their hours stolen by online distraction. Unless awake and aware, a life can be stolen by that which is unproductive and unimportant.

The last labour is not going to be easy for many. Can our teens tame the 'Cyber Cerberus'? Can they avoid the harm, the trivia and the addiction?

In suggesting the tasks detailed above, the aim has been to promote greater responsibility, skill and discipline into the lives of our sons and daughters.

However, that's enough about labours, tests and tasks for the moment. It's time to return to the central theme of encouraging heroic discipline into the lives of our children.

EXCELLENCE

More often than not, excellence is a product of discipline.

In his book *Bounce*, Matthew Syed suggests that one of the most important factors in fostering good performance in a student is whether they have been placed on a 'trajectory of excellence'.[4] There are many parents, teachers and coaches who have endeavoured to put children on a trajectory of excellence – however, to be successful, the children must agree to be partners in this process.

Syed reports on a study undertaken in 1991 by K Anders Ericsson, a psychologist at Florida State University. Ericsson studied three groups of violinists. One group was outstanding, another was good, and the last group was only of average ability. The finding that Ericsson made was that by the age of twenty, the outstanding group had put in 10000 hours of practice, the good group 8000 hours of practice, and the average group 4000 hours.

Syed also recounts an audacious human experiment by a Hungarian named László Polgár. Polgár advertised for a wife – he found one and married her in 1967, and then declared that any parent could produce a world champion. He proceeded to test this theory when his wife, Klara, provided him with three daughters, Susan, Sophia and Judit. Laszló's daughters became the greatest female chess players of all time.

The secret to outstanding performance at school is no different, in that high expectations, parental support and purposeful practice are essential.

The idea of 'purposeful practice' is particularly important. There is a natural tendency for children to want to show off what they can already do. This is much more attractive than the pain associated with exploring the limits of potential. Some children are 'clock watchers' when doing something like piano practice – when the hour is up, they're off to play. Job done, no worries.

No: the job isn't done.

Learning to play the piano for an hour every week can be useless if it does not extend a child's skill. Competence does not come with time, it comes from getting better. The two are not as closely related as some think. Therefore, no practice session should be concluded unless there is clear and demonstrable progress beyond that which was able to be done at the start of the lesson. The next essay needs to be of a higher standard than the previous essay. The next race needs to be run faster than the last. In other words, practice is not enough. It needs to be 'purposeful practice'.

Syed suggests that purposeful practice will only happen if a person makes a conscious decision to improve. They must have an intrinsic desire to do well. Practising only because 'Mum wants me to do this' will only work if Mum's shadow is falling across them, and that is unlikely, because mums are usually busy with other tasks. Therefore, our children need to be able to cope with the discipline of practice on their own.

AN EXAMPLE TO SHARE

THE OLYMPIC GAMES

If ever there was an arena that demanded discipline and practice, it is the Olympic Games.

In 393 AD, the ancient Olympic Games were stopped after nearly twelve centuries of competition by a spoilsport called Emperor Theodosius. He found his sensibilities offended by the pagan characteristics of the games. Some 1500 years later, a Frenchman named Pierre de Coubertin found himself concerned by the lack of vigour in the French military following their placing an uncomfortable second in the Franco-Prussian War of 1870. He agitated for the reintroduction of the Olympic Games, which led to the establishment of first modern Olympic Games. These were held in Athens in 1896.

The conditions enjoyed by athletes in 1896 were a little different from those of modern-day Olympians. For example, the swimming was not done in a pool of calm, crystal water – it was done in the frigid, turbulent swill of the Aegean Sea.

In 1892, Coubertin stated:

Let us export our oarsmen, our runners, our fencers into other lands. That is the true Free Trade of the future; and the day it is introduced into Europe, the cause of Peace will have received a new and strong ally.

Unfortunately, the cause of peace has not always been advanced by the Olympic Games. As far back as the 1908 London Olympics, Irish athletes refused to compete under the British flag. The Nazi Olympics of Berlin in 1936 saw the African-American Jesse Owens refute Hitler's notion of Aryan supremacy by winning four gold medals. Eleven Israeli athletes were killed by Palestinian terrorists at the Munich Olympics of 1972 and there have been countless other political spats promulgated at the Olympics over the past 100 years.

Nonetheless, the Olympic motto of *Citius, Altius, Fortius* (faster, higher, stronger), remains relevant to us all.

We need to remind our sons and daughters that things of great worth are seldom achieved without pain, so we must all get used to it, get on with it and be prepared to cope with a little discipline in our lives.

That said, it is also important to remember that even with disciplined training, our children will not always win. Little is more damaging than parents feeling crushed because their child did not win, and even more so when the child has done their best.

They will not always win. Even the Olympic Creed acknowledges this.[5]

THE OLYMPIC CREED

The most important thing in the Olympic Games is not to win but to take part, just as the most important thing in life is not to triumph, but the struggle. The essential thing is not to have conquered, but to have fought well.

In a speech to a high-school gathering some years ago, Microsoft founder Bill Gates shared a few realities of life, including the following:

A PHOTO TO TAKE

SOME LIFE TRUTHS

Life is not fair - get used to it!

The world won't care about your self-esteem.

The world will expect you to accomplish something BEFORE you feel good about yourself.

You will not make a hundred thousand dollars a year right out of high school and you won't be a vice-president with a car phone until you earn both.

Your school may have done away with winners and losers - but life has not.

(Although this advice was shared by Bill Gates, its original source remains unclear.)

Speaking of Bill Gates – don't think his success came easily. From the age of fourteen, Gates engaged in thousands of hours – often sixteen hours a day – programming computers when most people didn't even have one.

Bill Gates's story is told in Malcolm Gladwell's book *Outliers: The Story of Success*. The book makes depressing reading for those looking for shortcuts to success. *Outliers* will tell you that The Beatles had to play for five hours a night and perform 1200 times before achieving their musical breakthrough in 1964.

Gladwell comments on the work ethic of Asian children and explains why they dominate in terms of numbers going to selective schools in many countries. He found that traditional European farmers worked about 1200 hours a year, whereas their Asian counterparts would work nearer 3000 hours. Gladwell contrasted the work ethic of the east and west with two sayings. The first is from Russia:

If God does not bring it, the earth will not give it.

The second is from China:

No one who rises before dawn 360 days a year fails to make his family rich.

We sneer, of course, and say that life is not about being 'rich' – then we complain about being poor!

Gladwell goes on to describe the KIPP (Knowledge is Power Program) schools in the United States. It's challenging. Lessons start at 7.25 a.m. and continue until 5 p.m. On Saturday, tuition starts at 9 a.m. and finishes at 1 p.m. Each day includes ninety minutes of mathematics and ninety minutes of English. Students study many other subjects and every student must play a musical instrument. Not surprisingly, KIPP students do amazingly well at school and university.

This example of American industry runs counter to what Gladwell typically found in the western world. He found that early educational reformers in the United States were suspicious of too much schooling. This led them to eliminate Saturday schooling and introduce the long summer holidays. These measures – particularly the long summer holidays – are now reckoned to be an educational disaster for some students because they completely disengage with learning for several months of the year.[6]

Perhaps this judgement is too harsh. Maybe children are still learning in the long summer holidays; it's just that they're learning different things. Although, it is still true that success is seldom gained easily. The correlation between work and reward needs to be revealed to our offspring, who sometimes want the trappings of success without the discomfort of working for them.

AN EXAMPLE TO SHARE

An example of someone with terrific physical and mental discipline is Jessica Watson, who, at the age of sixteen, sailed solo, nonstop and unassisted around the world.

The brown scabs on the side of Jessica's boat, *Ella's Pink Lady*, when she returned told the story of her hardship more eloquently than any of her blogs.

Living with the possibility of catastrophe for that long would have terrified most people.

But this girl was tough – not so much physically as mentally. Colliding with a 63000-tonne cargo ship in sea trials a few weeks before setting sail around the world, contending with critics, bobbing back after being knocked flat several times by huge waves, surviving 210 days in a 10-metre boat, coping with 75-knot winds and 12-metre seas – that's a tough ask.

Reflecting on these challenges, Jessica told reporters that she had been pleased with her mental performance. This comment is interesting and suggests where most battles have to be fought – in the mind. Her success in this area led to her becoming Young Australian of the Year in 2011.[7]

FINALLY

Even with discipline, we may not succeed. But there may be other rewards – and these can be just as valuable. As it is said, the journey is often as important as arriving. We may not always succeed, but we can be enriched by the experience of trying to succeed. Some enterprises will end in failure. However, these failures can inform and give a better understanding of what doesn't work.

Discipline is needed to achieve success. Discipline is also needed to deal with failure. When met with failure, the discipline required will be that of remaining positive when what we really want to do is cry. At other times, the discipline required will be to engage in an exhaustive analysis of where you went wrong and to resolve not to repeat the failure next time.

SUMMARY

- A leader typically needs to have personal discipline if they wish to achieve anything much in life.
- Leaders need to take command and control of themselves before they command and control others.
- Aspiring leaders can help their cause by demonstrating mastery in something, and this will only happen if they are prepared to train.
- Rather like the Labours of Hercules, our children can be set tasks to perform in order to demonstrate they are ready for the responsibility of leadership.
- Children need to place themselves on a trajectory of excellence.
- Shortcuts usually lead to being short-changed in one's quest for attainment.
- Whether an Olympic athlete or a teenage adventurer, there are many role models that can inspire.
- Not all have won or achieved their goals, but the world is a better place for them trying.

An example to follow

Finding honest examples of good leadership is not as easy as it should be.

The memoirs of most leaders are curiously deficient in confessing to inadequacy and are often self-advancing. Other biographies grind through detail that may be of interest to the writer but is not nearly so fascinating to the reader.

Nonetheless it can still be an interesting exercise to read about leaders throughout history. Some people have made a stab at naming the greatest leaders. For example, Michael H Hart, a white separatist, produced a book in 1978 entitled *The 100: A Ranking of the Most Influential Persons in History.*[1]

Hart's top ten were:

1. Muhammad
2. Isaac Newton
3. Jesus Christ
4. Buddha

5. Confucius
6. Saint Paul
7. Ts'ai Lun
8. Johannes Gutenberg
9. Christopher Columbus
10. Albert Einstein.

Note the absence of women. In fact, Hart includes only two women in his 100. Queen Isabella is ranked sixty-fifth, and Queen Elizabeth I of Great Britain is ranked ninety-fourth.

One of the few books that honour female leaders is Deborah G Felder's book, *The 100 Most Influential Women of All Time*. This book has a very American orientation.[2] Have a look at her top ten:

1. Eleanor Roosevelt
2. Marie Curie
3. Margaret Sanger
4. Margaret Mead
5. Jane Addams
6. Mary Wollstonecraft
7. Elizabeth Cady Stanton
8. Susan B Anthony
9. Harriet Tubman
10. the Virgin Mary.

Not everyone will agree with this list. Those who have travelled a bit will know of the significance of the Virgin Mary to many people. From hilltop villages to great city cathedrals, Mary's influence is honoured throughout much of the world. This could not persuade Felder to advance her above nine other women, mostly American. Outside of America, many would be struggling to know the significance of half those in her top ten.

Another complicating factor is that history is written by the victors – and by Hollywood, which has turned some losses into victories. Apparently, America won the Vietnam War.

Our sons and daughters need to know that the examples of leadership advanced by their own culture may be a touch biased and that the 'bad guys' may, in fact, have more to teach about leadership than many of the 'good guys'. For example, look at Ho Chi Minh.

A STORY TO SHARE

HO CHI MINH (1890-1969)

VIETNAMESE COMMUNIST LEADER

Ho Chi Minh was born to country peasants in the French colony of Vietnam. His schooling in the city of Hue was not completed because he left to teach in a fishing community. After that, he travelled the world. Ho became a bus-boy in Saigon, a kitchen hand in London and a communist in Paris.

After reading the works of Karl Marx, Ho joined the communist party and became a militant. His activities included editing a communist newspaper, meeting Lenin, Trotsky and Stalin in Moscow, and setting up a revolutionary youth organisation in China.

Ho spoke Chinese, French, German, Russian, Japanese and English. All these languages were needed as he moved about the world advancing the communist cause - activities that earned him a death sentence from France and imprisonment by the Chinese.

Ho would often disguise himself as a beggar, peasant, monk or merchant. His covert activities included organising resistance to the Japanese in World War II, for they had taken control of Vietnam from the French. A string of organisations were set up by Ho, including the Indochinese Communist Party and the League for the Independence of Vietnam.

When Japan withdrew from Vietnam in 1945, Ho became Chairman of the Provisional Government and declared Vietnam to be an independent country. Unfortunately, some didn't agree. Vietnam endured a Chinese invasion from the north and a re-occupation of the south by the French.

After some time, the French persuaded the Chinese to leave, but Ho, now called Ho Chi Minh (He Who Enlightens) could not get the French to leave. In fact, the French decided to strengthen their hold on Vietnam and sent a French naval vessel into Haiphong harbour, killing 6000 civilians. This prompted the outbreak of war.

After many years of conflict, the French decided to draw the Viet Minh guerrillas out by establishing a stronghold in the fortress city of Dien Bien Phu. However, after smuggling Chinese cannon parts to the nearby hillsides, the Viet Minh pounded the French into surrender.

Despite winning the war, Ho Chi Minh was only given control of the northern part of Vietnam. The governance of the entire country was conditional on the outcome of democratic elections promised for 1956. However, the French, Chinese and Russian authorities decided not to hold the promised elections, so Ho's supporters – now called the Viet Cong – began guerrilla warfare to unify South Vietnam with northern Vietnam.

Because America wanted to contain the spread of communism through Asia, it provided military support to South Vietnam. American involvement increased to the extent that more bombs were dropped on Vietnam than on Japan and Germany during World War II, American casualties mounted and with them, a demand from many US citizens that their country stop its involvement in the war.

Ho Chi Minh turned up the heat on the Americans by launching the Tet military offensive, a campaign to overcome the American and South Vietnamese troops in the south of the country. The campaign was successful and this increased calls for peace.

Finally, the American President, Lyndon B Johnson, agreed to stop the bombing in Vietnam. However, his successor, Richard Nixon, continued the fight – but not for long. It was increasingly obvious that the war was unwinnable. America withdrew from the conflict in 1973. South Vietnam was eventually conquered by North Vietnam, and its capital, Saigon, was renamed Ho Chi Minh City.

Ho Chi Minh did not witness the surrender of Saigon in 1975, for he died on 3 September 1969. He is revered in Vietnam as 'Uncle Ho', the one who gained independence for Vietnam. Outside of Vietnam, his status as a leader is not always recognised. It should be.[3]

Much can be learned from studying famous leaders. However, the relevance of those described in history books may not be quite so great as looking at leadership examples that are local and contemporary.

There are many ways our sons and daughters can learn about leadership by studying individuals within their own community. Although these characters may not necessarily be listed in the *Who's Who*, their effectiveness as role models should not be doubted. For example, a study of those leading local sporting teams could be useful because most teenagers have been members of sports teams and can identify with the leadership challenges associated with their captaincy.

CAPTAINCY OF A TEAM

'O Captain! My Captain!' wrote Walt Whitman as he mourned the death of his President, Abraham Lincoln. This line of poetry was to be made memorable by the film *Dead Poet's Society*. In the film, Robin Williams plays a charismatic English teacher who allows his students to call him 'Captain. My Captain'.

In real life, captains can be a disappointment. Often the award of captain is given to someone who has a limited understanding of the responsibilities the role carries and even less understanding of the opportunities the role brings.

It seems that the only exercise a student must do in preparation for the role of a sport's captain is to ensure that their thumb is in excellent working order. Little is called for other than the ability to flick a coin in order to determine who will kick, bowl or serve first. Real captaincy calls for something a little more than the ability to toss a coin in the air.

A ROLE PLAY TO CONSIDER

Get your son or daughter to imagine they are the captain of a field hockey team. (If necessary, change the sport to make it more relevant.) What would they do in the following situations?

1. It is the grand final and the crowds on the sideline bear testimony to the importance of the game. You are having a hard time of it in the game; attack after attack has broken down because they have a very good player. At half-time, you are down two goals and team morale is not good. As captain, what do you say to your team?

2. The hockey game is still in progress and you continue to have no luck against the opposition player. You are aware that sitting on the sideline in the reserves is a new student who has not really proved herself but appears to be a reasonable player. Importantly, she is left-handed and could be able to handle the difficult ball-play on the left side of the pitch. Do you take yourself off and bring on the left-hander? What factors would influence your decision?

3. It is late in the game and the scores are locked. Then, your team gets a penalty right in front of the goal. There is a very real chance you will score from the penalty. The best person at taking the penalty is a rather excitable character – although not always reliable, his shots, if on target, are unstoppable. You are probably the second-best player to take the penalty. Would you take the penalty shot or allow your teammate to take it? Explain your views.

4. Your team loses the grand final in extra time. Your players feel dejected. What would you say to them?

5. At the tea and speeches afterwards it is your turn to say a few words. The game witnessed some poor umpiring; in fact, it would be accurate to say that strange umpiring decisions probably cost your team the victory. What would you say in the speech?

As well as role play, it can be helpful to go through the tasks a captain could undertake other than flicking a coin. If some help is needed, then share the following examples.

- You are aware of the importance of the next game, so instead of having the usual team briefing, you write a personalised note to each member of the team to encourage them.
- You are aware that a few of your players are not hitting the ball well. After school, you arrange for them to practise.
- One of the players is upset their mate is not in the side and starts a campaign to remove an existing player to make room. You speak to the critic and point out the damage being done.
- You are aware that the post-match speeches are beginning to sound the same, so you make a conscious effort to be more creative and interesting in your speeches.
- You are aware that there are some excellent young players in the grade below, so you go and watch them play. Then you have a word to your coach, who you feel may not be aware of the talented youngsters.
- A young player is promoted and takes the place of one of your best friends in the team. Your friend is upset, but you feel it is the right decision and tell them so.
- Because of the mud being brought into the change-room after training, you ask the players to remove their boots before they enter.

- Recognising that the school crowd is beginning to applaud opposition errors, you ask the principal to say a few words to the school about it at the next assembly.
- Each week you check the game plan with the coach and remind the team of the strategy to be adopted in the next game.
- After some ordinary refereeing decisions, you tell your team not to show their anger, because it is only going to get the referee further offside.
- At half-time, you ask your team which opposition players they think are the weakest. As the responses come in, you suggest a modified game plan that exploits these weaknesses.
- During the game, one of the opposition players is injured. You go over to check on the injured player and show support.
- During the game, there is growing frustration at the interpretation of one of the rules. You approach the umpire and ask for clarification.
- After the game, you deliberately encourage the player whose mistake cost you the game.
- You thank the opposition even though you thought they were lucky to win. You also congratulate their best player.
- After the game you discuss the things you think need to be worked on for the next game.
- Before the final game, you collect money from team members to buy a present for the coach.
- At the end-of-season lunch, you give a speech that provides an overview of the season and thanks all who have supported the team.
- You visit one of the members of the team recovering from an illness and bring them a video clip of the game they missed.

These examples are for illustration only and can be adapted to any sport. The goal of the exercise is to show that there is a lot more to captaincy than tossing a coin.

A PHOTO TO TAKE

> To lose the game on the field is
> unfortunate.
> To lose the game off the field is
> unforgivable.

There is no shame in losing a well-contested sporting competition, but to lose the respect of supporters is shameful.

Winning the game off the field requires good sportsmanship, thanking the opposition, leaving the change-rooms clean and ensuring that the after-match speeches are well delivered.

Another example of leadership that teenagers might well be able to relate to is that of a school prefect or equivalent leadership position.

AN ASSESSMENT TO DO

Although it's not realistic for all our sons and daughters to expect a leadership position at school, this should not prevent them from evaluating themselves against a job description of a student leader. These job descriptions can usually be obtained from the school.

If no such job description exists, it would not be difficult to write one. Shown on the following page is a job description of a school prefect. It could easily be customised to suit most leadership positions within a school.

Having obtained or written a job description, our aspiring student leaders could be invited to assess how well they could fulfil each aspect of the job. This diagnostic exercise can be valuable in highlighting areas of leadership that need to be worked on.

A JOB DESCRIPTION FOR A SCHOOL PREFECT

1. General expectations of prefects

	Weakness				Strength	
	1	2	3	4	5	N/A
Supports the school's mission and goals.						
Sets a good example both in and out of the classroom.						
Acts as an effective link between students and staff.						

2. Specific expectations of prefects

	Weakness				Strength	
	1	2	3	4	5	N/A
Remains active in the role after gaining the position.						
Is a strong presence in the school.						
Is reliable in doing their duties.						
Is proactive rather than reactive.						
Leads by example.						
Puts principles before popularity.						
Has a servant heart.						
Chooses to notice and deal with:						
- inappropriate dress						
- inappropriate behaviour						
- bad language						
- intolerance, racism, harassment						
- teasing, bullying, putdowns						
- litter and graffiti						
- known trouble spots						
- conflict.						
Is a moral leader.						
Is compassionate.						
Spends time with and helps:						
- the younger student						
- the new student						

- the different student						
- the lonely student.						
Does not turn a blind eye to inappropriate behaviours by:						
- students in general						
- friends in particular.						
Is punctual for duty.						
Is present for duty.						
Is diligent on duty.						
Looks and sounds like a leader by:						
- giving firm, clear instructions						
- using good body language and posture						
- making good use of voice and language.						
Acts like a leader in the following ways:						
- Is decisive and clear.						
- Is thoughtful.						
- Is fair.						
- Is consistent.						
- Uses initiative.						
Helps out with school events in the following ways:						
- Is high profile and observant.						
- Directs and controls well.						
Makes good use of punishments using neither too many nor too few.						
- Uses punishments that are constructive.						
- Uses punishments that are fair.						
- Uses punishments that are consistent.						
Makes good use of support staff including:						
- the principal						
- staff.						

This exercise suggests there is value in finding out the skills looked for in a desired leadership role. Thereafter, work can progress on developing these skills.

WHAT REALLY IS LEADERSHIP?

'I don't know how to define leadership but I know it when I see it.'

There are some indefinable qualities to leadership. Therefore, we need to have sympathy when some struggle to define leadership. The task is not made easier when: leaders are not leading, definitions of leadership are changing, and leadership is now being expressed in many different ways.

Leaders are not leading

As we have seen, some of our contemporary leaders can be a disappointment. Just when we think we have found a great role model, they often let us down.

One only has to look at the disconnection between what a politician promises and what they deliver. Let's have some fun!

Clearly, there are now many sorts of political promise. There is the bog standard:

Promise: *Explicit undertaking. Declaration of intended way forward. Commitment to an action.*

Given that many political promises are as reliable as a second-hand lawnmower, we need more nuanced types of promise, such as:

Promatoe: *This stands for PROMise MAde TO get Elected. These are non-binding promises.*

There could also be:

Prombroke: *This is a promise that is able to be broken due to imperatives neither suspected nor known when the promise was made.*

In addition:

Promonant: *A whopping great big promise that is an absolutely, positively, cross-my-heart-and-hope-to-die sort of promise that is only broken sometimes.*

To this could be added:

Promisquous: *An immoral, unrestrained sort of promise that creates lots of immediate advantage but might be regretted in the long term.*

Also:

Promenade: *A promise paraded and promoted for show only.*

And:

Promoshun: *A promise made for puffery and publicity. It is given with a set of steak knives.*

Enough! We shouldn't get too cynical about our politicians. After all, they are merely representatives of the people, and we are not always renowned for an ability to keep promises.

Definitions of leadership are changing

With growing frequency, people are defining leadership as management. This is wrong and serves to confuse what leadership is. Being a leader implies having a charismatic quality an ability to influence others to follow. 'Manager' implies a capacity to deal with bureaucracy and enforce an adherence to procedures. Here are some other basic differences:

- Managers tend to maintain. Leaders tend to innovate.
- Managers are supervisory. Leaders are visionary.
- Managers have authority. Leaders have influence.
- Managers generally like order. Leaders may create chaos and disturb with new possibilities.

It is easy to romanticise leadership and dismiss management. Management has a legitimate place in society, and those who deal with administration and policy are important. Coordination and supervision are also important, as is the day-to-day overseeing of an organisation.

A new form of leadership

In recent years there has been a trend away from individual leadership to a style of leadership with a heavier accent on teamwork.

Old style of leadership	New style of leadership
One person has the solutions.	The team has the solutions.
Accent on individualism.	Accent on collaboration.
The leader is empowered.	The team is empowered.
The leader is at the top of the organisational pyramid.	The leader is at the centre of a collaborative group.
Autocratic.	Democratic.
Hierarchical.	Less hierarchical.
Dictator.	Facilitator.
The leader creates a sense of dependency.	The leader creates a sense of empowerment.
More mechanical and impersonal.	More relational and personal.
The leader is served.	The leader serves others.
The leader values conformity.	The leader values diversity.
The end matters more than the means by which it is achieved.	The means by which objectives are met are also important.

Leadership can be expressed in different ways

It is important to recognise that the expression of leadership can vary. For example:

Leadership style	The Enforcer	The Boss	The Friend	The Colleague	The Model	The Coach
	Sets rules and is keen to see they are enforced. Monitors closely to ensure tight control.	Establishes the mission and goals. Sets standards and protects them.	Promotes friendship. Likes to avoid confrontation.	Employs democratic principles and encourages the group to reach agreement.	Leads by example and expects others to follow. Responsibility is taken from those who fail to perform.	Works for long-term success by developing individual and group skills.
Aims for	Compliance	Standards	Harmony	Democracy	Imitation	Development
Effective when	Obedience is essential.	There is a need to unify a group and give it direction.	Cohesion and peace are needed in a group.	The group is made up of competent members.	The group respects its leader.	The group wants to improve itself.
Not good for	Encouraging creativity.	Encouraging democracy.	Times when discipline and correction are needed.	Times when clear responsibility is needed.	Groups without a gifted leader.	When time is short.

Most leaders employ a range of leadership styles. Some of these styles are less readily identified with leadership than others, but they are still legitimate expressions of leadership.

AN EXAMPLE TO SHARE

ERNEST SHACKLETON (1874-1922)

When one reads of Ernest Shackleton's epic voyage to the Antarctic on the *Endurance* in 1914-1917, it is clear that Shackleton employed all the above-mentioned leadership styles. For example:

- **Enforcer:** Threatening a rebellious team member with disciplinary action when his leadership was challenged.

- **Boss:** Ensuring strict discipline was maintained even when his ship was trapped in ice.
- **Friend:** Not abandoning his friends marooned on Elephant Island, but setting out to rescue them.
- **Colleague:** Participating in pageants and festivities with his crew on board the *Endurance*.
- **Model:** Not asking his team to do tasks he was not prepared to do himself.
- **Coach:** Based on his previous experience in Antarctica in 1901-1903, training his team and advising them on how they might best survive.[4]

Different situations call for different leadership styles. A good leader is able to choose the most appropriate style for a situation.

THE UGLY SIDE OF LEADERSHIP

There are many people in leadership positions who do not have any leadership qualities. This is because leadership positions can be gained through inheritance, favouritism, passing exams, money, making friends, and luck – to name but a few.

Even when leadership positions are gained by genuine leadership skills, these skills can be accompanied by less desirable qualities, such as greed, cruelty, neurosis, insecurity, egocentricity, ambition, vanity, ruthlessness, fearfulness and intolerance.

An example of flawed leadership is Napoleon Bonaparte. He was an undoubted leader, but he also suffered from an inferiority complex due to his relatively low birth status. He was moody, manipulative and ambitious. He was vain, self-absorbed and dismissive. He was also a magnificent leader.

People are a complex mix of attributes – some good and some bad. No leader has been without some flaw.

Knowing this can come as some relief to a teenager who is constantly being challenged to have a perfect body, great ability and a blameless lifestyle. A weakness in one area should not be allowed to disqualify him or her from leadership. Indeed, an imperfection can have the benefit of keeping us humble and making us more tolerant as leaders.

That said, it is as well to know what our flaws are and not believe all our own press. For those not sure what their flaws might be, asking close friends and those who love you enough to tell the truth can be enlightening.

In order to prevent this exercise from becoming too negative, the enquiry could be more general, such as: *What three things do you like best about me? What one thing would you like to change about me?*

Radicalisation

A tragically relevant example of good and bad leadership influences lies in the growing problem of radicalisation. Extremism has torn families apart, and seen too many going overseas to fight in a war that leads to them being killed.

Several parents claim the drift of their children into extremism was something they just couldn't stop. Is this true? The answer is: sometimes. Parents can be powerless in some things. However, there are things parents can do.

The radicalisation of the young is much more likely if:

- The parents are radicalised.
- The family comes from a country that is torn by religious extremism.
- There is a strong family affiliation with a dominant culture.
- A strict religious adherence is observed.
- Youth groups are established that are influenced by radicals.
- They feel disconnected from and rejected by mainstream society.
- They are attracted to the excitement of guns and war.
- They have a boyfriend or girlfriend who has been radicalised.

- They already have a history of going against mainstream authority.[5]

Having noted the above, it needs to be said that there are many exceptions to this stereotype. It is entirely possible to be radicalised when none of the situations described above is evident.

The best antidote a parent can use against radicalisation of their children is to focus on the following:

- Foster a culture of non-extremism in the home.
- Choreograph friendships with people who are known for their balanced and moderate views.
- When discussing religious and political issues with the family, do so in a balanced and informed manner.
- Encourage a positive engagement with mainstream culture.
- Remain in constant conversation with your children.
- Do what they can to prevent family association with known radicals.
- Monitor children's social media chatter by becoming part of it.
- Worship at a location free from religious extremists.
- Deal with any radical leanings as soon as they are detected.
- Use expert counselling services if required.

There is no surefire way to prevent radicalisation. However, it is far less likely in a loving home that enjoys open communication and the honest sharing of opinion.

The positive side of leadership

Although there are many examples where the expression of leadership is corrupt and inappropriate, there are several examples of leadership that are wholesome and inspiring. Often, one does not need to go outside of the home to witness outstanding examples of leadership. It can be seen in a servant-hearted mother. It can be seen in a faithful father. It can also be seen in the courage of a grandparent who is battling cancer.

To read about the qualities associated with leadership is to read about the best qualities that can be found in a person.

A TASK TO CONSIDER

Share the following list with your sons and daughters. Ask them whether anything else should be added.

Qualities of a true leader

Some of the desirable qualities of a leader are:

- Creative
- Problem solver
- Prepared to take calculated risks
- Assertive in a positive way
- Courageous
- Charismatic
- Determined
- Responsible
- Has an aura of authority
- Faithful and reliable
- Positive and constructive
- Fair and consistent
- Fulfils expectations
- Respects the rights of others
- Gives praise and uses criticism constructively
- Capable and able to cope
- Searches for self-improvement
- Tactical
- Ethical/moral
- Loyal
- Has good communication skills
- Has a sense of humour and good interpersonal skills
- Empathetic, caring, approachable and friendly
- Models the behaviours expected of others
- Has the gift of firm yet relaxed control
- Empowers others
- Self-disciplined
- Observant and intuitive
- Proactive
- Learns from mistakes
- Good team player
- Contributes well to the synergy of a group
- Aware of their obligations
- Has a calling

- Accessible, visible
- Willing to go the extra mile
- Committed and involved
- Has a servant heart

In a world all too ready to trumpet failure and trivialise success, it can be useful to keep a 'book of blessings'. Whether digital or in print form, great encouragement can come from recording good examples. Some people collect stamps. Others collect Facebook friends. Why not collect good examples? Record online links to stories that inspire you. Scrapbook those rare newspaper stories that encourage. Share not only what was bad about your day, but what was good.

It can also be a lovely thing to encourage good leadership by acknowledging it when it is seen. An email, phone call or letter to someone who displayed any of the qualities described above can bless the recipient and help generate ongoing expressions of good leadership.

There are many examples of good leaders and there are many examples of bad leaders. An online search will provide leadership stories to both warn and inspire. Typing 'Great leadership stories from the movie world' into your favourite search engine can yield rich dividends, as would 'Examples of good leadership found in films'.

A STORY TO SHARE

ODETTE SANSOM (1912-1995)

Odette Sansom's father was a bank official who had distinguished himself in World War I in which he won the Croix de Guerre and lost his life. Odette lived with her widowed mother in Boulogne before marrying an Englishman, Roy Sansom, with whom she had three daughters. When the Germans took control of France, the Sansoms moved to

England, where Odette volunteered her services to the British Special Operations Executive (SOE). This clandestine organisation specialised in working behind enemy lines. Odette was schooled in firing Sten guns, throwing grenades, resisting interrogation and learning Morse code. The cover for her work was the First Aid Nursing Yeomanry, affectionately known as 'Fany'.

It was not long before Odette was sent to Gibraltar. She sailed in a two-masted felucca, which landed her secretly on the French coast at Cassis, near Toulon. Odette was joined by Captain Peter Churchill, and they assumed the cover of a married couple as they worked behind enemy lines. However, Odette and Peter were soon captured. They were sent to Fresnes Prison in Paris. Odette was tortured. Her toenails were pulled out and she was burned with a red-hot poker, but she remained silent. A frustrated enemy then condemned her to death. However, the sentence was not carried out because the Germans suspected, incorrectly, that she might be related to the British Prime Minister, Winston Churchill. Odette was locked away in Fresnes Prison, where she was interrogated for a further eight months.

Odette was joined by six other captured SOE women and taken by train to Karlsruhe. From there, three of the women were taken to the Natzweiler-Struthof concentration camp and shot. The other three were taken to Dachau and shot. After being tortured again, Odette was moved to the Ravensbrück concentration camp and put in an underground cell. Her captors turned up the central heating until it was fearfully hot and deprived her of food. After this, the Germans took her to an above-ground cell whose window faced the execution ground and crematorium.

Towards the end of the war, when the concentration camp was about to be liberated by the Americans, the Camp Commander took Odette to the American lines, hoping to win favour by 'rescuing' the woman he believed to be Winston Churchill's niece by marriage. His initiative did not work. He was sentenced and hanged, as were most of the senior officials of Ravensbrück.

Odette returned to England and, having divorced her husband, spent some time with her three daughters before marrying Peter Churchill. After divorcing Churchill in 1956, she married Geoffrey Hallows in the same year.

Odette Sansom was one of fifty SOE women sent to operate in France during World War II. Fifteen of this group were killed.[6]

The story of Odette Sansom inspires because of her extraordinary bravery. She was prepared to go to great lengths to tackle an evil, even to the extent of putting duty to country before family responsibilities. For any aspiring leader who is doing it tough, Odette's story can serve as an example of how to cope. It also encourages us, because she was not perfect - and neither are we.

FINALLY

Odette Sansom's story brings us back to where we started this chapter. It reaffirms that there exist many examples of good leadership. There are examples of men and women – fictional and real, contemporary and historical – who can inspire our sons and daughters.

However, the most powerful example our sons and daughters are likely to experience is the example given by their parents and by the values adopted in the home.

Choosing family values is best left to individual families to decide. A useful strategy is to have the whole family gather to agree upon the general principles it wishes to live by. The family might come up with something like the following.

Our family believes that our home is a place in which:
1. Love will be expressed in word and deed.
2. Unique strengths and differences will be encouraged.
3. Everyone in the family is precious.
4. Increased freedom should be linked to evidence of increased maturity.

5. Family members have a responsibility to protect each other and the good name of the family.
6. All should contribute to household chores.
7. Telling the truth is important.
8. Sharing how we feel is important.
9. Contributing to family wellbeing is important.
10. Rights and privileges are earned.

Okay. You can probably do better. Good. By so doing, we can ensure that our homes model the example our children need.

SUMMARY

- Finding good examples of leadership is not as easy as it should be.
- Such examples that do exist are often culturally biased or unbalanced in some way.
- Although history has many good leadership examples, case studies exist that are closer to home, such as the role of a sports captain in a school team and the role of a school prefect.
- Undertaking role play can be a useful way to exercise leadership skills.
- Finding examples of leadership is complicated because: leaders are not leading, definitions of leadership are changing, and leadership is now being expressed in many different ways.
- We need to inoculate our children against the power of radicalisation.
- Use of the world of film and the world of fiction can be an effective means to study leadership.
- The home is the best place to model leadership.

A villain to conquer

Any leader worth their salt needs a villain to conquer, a scourge to get rid of, a danger to diffuse. Superman would have been remembered only as the mild-mannered reporter Clark Kent were it not for a steady procession of villains who caused him to dash into a phone booth and emerge in a fetching pair of tights and a big red cape.

The world has no shortage of baddies to be put in their proper place. At the macro level, there are the sorts of injustices reported in the media. Atrocities of one kind or another are all too common. When nations, tribes and cultures war against each other, the impact on their people can be massive. The redeeming work by teenagers must necessarily be limited to such things as supporting organisations such as the United Nations and the International Red Cross in their work.

At the micro level, there are also countless wrongs that the young hero or heroine can assist with righting. For example, they can challenge the cyber bully, report the cheat and counsel the person who is spreading vile lies.

Most teens have a heightened sense of justice. 'It's not fair!' has been uttered from the lips of more than one adolescent. However, although not short of an opinion on what is right and what is wrong, some can be short of motivation to do anything about it.

Villainy is not difficult to find. What is more difficult to find is the person who will step in and try to do something about it. Even for children, many opportunities exist to right a wrong. For example:

- A person being bullied can be supported.
- Someone distributing drugs can be reported.
- Graffiti activity can be stopped.
- Shoplifting can be discouraged.

As one reads the above, there is more than a touch of the 'goody two-shoes' about it all, and even a hint of the 'dobber'. However, this should not prevent these wrongs from being tackled. So, how do teenagers go about this?

If our children become aware of activity going on around them that is not legal, the burden of this knowledge can be significant. Children, as well as adults, have an obligation to report any illegal activity to the appropriate authorities, including the police. How to report such matters, when to report such matters, and to whom such matters should be reported all need to be properly understood.

If further advice on whether a matter should be reported is needed, there are people to talk to, such as the Kids Helpline 1800 55 1800 or Police Assistance Line 131 444.

If done properly and through the right channels, tackling an injustice can bring a right conclusion to a wrong situation. Despite the appeal of taking a gung-ho approach to fighting the evils of the world, our teen heroes and heroines may need to be reminded that despite some undoubted strengths, they do not have the powers of Wonder Woman or the strength of the Incredible Hulk. However, they are not without a capacity to deal with an injustice if they use the right resources and obtain the help of those trained to deal with such matters.

A CONVERSATION TO HAVE

'What if' conversations can be useful when exploring what a teen would do if confronted by various forms of villainy.

- 'With one school student in six reporting they are bullied, what would you do if you were bullied? What would you do if you saw someone else being bullied?'
- 'They reckon that ice is becoming an epidemic. What would you do if someone offered you ice? What would you do if you knew someone was dealing ice in your school?'
- 'There are some sleaze-balls who are not school students wanting to crash the schoolies celebrations to have sex with the girls. What would you do if you felt one of your girlfriends was being pressured into sex at a schoolies party?'

The 'what if' scenarios can be adjusted to make them even more age-appropriate. Customised sensitively, such discussions can remind our teens that although they may not have a natty cape and the ability to fly at supersonic speed, they do have the capacity to bring about justice. They must also understand that justice will not flourish if people turn a blind eye to the evil they see around them. We need to inoculate our children against this by heightening their sense of responsibility.

A STORY TO TELL

ROSIE BATTY (1962–)

The story of Rosie Batty, Australian of the Year in 2015, is worth sharing for many reasons, not least because it tells of a normal person who was prepared to confront villainy with a courage that made her a household name.

On 12 February 2014, Rosie's estranged partner, Greg Anderson, killed their son, Luke, by beating him to death near the cricket nets of Tyabb oval in country Victoria. The police were alerted to the assault and on arrival were compelled to shoot Anderson. Anderson died in hospital the next day.

Over the thirteen years prior to his death, Anderson had developed a history of domestic violence. At the time of his death, he had four warrants out for his arrest and eleven criminal charges against him. Despite this history, Anderson was not in jail and was free to enact further harm.

The murder of a son would have crushed anyone, and Rosie was devastated. However, she carried on, and with great determination used her tragedy to help tackle the scourge of domestic violence nationally. With the life of a woman lost almost every week to domestic violence in the country, Rosie's campaign gained much support. She became a fearless crusader for the better protection of women in abusive relationships.

When Rosie was announced as Australian of the Year in 2015, there was a standing ovation. She had alerted a nation to an evil to which it had blinded itself. Domestic violence had been happening for generations, but only with Rosie Batty's voice came a national initiative to do anything about it.[1]

The question prompted by Rosie's story is whether we have the courage to stand up against evil.

INSTITUTIONAL VILLAINY

When there is a pervasive evil in the land, real courage is required to tackle it. Institutional villainy still exists, even in the comfortable communities we live in. It's just that we don't see it – or, if we do, we have become so accustomed to it that we accept it. When one is part of an institution, it can be difficult to see the things that are wrong with that institution.

There are none so blind as those who will not see, and there are many who will not see because being blind works to their advantage. History gives many examples of reform being slowed because it was not profitable to alter the status quo. For example:

- To have seen the evil in slavery was to lose money.
- To have seen the evil in apartheid was to lose power.
- To have seen the evil in corruption was to lose money and power.

It has been suggested that in a nation that is blind, the one-eyed man can be king. A society that has become blind to an evil needs a Rosie Batty, someone who can stop people from stumbling sightless into further harm. We need our young people to be able to identify an evil and be prepared to do something about it. We need them to be prophets of their time, to interpret the signs and make a moral assessment of what is right.

> *Thus conscience does make cowards of us all;*
> *And thus the native hue of resolution*
> *Is sicklied o'er with the pale cast of thought*
> William Shakespeare (*Hamlet* – Act 3, Scene 1)

Abolition of the slave trade

Slavery has been in existence for thousands of years and remains prevalent in some parts of the world today. In the nineteenth century, slavery was common. Slavers would raid villages in Africa and forcibly take people to Central and North America where they would be sold to the owners of plantations to work on their farms.

One would have thought that at some point in the process – of going to a village to terrify and capture its people; of locking the survivors in chains; of burning, raping and killing; of separating children from parents, husbands from wives; of herding humans like animals into ships and cramming them into unimaginably foul, dark spaces; of taking them on a sea voyage during which as many as half would die; of beating and abusing them on a daily basis; of selling them like furniture to a master who would brand them and force them to work long, hard hours doing dull, repetitive work for no pay; of stripping them of rights, respect and hope – someone might have said it was wrong. But, no.

People would go to church on Sunday and buy slaves on Monday. Slavery had become generally accepted by western society because it offered enormous wealth to plantation owners, factory owners, ship owners and anyone connected with the industry.

How could a society that considered itself civilised have accepted slavery? The answer is complex, but the reasons are probably not so different as to why unacceptable practices still go on today.

These reasons include: greed, self-interest, moral blindness, ignorance and inertia.

Over a fifty-year period from 1680 onwards, two million slaves were transported from Africa to the West Indies and North America. The powerful pro-slavery lobby caused the British Government to resist banning slavery for a very long time.

It can be an uncomfortable moment when a community is required to recognise an evil within it. Stout opposition can be expected, as shown by the following examples of two anti-slavery campaigners.

TWO STORIES TO SHARE

WILLIAM WILBERFORCE (1759-1833)

At age twenty-one, William Wilberforce was elected to the British Parliament. Seven years later, in 1787, Wilberforce agreed to lead the parliamentary abolition movement after being invited to do so by the prime minister, William Pitt the Younger.

An anti-slavery presentation by Wilberforce to the Privy Council in 1788 was sabotaged by key witnesses changing their testimony at the last minute and supporting slavery. The following year, Wilberforce presented an Abolition Bill to Parliament but, despite a brilliant speech, opponents used delaying tactics to block the Bill for two years.

In 1791 the Abolition Bill was defeated when less than half the MPs stayed in the House to vote. In the following year another Abolition Bill was introduced and was passed by Parliament but only after it was made ineffectual by adding the key word 'gradual'. In other words, the Parliament only agreed to a gradual abolition of slavery. Slavery continued much as before.

Wilberforce reintroduced the Abolition Bill time and again throughout the 1790s without success. Support for the abolition of slavery actually dropped. However, Napoleon's support of slavery and Irish MPs' lack of support for slavery, eventually began to strengthen the call for its abolition.

The Abolition Bill failed in 1804 and 1805 but was passed on 23 February 1807, at which time Wilberforce was given three cheers and rousing applause in Parliament. Slave trading was now illegal on British ships, but slave ownership was still legal. So began the second half of the campaign, which was to free existing slaves.

There was strong government resistance to the emancipation of slaves. The situation was not improved when failing health forced Wilberforce to resign as an MP in 1825. He handed the campaign to emancipate slaves to Thomas Buxton.

The Emancipation Bill was finally passed on 26 July 1833. Three days later Wilberforce died.[2]

HARRIET TUBMAN (c.1822-1913)

Harriet Tubman was born a slave on a plantation in Maryland. In 1844 she was forced by her owner to marry another slave, John Tubman.

Five years later she decided to escape and find her way to the north of America, where slavery had been abolished.

Harriet escaped with her two brothers, but they were too fearful to go through with the plan and returned. Alone but using her natural wit, Harriet evaded capture and finally made it to the north where she could be free. After establishing herself in the north and getting a job, she covertly returned to the slave states in the south to help other slaves escape.

Harriet made no fewer than twenty trips back to the south and each time brought back with her a group of slaves seeking freedom in the north. Some 300 slaves were rescued by Harriet, earning her the title of 'The Moses of Her People'.[3]

The slavery issue was to split the American nation. The northern states were anti-slavery and the southern states were supporters of slavery. This caused the nation to war upon itself. The American Civil War lasted from 1861 to 1865 and was eventually won by the north. This resulted in the Emancipation Proclamation by President Abraham Lincoln in 1863 and the prohibition of slavery throughout America two years later.

A QUESTION TO ASK

A good question to ask our sons and daughters is whether they think an evil exists that society is doing too little about.

Examples might include:

- Poverty and wealth distribution.
- Domestic violence against women and children.
- Ownership of mineral wealth.
- Racism.
- Treatment of refugees.
- Global warming.

- Unhealthy food additives.
- Obesity.

STANDING UP TO BULLIES

Whether any of the topics above ignite the passion of our teens is not certain. What is certain is that most children will experience, witness or perpetrate some form of bullying. Here is a societal evil that can be tackled. It will take courage and it may take time, but it is within the reach of our sons and daughters to take a stand against bullying.

In advocating for children to make bullying one of their 'causes', it is not suggested that they should become 'caped crusaders' dashing around the place getting rid of bullies. Such heroics can make the situation worse. What is being advised is that they learn to use the available resources to ensure that bullying is minimised in their community.

Is the task of getting rid of bullying difficult? Yes. Getting rid of slavery wasn't easy either. But people did it!

What is bullying?

Bullying is the deliberate intention to harm someone who does not have the power to stop it. Bullying, harassment or any form of discrimination is immoral and interferes with the right of a person to feel safe and valued.

Bullying takes many forms. It can be:

- Face-to-face, such as fighting, pushing, taunting, insulting, embarrassing, intimidating and invading personal space; and be-hind-the-back such as writing threatening or offensive messages, sending distressing emails or writing anonymous hurtful notes.
- Individual, such as a person mocking or teasing someone; and collectively by such means as social exclusion or a hate-group recruitment.
- Physical; and psychological.

- Sexual harassment, which involves behaviours such as unwanted sexual touching, inappropriate joking, exposure, making sexual advances or demeaning someone due to their sexual orientation.
- Racial harassment, which involves behaviours such as social exclusion, teasing, taunts and threats based on another person's race.
- The causing of hurt by traditional methods such as punching, kicking and spreading hurtful rumours; and the causing of hurt by contemporary means such as cyber bullying, sexting, engaging in identity theft or by trashing someone on social-networking sites.

The key features of bullying are that it causes hurt and distress and is repeated and involves the use of power in an unfair way.

Bullying need not always be done by the older or stronger. 'Bullying up' is bullying done by the smaller, the younger and the weaker, who either use anonymous means to bully, such as cyber bullying, or overt means to bully, knowing that any retaliation would make the provoked person look like they were the bully.

For behaviour to be classified as bullying, it needs to involve repeated actions that are designed to cause hurt. Not having friends or being unpopular isn't necessarily a sign that someone is a victim of bullying. It may simply mean a person lacks interpersonal skills. There is a difference between bullying behaviour and what can be described as normal interpersonal conflict.

CYBER BULLYING

Cyber bullying occurs when hurt is caused via modern technologies such as the internet and other forms of social media, or through the use of smartphones and other mobile devices.

Modern technologies empower the individual, even the most unlikely of individuals, with an immense capacity to cause harm.

They are also an attractive means of bullying because they can, under certain conditions, be carried out with relative anonymity.

Cyber bullying can be particularly damaging because of the capacity it has to humiliate, hurt and harm a person in front of a huge 'audience'. It can also be done quickly and easily. On an impulse, a person can wreak emotional havoc on another and do so before the voice of reason hints at the inappropriateness of the action.

A further problem with cyber bullying is that the bully is often unaware of the extent of the harm they are causing because cyber bullying seldom occurs face to face. The feedback is muted by distance, so the perpetrator is protected from understanding of the awfulness of their behaviour.

Examples of cyber bullying include:

- Sending hateful or threatening comments or pictures via mobile phone or the internet and through social-networking sites such as Facebook.
- Using modern technologies to engage in the social exclusion of someone and in hate-group recruitment.
- Stealing someone's identity in order to harm them.
- Putting pressure on a person to send revealing or compromising pictures of themselves.
- Covertly filming, recording or taking a picture of someone and posting the images on the internet to cause hurt.
- 'Outing' and disseminating confidential information about someone.
- 'Flaming' and multi-messaging to clog up a person's electronic system to cause them distress.
- Using aliases and pseudonyms in chat rooms and on social-networking sites in order to harass and upset others.
- Engaging in cyber-stalking and the invasion of privacy.
- Referring to a school or workplace in a negative or disparaging way on the internet.

SEXTING

Sexting is another expression of cyber bullying.

Sexting is taking sexually explicit photos and making them available for others to see via a carriage service such as mobile phone or computer.

Sending explicit images of anyone, including yourself, is a crime if you are under the age of eighteen. If the person in the picture is under the age of sixteen, it can be a very serious crime.

HOW TO RESPOND IF BULLIED

If our sons and daughters are being bullied, it is important that they talk to an adult who is in a position to help. There can sometimes be reluctance to report bullying because it is embarrassing to admit you have become the play-thing of bullies. Furthermore, there can be a fear of being labelled a 'dobber'. Some victims of bullying may not want to report bullying because they feel it might only make matters worse. These fears are understandable but must not prevent our children from reporting bullying behaviour.

Other than telling a responsible adult about the bullying, our sons and daughters can obtain further help from:

- Kids Helpline: 1800 551 800; www.kidshelp.com.au
- Lifeline: 13 11 14; www.lifeline.org.au
- Bullying. No way!, www.bullyingnoway.gov.au

Victims of bullying can also benefit from thinking through why it is they have been targeted. This might result in action points such as the following:

- Reviewing behaviour and body language. If you look like a victim you can become a victim. Squared shoulders and a smile can do much to deter a bully.

- Identifying trouble spots. There are probably places that are high-risk areas for bullying. Avoid them.
- Developing your 'emotional quotient'. This includes the ability to read body language, to sense mood, to be intuitive and empathetic. Such skills not only make you less of a target, they can enable you to see where a situation may be heading. Early detection of possible bullying can provide options for avoiding it.

Sometimes bullies like to bully because it entertains or gives them a sense of power. If this is the case, then remedial action points might include the following:

- Try not to get angry or show that you're angry when bullied. If your anger is obvious, the bully has the satisfaction of knowing that they have controlled your emotions.
- Admit to imperfections. It can send positive messages about you having a realistic understanding of yourself.
- Use inoffensive humour. Bullying can be blunted by a good laugh. The capacity to laugh at yourself can create a bond with a group that might otherwise remain hostile.
- Surround yourself with good friends. Those with strong friendships are usually less of a target for bullies.
- Try not to retaliate because this can often inflame the situation.
- Remind yourself that it is the bully who has the problem, not you. Try to think through what inadequacies the bully might have that cause them to behave as they do.

HOW TO RESPOND IF WITNESSING BULLYING

If any of our sons and daughters witness bullying, encourage them to do the RITE thing:

R RECOGNISE that bullying is going on. Don't ignore it. If it's meant to be 'harmless fun', then people should be laughing. If they're not, it could be bullying. Is there a power imbalance? Is it being repeated? Is someone trying to cause hurt to another? If any of these are true, then recognise that it could be bullying.

I INFORM the bullies that you want them to stop. Do this in a polite but firm way. This is the time and place where the hero or heroine is unmasked. Why? Because telling a bully to stop can take a great deal of courage. There can also be unpleasant consequences. You can become a target of bullying. However you can also be revealed as a leader who has the courage to do something when everyone else is hiding in each other's shadows and accepting that which should be rejected.

T TALK to the victim and reassure them. Let them know they have an advocate, someone 'in their corner'. It is also important to TELL a responsible adult about the bullying. Those they inform must be able to help, or have the means to obtain help to stop the bullying.

E EVALUATE the situation. If it does not improve, try another tactic. Sometimes the bullying can be stopped by suggesting to the bully that serious trouble can result. At other times the best way to stop the bullying is to divert the bully to another activity that is harmless. If all else fails, get help from a responsible adult.

It's not easy for young people to deal with bullies, particularly if they happen to be their friends, or are in the same year group at school. This is where true grit is needed. This is where most people fail. This is where the true leader emerges.

THE IMPORTANCE OF A BROAD MIND

Many issues are not as clear-cut as bullying in terms of morality. For example, the Jewish occupation of Palestinian lands is a complex moral issue. Western military activity in Afghanistan is another example. Different people can have different opinions about the morality of such issues.

Another complicating issue is whether circumstances can ever explain or excuse evil. If the drug pusher was an addict, does this excuse them? If the bully was the product of an abusive upbringing, does this excuse them? If the thief needed money to buy food, does this excuse their behaviour?

A DEBATE TO HAVE

Because some of our young people see moral issues in black and white, it can be enriching to get them to explore issues where there are 'shades of grey'. For example, should the rich pay higher taxes than they do at present? Should the government help fund private schools? Should refugees be discouraged from settling in your country?

When talking to the father of one of my students some years ago, he said that he had been brought up in a family that required each child to lead a debate at dinner time about some aspect of the news. This habit probably explained why this family was part of a dynasty of strong and effective politicians.

A good way to explore shades of grey is to introduce our sons and daughters to Socratic debate. This involves them having to argue something from one point of view for a few minutes and then argue the same topic from the opposite point of view for an equal period of time. In ancient times, an issue would be debated by two people seated on two chairs in opposite corners of a room. One person would argue one point of view. The other person was required to argue the opposite point of view. Sometimes, the roles would then be reversed. The decision as to who would argue what position was decided by the toss of a coin.

You could undertake a similar exercise in the home. Get the family to argue a matter from one perspective, then from the opposite point of view. Such an exercise can reinforce the fact that there are more than fifty shades of grey!

A MIND EXPANDED BY POSSIBILITIES IS LESS LIKELY TO BE SHRUNK BY PREJUDICE.

Socratic debate was the precursor to modern debating. Many schools have active debating clubs. Although not everyone's cup of tea, why not encourage your sons and daughters to get involved with debating?

If no club exists, or if there is no inclination to join such a club, then let the dinner table become the Socratic debating chamber. Pluck a few topics from the newspaper or the TV news, and discuss them over the meat and three veg.

TRUTH AND CONSENSUS

It can take real leadership to determine what is true when the majority do not agree. Just because one opinion is held by a large number of people does not make it accurate. Accepted policy and opinion needs to be tested, but they need to be tested with integrity.

Albert Einstein (1879–1955) was one of the most brilliant physicists who ever lived. Being German but born of Jewish descent, Einstein had to flee Germany when Hitler came to power in 1933. Einstein wrote a number of papers that were to have a revolutionary impact on the world's understanding of physics. Of these, probably the most significant was his Theory of Relativity.

Hitler organised 100 Nazi professors to publish a book condemning Einstein's Theory of Relativity. When this was pointed out to Einstein, he remained optimistic, arguing that if he had been wrong, one professor would have been enough.[4]

What this story teaches us is that there is a difference between truth and consensus. It is important that our children recognise that people do not always combine to produce the right response. Just because most members of a gang think something is okay does not necessarily mean it *is* okay.

Some twentieth-century German Christians supported Hitler. Some twenty-first-century Muslims support terrorism. In the eighteenth century, half of America supported slavery. Two centuries earlier, large gatherings of learned people got together and affirmed that the world was flat.

DIFFICULT PEOPLE

Not all those we dislike are villains. Many of those we are tempted to condemn as the embodiment of evil may, on sober reflection, only be irritating. That said, difficult people exist, including the following:

- **The Narcissist**: Narcissism is self-love and it is a condition that has been identified as a growing problem in contemporary society. It produces individuals who have inflated opinions of their abilities and strong feelings of entitlement. Such people are often deeply sensitive to criticism and can be insensitive to others. They can exploit others for their own advantage and some have real difficulty submitting to the authority of others.

- **The Delicate Flower**: There are those who are infuriatingly pathetic, whose colds are always flu, whose headache is meningitis, whose wounded pride is a catastrophe. They find it hard to bounce back. They wallow in gloom and self-pity. They collapse unless they are fed with an hourly dose of praise. Their courage is not strong and they can be given to thinking they are the victims of unfairness.

- **The Indulged**: The indulged person can be quite similar to the Narcissist and the Delicate Flower. They still subscribe to the view that the universe must revolve around them and they can get very touchy should anyone dare suggest that they, like everyone else, must revolve around the sun. Such people do not readily submit to authority and can be petulant if they do not get their own way. For this reason they often do not make good team players.

- **The Show Pony**: Some people present very well. They look magnificent and carry an aura about them that is appealing, but thereafter they are a disappointment. They can make extravagant promises but fail to keep them. At other times they seek attention and then, having got it, fail to keep it. Some can be rather loud and dominate conversations with volume rather than with wisdom.

- **The Cynic**: There are people who are spectators in life, who like to watch and comment, but never get involved. Sometimes these people have been 'passed over' in favour of others and their bitterness is expressed in continual criticism.

- **The Bully**: A few people are wired in a way that requires them to control others. This control is manifested in many ways, including emotional manipulation and physical intimidation. Sometimes the bully is merely hiding their own insecurity. At other times they are reflecting a past in which they were subject to bullying. Bullies can be dangerous and vindictive.

- **The Manipulator**: There are some people who are very private and naturally not given to being up-front on issues. They keep their options open and generally work secretly to achieve their ends. Often they involve themselves in schemes that are shrouded in secrecy. Loyalty is generally not strong. They work in the twilight zone of what is moral and they organise things to their own advantage.

- **The Chaotic**: Some people are a disaster area in terms of organisation. They are late, they are missing things, they have forgotten things. Even their speech can be a jumbled mass of words the listener has to sort out. These people need organisational training, memos, lists, set procedures, clear protocols and routines.

- **The Martyr**: There are a few people who have a perpetual cloud of gloom over them. The glass is always half empty and never half full. For them, life is unfair. They suffer and do not mind other people knowing it. Care is needed when handling such people because some have legitimate reasons for being in this state.

- **The Cheeky**: This describes the cocky individual who teases and challenges authority. They use humour and fun as a way to test, probe and irritate. No action is particularly offensive but collectively their behaviour can undermine the standing and authority of others.

Of course, none of our children would be the embodiment of any of the above, but there might be a smidgeon of some of these qualities. Imperfection is to be found in all of us. For this reason, a leader needs to be able to handle those that get up their nose and they need to check that they are not causing the same problem for others.

HOW TO DEAL WITH DIFFICULT PEOPLE

Leaders have to deal with all sorts of people. Some will be a delight to associate with. Others will be a challenge. It is not always possible for the leader to avoid the latter. Therefore, a number of coping mechanisms have to be learned.

- *Be firm*

Sometimes the iron fist is needed but it should always reside in a velvet glove. Remain firm on those things that you should be firm on, but be prepared to negotiate on those things that you are happy to negotiate. Being firm does not mean being unreasonable, bullish and blinkered. It means you've arrived at a carefully thought-through position.

- *Don't rush in*

It's not only important to arrive at a clear opinion on things, it's important to say when you haven't. Don't be tempted to give an opinion on issues you need to think through further. It is far better to say, 'Thanks for your thoughts, I'll get back to you.' This will give you time to reflect on the issue free from the clamouring voices of lobbyists.

- *Avoid being sidetracked*

It is easy to be sidetracked. Some people like to take the heat off themselves by saying something like, 'You always pick on me . . . what about her? She was doing it too.' The sort of response required in these situations will vary but it might need to run along the lines of, 'I'm happy to deal with the fairness issue in a minute, but at the moment I'm talking about your treatment of the cat.'

- *Be forensic*

A leader needs to have the mind of a detective and should seek not only to notice what is happening but notice *why* it is happening. For example, poor behaviour may be the result of pure bloody-mindedness; on the other hand the behaviour may have its genesis in tiredness, inappropriate parenting, pressure from a gang, or a host of other reasons. It's important to try to understand the reasons behind the actions.

- *Use leverage*

A good way to get people to comply with you as a leader is to use leverage. This is not about blackmail or threats. It's about knowing what the person values and using that to get them to comply.

- *Check your prejudices*

We all have prejudices. It's important to know your prejudices and be able to take these into consideration when dealing with a matter. We are all prisoners of our past and need to be aware of the influence the past has on our judgement.

- *Be unconventional*

Sometimes it can be good to take a novel approach. For example, when someone is bracing themselves for a telling-off, it can be very effective to do the opposite: 'Listen, Jill, you have sporting skills I could only dream of and you should be the captain of our team. But it's not going to happen if you're continually late for training.'

- *Listen, then speak*

We have been given two ears and one mouth. Therefore, we need to listen twice as much as we speak. Sometimes it can be hard to listen. Anger can block our ears, and preoccupation with crafting a withering response can prevent us from listening to what is being said.

- *Avoid shaming*

Shaming people rarely works and is generally ineffective in bringing about change. 'You bloody idiot, you ought to be ashamed of yourself' – this sort of broadside seldom achieves much more than to increase anger levels.

- *Avoid stereotyping*

'You *always* do this.' 'You *never* think before acting.' Generalisations such as this are not helpful.

- *Tough love*

Tough love is sometimes necessary: 'Despite being your friend, if you do this again, I'm going straight to the boss.' It can be hard to say these sorts of things but it's sometimes necessary to do so.

- *Be honest*

Not many people wish to put a relationship at risk by saying something that needs to be said, but being a faithful friend can sometimes require that we do.

Having noted the above, it's worth remembering that there is a touch of imperfection to be found in all of us. We all collect a bit of muck in our lives.

A PHOTO TO TAKE

WE ARE WHAT WE FEED

A Native American chief was approached by one of his warriors who was troubled by the conflict going on in his life between wanting to do good things and wanting to do bad things.

The warrior explained it was like having two dogs in his head fighting each other for control. One was a bad dog that would snarl, steal and be vicious. The other was a good dog that was loyal, friendly and obedient.

The warrior asked his chief which of these two dogs would eventually win.

After some thought, the chief gave his answer. He said the dog that would win would be the dog the warrior fed.

If our sons and daughters spend time with that which is violent, degrading and wrong, they will feed the bad dog. If they spend time with those whose morality damages themselves and others, they will also be feeding the bad dog. On the other hand, if they feed their minds with enriching stories and their lives with experiences that inspire and strengthen, they will be feeding the good dog.

CHOOSING THE RIGHT FRIENDS

One of the best insurances against moral failure in our sons and daughters is to ensure they have the right friends. If our children associate with villains, they're more likely to become a villain. If they associate with good people, they're more likely to become a good person.

If lying down with dogs will give you fleas, a close association with those who are wise, creative and informed is likely to yield great benefit. More than one leader has received inspiration and support from good friends.

Those who are true friends will not only encourage during periods of adversity, they will keep a leader's feet grounded when things are going well. Many great leaders have survived only because they have chosen a wonderful life partner who rolls their eyes when others are clapping.

STANDING UP TO YOUR FRIENDS

Even with the best friends in the world, we can still be led astray. There will be times when friends can be wrong.

In one of the closing scenes of *Harry Potter and the Philosopher's Stone* by JK Rowling, there's a banquet at which the Hogwarts School of Witchcraft and Wizardry House Cup is awarded. The headmaster, Professor Dumbledore, awards a number of last-minute points, which causes Harry Potter's House, Gryffindor, to tie with their rival House, Slytherin. It is then that ten extra points are awarded by Dumbledore to Neville Longbottom. This wins the cup for Gryffindor. Dumbledore explains the extra points by saying that although it takes great courage to stand up to enemies, it takes even more courage to stand up to friends.

SURVIVING THE VILLAINS

There are some individuals who do not have an enemy in the world. Unfortunately, rather too many of us acquire if not actual enemies, then people who don't like us. This can happen for good reasons and bad.

When I see litter, I tend to pick it up, even in city streets. It drives my children mad! When leaving a public toilet, I try to make it a nicer place to enter than when I arrived. People do not seem to mind sitting next to me at a dinner table. Yet, despite these sparkling endorsements, when taking over the headship of a school, there were calls to have me sacked. At the end of my headship, there were calls to have me sacked. In the middle of my headship, there were calls to have me sacked. I've experienced anonymous letters to the School Council, leaked stories to the media, libellous identity theft, slanderous gossip and character assassination in the press.

All this goes to show that if you're in a position of leadership, you're probably going to make enemies. Therefore, survival skills are needed.

When we are hurt by enemies, it can be painful. However, if we are not careful, this is only the first generation of hurt. Thereafter comes the second generation: we can burn with anger and indignation, or we can fret, become withdrawn and generally messed up. Then comes the third generation of hurt: we don't sleep well, we don't eat well and we become very dull company. This results in a drying up of social engagements. Then the fourth generation of hurt arrives complete with its sedatives and anti-depressants.

Those who hurt us not only inflict pain once, they can inflict pain again and again. This makes early intervention and expert professional help essential. However, there are things we can do, chief of which is to control who it is that we allow to mess with our mind.

If unpleasant people are allowed to control our mood, we're not being clever. Don't empower enemies any more than can be helped. They have done enough damage through their initial meanness – don't let them do any more.

If anyone is going to be allowed to influence your mood, let it be good people, not bad people.

Easy.

Actually, it isn't easy – so be prepared to seek medical help if periods of discouragement become prolonged and low morale begins to morph into full-blown depression.

PERSONAL ATTACKS

Margaret Thatcher was the first woman to lead a major western democracy when she became Prime Minister of Great Britain in 1979. Her plan to recover the economic prosperity of Britain and halt the nation's slide towards socialism was brave but brutal. During her eleven years as prime minister, Thatcher took on the trade unions in a bitter showdown, privatised government industries and cut taxes for the wealthy.

Understandably, Thatcher made enemies. The British miners went on strike for a year and the Russians called her the 'Iron Lady'. In her dealings with her enemies, she remained tough and uncompromising, as the Argentines found out in 1982 when they tried to take control of the Falkland Islands.

Margaret Thatcher said she tolerated the personal attacks because it signalled her enemies did not have any good arguments left.[5]

One does not have to be prime minister to suffer attacks of a personal nature. Our children can also suffer such attacks. These can be intensely hurtful. However, it can be helpful to remember that those who engage in such attacks often do so in a wilfully unbalanced manner. When you know what you are like and those who matter in your life know what you are like, that should be sufficient assurance. There is no need to take on board the malevolent opinions of others.

FINALLY

While recognising that all people have rights, it needs to be recognised that all people also have responsibilities. Yes, we must love the sinner, but we must still be allowed to hate the sin.

There is a place for moral outrage. There is a place for heroes and heroines who are prepared to stand against those things that harm us.

SUMMARY

- Leaders need a villain to tackle and a cause to adopt.
- Teens usually have a heightened sense of justice but sometimes need motivation to take steps to get rid of injustice.
- Dealing with illegal or immoral activity needs to be done in accordance with the law and through the proper authorities.
- 'What if' conversations can be useful in getting our sons and daughters to consider what they would do in situations when bad things are happening.
- Institutional wrongdoing has existed in the past and exists in the present. This can provide causes for our teen leaders to tackle.
- Bullying is an ever-present problem and represents a contemporary evil that needs to be addressed.
- Care is needed when identifying wrongdoing. Moral issues are not always black and white. Learning the art of Socratic debate can improve an understanding of different opinions on moral issues.
- There is a difference between truth and consensus.
- Degrees of villainy exist. Some people can just be difficult to cope with.
- Choosing the right friends can help our sons and daughters do the right thing.
- There may be times when it is necessary to stand up to one's friends. This can be more difficult than standing up to one's enemies.
- Enemies can harm and this harm can reverberate a long time.
- There is a time for tolerance, but there is also a time for moral outrage.

A calling to hear

There have been times when many of us have stopped and wondered, *What is it that I have been put on this earth to do? What's the point of everything? Life seems to be an unending cycle of births and deaths — is there anything I should be doing in between?*

Whether it is the maudlin mood that follows a night of revelry, a coffin sliding through a curtain to be burned, or lying on your back looking at the stars, there are moments when we ask ourselves what life is all about.

It is a good thing for our sons and daughters to think about what's important in life. What legacy do they want to leave? What is their calling?

These are difficult questions for us to answer, let alone a child whose head is full of cottonwool and play. We need to be realistic. Youthfulness and a rapidly changing world prevent most teens knowing what their destiny is with any degree of certainty.

For many, any confessed goal will be little more than, 'eat, drink and be merry'. They want to cram as much fun as possible into their life. For others, their goal will be to fulfil their biological design by raising a family – all while balancing a corporate career, keeping in touch with 1000 Facebook friends and ensuring the private yacht is well stocked with rum and Coke.

These are not unreasonable goals – but they *are* goals. They are not a calling.

A CALLING

A motivation to do something for oneself is ambition. A motivation to do something for others is a calling.

Ambition is not a bad thing. But it's not a calling. A calling needs to be of general benefit to society.

The stated purpose of one of the schools I was privileged to lead was described as:

> *Providing an education that is not for the exclusive benefit of its students, but for the entire community.*

This is the essence of this chapter. What is it that our sons and daughters can do that benefits the wider community? What sort of service can they render? What are the causes, convictions and callings that are going to lift them from a preoccupation with self?

CAUSES, CONVICTIONS AND CALLINGS

The religious reformer Martin Luther (1483–1546) once stood before his critics and said, 'Here I stand, I can do no other.'

Where do we stand on the key issues of life? One of the criticisms of some youth today is that they do not know what they believe. Even more alarming is that many appear happy to stay in this state and progress through life without a cause, without a conviction and without a calling.

A **cause** is a project, political viewpoint, creed, charity, organisation or any initiative that encourages people to support it.

A **conviction** is an opinion, a persuasion that a particular initiative is worthy of support.

A **calling** is a beckoning, a compulsion to do something that is worthwhile.

Indifference and ignorance are probably the main reasons some people have difficulty identifying a cause, developing a conviction or hearing a call.

Indifference is born of a preoccupation with self. There are some whose concerns are limited to getting rather than giving. Ignorance is born of not knowing what is going on. There are some whose knowledge of the real world is irresponsibly limited.

These afflictions are by no means limited to the young. We all have to wrestle with selfishness. Because of this, the witness we offer our children in dealing with this beguiling problem is probably the best instruction we can give.

SOME IDEAS TO CONSIDER

ENGAGING WITH CURRENT AFFAIRS

For our sons and daughters to become aware of a cause, develop a conviction or hear a call, they need to be listening. They also need to be watching – and doing whatever is necessary to become informed.

A great way to do this is to get them to watch the news on the television and/or to read the newspaper. If having dinner interferes with the former and competition for the newspaper frustrates the latter, treating your teenager to an online subscription to a reputable newspaper is a great idea.

Having encouraged reading about, and engagement with, current affairs, it can also be useful to have a conversation about what's going on in the world. This is not going to happen if meals are taken in the solitude of bedrooms or eaten in silence around the TV. It is going to happen if there is intelligent and informed communion around a dining table devoid of electronic distraction.

Although they will deny it, our children will take their lead from parents. If we chat about the rights and wrongs of what is going on in the world, if we have the photo of a sponsored child on the fridge, if we ask our children to cook sausages at a fundraising function, they are more likely to adopt a cause, develop a conviction and hear a call.

That said, it is important that the causes adopted are theirs and not ours. We need to stimulate. They need to choose. They need to be motivated by a cause that is their own. They need to be encouraged to think through what it is that:

MAKES THEM TICK
MAKES THEM SICK

Then they need to do something about it.

IF YOU CARE ABOUT NO-ONE, NO-ONE WILL CARE ABOUT YOU.

EMPATHY AND COMPASSION

Some people are unable to hear a call of distress. They move about their daily business so distracted by issues relating to themselves that they are unable to accommodate issues relating to others.

Some do hear the call of distress, but do nothing because they lack empathy and compassion.

Choosing to help requires a conscious choice. It is a choice some people are not prepared to make. They prefer to live in their small corner while others, and their problems, are required to live in their small corner. Indifference, a callous disregard for any who are not friends or family, emotional exhaustion, fear of involvement, busyness, low emotional quotient, fatalism . . . there are many reasons we do not help.

GOOD AND BAD SILENCE

It is necessary for our sons and daughters to know the difference between good and bad silence. This is because silence is not always 'golden'. It can be yellow – the yellow of cowardice.

There is a time to speak, particularly when our voice can bring justice and take away pain. Our silence can encourage the bully to taunt again, the thief to steal again, the drug addict to use again. We need to know that those who remain silent allow these people's actions to become a habit, their habit a character and their character their ruin.

This is a tragedy when, by breaking the silence, the bully can be treated, the thief can be reformed and the drug user counselled.

There is a time to get involved. There is a time to care. There is a time to speak up.[1] We should be encouraging our children to make a difference and to leave the world a better place.

A PHOTO TO TAKE

There are three types of people in this world:
Those who drop litter.
Those who neither drop litter nor pick it up.
Those who pick up litter.
What sort of person are you?

THE IMPORTANCE OF TAKING NOTICE

Not noticing the small things can become a habit that prevents us from noticing the big things. Even less forgivable is when people point something out to us, something that could improve a situation or save a life, and we still do nothing about it. This can have disastrous consequences.

A STORY TO SHARE

Admiral Sir Cloudesley Shovell should have listened to the warning given by the young seaman. Instead of listening, he decided to hang him. It was expressly forbidden for a seaman to engage in the secret calculation of a ship's position. This explained why the seaman's body was now swinging lazily at the yardarm. There was nothing like a hanging to get the men to behave.

It was unfortunate that not many could actually see the body due to the troublesome fog. Returning from fighting in the Mediterranean against the French forces, Sir Cloudesley Shovell was comforted that his officers had placed his fleet of five ships safely west of Ile d' Ouessant, whereas this impudent sailor had spoken up and warned they were in danger of being wrecked on the rocks of the Isles of Scilly off Great Britain.

It was 22 October 1707 when the Admiral's thoughts were interrupted by a terrifying jolt and the splintering of timbers as his flagship, *Association*, struck the rocks off the Isles of Scilly. Four of the Admiral's ships were wrecked and 2000 men perished. Sir Cloudesley Shovell was one of only two survivors to be washed up on the shore. Unfortunately for the Admiral, his miraculous escape did not last long, because he was murdered by a woman who fancied the splendid ring on his finger.

This shipwreck motivated the passage of the *Longitude Act* of 1714 through the British Parliament. The sumptuous prize of £20 000 was to be given to anyone who could devise a 'practicable and useful' means to determine longitude, an essential measurement to fixing a ship's position at sea. The motivation of this prizemoney was to compel an English clockmaker by the name of John Harrison to devote his working life to designing an accurate timepiece that solved this problem.[2]

Sometimes, it takes a tragedy to get people to listen.

Some of our sons and daughters feel they might buy into unwanted trouble if they dare to speak up about a situation they believe is dangerous, wrong or inappropriate.

At other times, it is not fear that causes inaction. It is a learned helplessness — a sense that they have neither the power nor the influence to change the situation for the better.

A further problem can be apathy and ignorance. Many are simply not inspired to do anything to improve the world. Many are not aware of causes desperate for support. Many have not developed a political understanding of what is necessary for reform.

POLITICAL CONVICTIONS

A knowledge of politics provides a source of power, a way to advance a personal cause, calling or conviction.

Quite apart from this, if we want our sons and daughters to vote in an educated and intelligent manner, they need to be informed. We get the politicians we deserve. If we fall for the political hype, if we vote out of ignorance, and if we are stupid in our decision making, we reduce our mandate to complain about our elected representatives.

In their teen years, our sons and daughters should begin the process of developing political convictions. Their early years will probably see an adoption of the political views of their parents. However, somewhere along the journey of growing up, they need to develop their own opinions. To do this responsibly, they need to understand a few concepts related to politics.

Democracy

- Power is shared equally among all people.
- Generally associated with majority rule.
- Government is exercised directly by the people or by elected representatives.
- Tends to celebrate individual rights and 'natural law' (that which is morally fair and right).

Autocracy

- Power is given to one supreme leader.
- Often linked to very powerful people who are able to control others.
- Sometimes associated with dictatorship – absolute rule by one person.
- Often linked to the principle of a God-given right.

Neither system is without the capacity to be corrupted. As one unknown wit noted: 'It's not the voting that's democracy, it's the counting.'

Socialism

- Left-wing political orientation.
- Sometimes linked to communism, which seeks a classless society in which everyone is equal.
- Promotes control of production by an elected government that runs it for the benefit of everyone on an equal-share basis.
- Tends to be strong on social-welfare issues.
- Often associated with collectivism and totalitarianism.

Capitalism

- Right-wing political orientation.
- Economy is driven by a profit motive and characterised by private ownership rather than government ownership.
- Usually related to free enterprise – i.e. if you work hard you earn more; if you are successful you earn more.
- Rewards individual effort.
- Often linked with individualism and the protection of individual rights.
- Also linked with liberalism and a free-market economy in which the strong thrive and the weak do not.

Some political and religious terms are often misunderstood by teenagers. For example, two frequently misunderstood terms are anarchism and pacifism.

Anarchism

- Wants governments abolished, because governments are seen as organisations dominated by the powerful and privileged.
- Prefers society to be run by people cooperating with each other in a voluntary fashion.
- Places great faith in human nature being naturally good.
- Has developed a reputation for violence because some anarchists use terror to try to promote their views.

Pacifism

- A belief that no matter what the situation, war is inappropriate.
- Pacifists value each individual and respect human life.

Anarchism is not the opposite of pacifism. The opposite of pacifism is war-mongering. The opposite of anarchism is centralised government.

Examples of other frequently misunderstood political terms include fundamentalism and liberalism.

Fundamentalism

- Wants a return to foundational beliefs.
- Does not want beliefs compromised by liberal influences.
- Often associated with an extreme or uncompromising position.
- Sometimes seen as traditional and adhering to strict rules that others might see as out of date.

Liberalism

- Emphasis on individual freedom.
- Sometimes seen as more human-centred than God–centred.

- Stresses individual rights and free thinking, and supports an absence of rules and regulations.

AN EXERCISE TO COMPLETE

A way to encourage our sons and daughters to reflect on their political standpoint is to invite them to evaluate where they stand against a number of political criteria. Here is an exercise that can help this process.

MY POLITICAL ORIENTATION

Place an 'X' on the line where you estimate your political opinion to be:

Left-wing	Right-wing
I generally like change.	I generally like the status quo.
I am attracted to democracy.	I am attracted to rule by the strongest.
I am attracted to a classless society and equal wealth.	I am attracted to free enterprise and reward for effort.
I am attracted to production and services being run by the government.	I am attracted to production and services being run by private enterprise.
I am attracted to socialism.	I am attracted to capitalism.
I support the idea of government providing the help.	I support the idea of self-help.
I believe there should be more individual freedom.	I believe there should be some limitations on individual freedom.
I believe many traditions and customs are outdated.	I enjoy traditions and maintaining past customs.

If the crosses tend to be more towards the left-hand side, this indicates a political view that is more socialist, democratic and left-wing.

If the crosses tend to be more towards the right-hand side, this indicates a political view that is more conservative, capitalistic and right-wing.

POLITICAL VIEWS CAN CHANGE

It is important to note that political views may change over time. Benito Mussolini (1883–1945) is generally known as a right-wing Italian fascist and an aggressive and authoritarian dictator of Italy. What is less well known is that Mussolini was born the son of a socialist blacksmith, and as a young man described himself as a socialist. Mussolini's views changed during World War I, which saw an upsurge in Italian nationalism. This led Mussolini to change from left-wing thinking to right-wing thinking.[3]

In a similar manner, a teenager's political convictions will probably change over time (but hopefully not with such disastrous consequences). This is not just the product of becoming better informed. Change can result from a political party selecting a different raft of policies.

A STORY TO SHARE

AUNG SAN SUU KYI (1945–)

BURMESE POLITICAL ACTIVIST

One of the best contemporary examples of a woman with a true calling is the democracy campaigner Aung San Suu Kyi, who has, for several decades, sought greater political freedom for her people in Myanmar.

The country of Myanmar was once called Burma. It is a nation of over 45 million people that, since the turn of the century, has been ruled by a military dictatorship.

The daughter of General Aung San, a national hero in the battle for Burma's independence, San Suu Kyi studied politics at Delhi University. Between 1964 and 1967, she studied for a Bachelor of Arts in Philosophy, Economics and Politics at Oxford University. Thereafter, San Suu Kyi worked at the United Nations Secretariat before marrying a British academic, Dr Michael Aris, in 1972. The couple had two sons. Alexander was born in 1973 and Kim was born in 1977.

San Suu Kyi took the painful decision to move away from her husband and children in order to involve herself in the advancement of the pro-democracy movement in Myanmar. She was caught up in the popular uprising of 8 August 1988, but this uprising was suppressed by the ruling party and its military backers.

San Suu Kyi called for democratic government and formed the National League for Democracy (NLD). On 18 September 1988, the Burmese military seized power and placed San Suu Kyi under house arrest. Despite her detention, in 1990 the NLD won 82 per cent of the seats in a landslide victory, but the military refused to recognise the results.

In 1991, San Suu Kyi won the Nobel Peace Prize. Continually threatened and harassed, she was not released from house arrest until 1995. Midway through her house arrest, San Suu Kyi was offered freedom if she promised to leave both politics and Myanmar. She refused.

Many frustrating years followed. Despite being the people's choice as leader, this privilege was frustrated by the military.

It was not until 2015 that the people's choice was recognised. This gave the NLD the mandate it needed to control government. Subsequently, power-sharing talks have taken place with the military. Controlling parliament was one thing. Controlling the country was another.

Although Aung San Suu Kyi is now virtually free, her political activities are carefully monitored. Therefore the world still watches and wonders at the eventual outcome of her work as a political leader.[4]

GOAL SETTING

Setting goals can be a useful exercise because it gives momentum to a calling. As the old saying reminds us: *We don't plan to fail, we just fail to plan.*

Although goals relating to political reform may be off the agenda for most of our sons and daughters, it doesn't mean other goals can't be decided. For example, it would be difficult to argue that there was not some benefit to thinking through what they want to achieve in life.

Goal setting can be useful in realising both ambition and a calling. Whether it be for oneself (an ambition) or for others (a calling), the process of working out your goals starts by asking what it is you want to achieve. If our children need this to be clarified a little more, get them to think through what they want to achieve for themselves:

- Academically (school grades, exam results, etc.)
- Physically (health, fitness, etc.)
- Socially (friendships, relationships, etc.)
- Spiritually (morals, faith, etc.)

After this, ask them to consider what they want to achieve for the benefit of others. World peace and the eradication of all cancers are both admirable, but it might be helpful to set smaller goals to start with. These can be seen as steps to the big goals. In other words, encourage the setting of goals that are:

A **Achievable:** Be realistic. Eradicating cancer may be beyond them, but raising money for cancer research is not.
B **Believable:** Encourage them to set goals that stretch them but are not unrealistic. Raise $10 000 rather than $1 million.
C **Conceivable:** Remaining positive and optimistic is important. Think through what can to be done to achieve the goal. For example, the money for cancer research could be raised by making it a whole-school project or by organising a charity run.
D **Desirable:** Goals are hard enough to realise without being hampered by indifference. Make sure there is ownership of the goal, rather than inheriting the cause from others. Is it cancer research they want to support, or is it the issue of child soldiers, refugees in detention centres, the destruction of the Great Barrier Reef, or something else?

Thereafter, it is time to build a GATE.

This involves:

- Thinking through ways and means the goal will be achieved.
- Timetabling activities that will help meet the goals.
- Monitoring progress.

A PHOTO TO TAKE

STEPS TO SETTING A GOAL

G – Set a realistic goal.

A – Think of Activities that will help meet the goal.

T – Timetable those activities.

E – Evaluate how well you are going in meeting the goal.

BUILD A GATE

Goals may be set each day, each week, each term, each year or for a lifetime.

Some goals can be very big, but they should not be dismissed as impractical. The journey of a thousand miles begins with a single step. The writing of a book begins with a single word, and the ability to run like the wind begins with the first training session.

A TASK TO PERFORM

Have your children draw up their goals for the year. This can be done on a laptop, printed off and stuck on the mirror, or they can be punched into a mobile phone. These goals can be academic, social, physical and moral/spiritual.

However, setting goals is just the first step. What is a touch more challenging is taking the second step of working out what needs to be done to reach those goals.

Even more painful is timetabling those activities into the week. This is getting the rubber to hit the proverbial road.

Then – just so you know you are on track – what are the 'check marks' that will be used to see if you are succeeding?

Goals. Activities. Timetable. Evaluation. GATE.

Finally, make a few trusted friends or family aware of your GATE and get them to keep you on track with occasional enquiries as to how it is all going.

ACHIEVABLE STEPS

Some goals can be more than a touch daunting. However, 'hairy audacious goals' (HAGs) can be realised.

One of the most effective ways of coping with an ambitious goal is to break it into achievable steps. For the alcoholic to stay sober, they must avoid alcohol one day at a time. A patient suffering brain damage may have to endure months of rehabilitation. The goal to walk or talk again can be remote and far too difficult, but there are many tales of those who have recovered remarkably well by taking one small step at a time.

Optimism is a big factor, together with the right mental state that refuses to give in. The first weeks of rehabilitation might be to try to move a finger, or make a sound. In later weeks it might be to move a limb or say a word. Later still, the goal might be to walk, talk, run and sing.

As it has been said: *The way to eat an elephant is one mouthful at a time.*

Success will not be granted to everyone. Even the most optimistic can be injured by the cruel hand of fate. Yet it is important to give a dream a go and test whether it might be realised.

A STORY TO SHARE

ROALD AMUNDSEN (1872–1928)

An example of someone who understood the importance of breaking a big goal into a number of achievable steps was the Norwegian explorer Roald Amundsen. He would never have been the first person to reach the South Pole if he had not broken the expedition into stages.

The race to be the first to reach the South Pole was a close-run thing. Amundsen got to the South Pole on 16 December 1911, a month ahead of the British party led by Captain Robert Scott.

One of the reasons Amundsen succeeded was his meticulous planning. In 1910, Amundsen sailed in the *Fram* from Europe, and in January 1911 he set up a base at the Bay of Whales in the Ross Sea. Amundsen then set up food and supply depots along his proposed route at latitudes 80°, 81° and 82° south. These depots were better positioned and better spaced than those of Scott, whose party was to perish on their return journey just a few kilometres short of one of their supply depots.[5]

GOAL SETTING IS GOOD, BUT GOAL GETTING IS BETTER.

STEPPING OUT

Careful planning is good, but not if it needlessly delays commitment.

An abundance of care can disguise an absence of courage.

Stepping out is not always easy. Some can become paralysed by the thought of action, or so mesmerised by the options that they fail to take any. But we must remember that in the end, a person must do something if they want to achieve something.

THINGS CAN STILL GO WRONG

Setting goals does not guarantee achieving goals. Worthwhile goals can be frustrated by circumstances over which a leader has no control.

TWO STORIES TO SHARE

DAWN FRASER (1937–)

Dawn Fraser is one of the greatest swimmers of all time. Born in Sydney and one of eight children, Fraser's elder brother Don taught her to swim. When Don died of cancer at the age of twenty-one, Fraser did not give up. Harry Gallagher began to train her and Fraser went on to win eight Olympic medals and set thirty-nine world records in swimming.

At the Rome Olympics in 1960, Fraser won the 100 metres in her third consecutive Olympics. It might have been four consecutive Olympic wins had not the Australian Swimming Union banned Fraser for ten years after she was caught skylarking and trying to souvenir a Japanese flag from the grounds of the Japanese Imperial Palace. It defies belief that the Australian Swimming Union would have taken this decision and frustrated the life goals of its greatest athlete. But these things happen.

In an encouraging twist of fortune, Fraser's popularity and fame were only increased by the ban. She was awarded an MBE in 1967, voted Australia's greatest female Olympian in 1988 and named an Officer of the Order of Australia (AO) in 1998. Despite frustrated goals, Fraser has continued to serve her sport and her country. One of her main interests is working as an ambassador for the disabled.[6]

Someone else who failed, but failed gloriously, was Simón Bolívar. Unlike Fraser, whose goals could probably be described more as an ambition, Bolívar had a very clear calling.

SIMÓN BOLÍVAR (1783-1830)

Actually, his name was more impressive than Simón Bolívar - it was Simón José Antonio de la Santísima Trinidad Bolívar y Palacios. A great swordsman and horseman, Simón Bolívar felt called to help free South America from the oppressive rule of Spain.

His early years - a wild life of indulgence in Europe and a few years in the Venezuelan militia in South America - did not suggest that Bolívar was going to achieve much. However, the death of his wife, María Teresa del Toro, changed things.

It is strange how tragedy can cause a person to alter their priorities and shift from self-indulgent living to developing an interest in more worthy causes. Simón Bolívar's cause became the freeing of Venezuela from suffocating control by Spain.

In 1811, Bolívar, together with General Francisco Miranda, raised a rebellion and took control of Caracas in Venezuela. The Spanish responded by taking Bolívar and Miranda captive and regaining control of Caracas. Miranda died in prison but Bolívar escaped to the island of Curaçao, where he managed to stay alive by begging for food.

Bolívar then escaped to Colombia, where he raised an army of a few hundred individuals. However, this army was big enough to remove the Spanish from Tenerife, Mompós and four other towns. In 1813, Bolivar went on a ninety-day march during which he won six major battles. Again he advanced on Caracas. This time, the city surrendered without a fight.

During Bolívar's triumphal entry into Caracas, twelve maidens in white pulled his chariot through the streets. Flowers were scattered before him and he was proclaimed 'Liberator'. It was a title that upset the Spanish. Fresh troops were sent from Spain and fourteen years of incessant warfare followed.

There were defeats. There were victories. The most significant achievement by Bolívar's forces was to march across the continent from Ciudad Bolívar on the Orinoco River to the Andes mountains - and then climb these mountains. The toll was great on the exhausted army: 3000 started the march, but only 1200 survived it. After three days' rest, this rag-tag group then defeated a veteran Spanish army and by so doing broke the Spanish stranglehold on South America.

Whole countries were liberated. With the Spanish surrender at Callao, Peru, the last Spanish flag was hauled down from a South American flagpole. After 500 battles, Venezuela, Bolivia, Peru, Ecuador and Colombia were liberated. Bolívar had freed a significant part of a continent.

Bolívar's vision did not stop at liberation. He set up governments. He established constitutions. He set up guidelines for his newly liberated countries.

Unfortunately, the liberated countries then rejected Bolívar's models of government and dictatorships emerged. Discouraged and exhausted, Bolívar left his beloved South America.

While on a voyage to Jamaica, Bolivar's health deteriorated. He was taken from his ship to the Colombian shore to live out his last few hours. Bolivar died on 17 December 1830.

Twelve years later, Bolívar's body was brought back to Caracas. A naval fleet carried his remains in great solemnity. It was a fitting tribute to a man whose calling was to free a continent.[7]

A VISION

Some people develop a calling because they develop a vision.

Visions are usually things seen in the mind. A vision can be a person's dream, design and desire; it can be the image of a longed-for objective, a completed goal, a changed situation.

Other visions are fuelled by supernatural sources. These have variously been linked to God, the Devil and a range of other forces, including the suspect fish eaten for dinner.

For whatever reason, some people have felt themselves guided by a vision to do something.

Joan of Arc lived in the village of Domrémy in Lorraine, France. From 1424 onwards she saw visions and felt herself called to rescue France from the English and help the Dauphin become the crowned King of France.[8]

Constantine (c. AD280–337) was won over to Christianity by two visions he had when preparing to battle his rival, Maxentius, for absolute control of the Roman Empire. The first vision was a fiery cross in the sky under which were the words:

In hoc signo vinces
(In this sign you will conquer)

The second vision came as Constantine prepared to attack Rome. He was told to have the Christian monogram painted onto the shields of his men:

Iesus, hominum salvator
(Jesus, the saviour)

When Rome fell to Constantine's troops, it resulted in the first Christian to sit on the throne of the Roman Empire.[9]

It would not be fair to expect our sons and daughters to develop a vision along the lines of those of Joan of Arc or Constantine, but they are able to develop a vision for their future. A good way to advance this vision is to give guidance on how to select a career.

Most careers do not fall into people's laps. They are obtained because the person takes command and control of the variables influencing career acquisition. This requires initiative. It also requires the ability to work towards a deferred reward.

Chosen careers and leadership positions need to be planned for. Significant goals of this nature are only achieved after a great deal of preparative activity. Chief among these activities is careful thought.

Our children are likely to have many careers, several of which do not even exist at the moment. However, thinking about future careers can still be a worthwhile exercise.

AN EXERCISE TO COMPLETE

Employability is influenced by many things specific to a job. For example, an airline pilot needs good eyesight, a capacity to master a great amount of technical material, excellent hand-eye coordination and advanced leadership skills.

Expecting our sons and daughters to develop competencies that are specific to a career is not always wise. Teens are likely to change their minds several times in relation to a career, and a great number of future career openings remain unknown at present.

Therefore, it might be better to encourage our sons and daughters to consider the more general qualities future employers might be looking for. For example, they could be invited to rate themselves on a scale of 1 to 10 (with 10 being the highest score) on the following sorts of employment qualities.

AN EVALUATION OF MY EMPLOYMENT QUALITIES

Honesty and integrity	/10
Work ethic	/10
Creativity	/10
Reliability	/10
Problem-solving skills	/10
Good teamwork	/10
Intelligence	/10
Initiative	/10
Teachability	/10
Resilience	/10

Having undertaken this exercise, a general question can be asked as to what they might do to improve their employability.

YOUNG LEADERS

Some might be tempted to think that encouraging the young to think about a career is difficult enough without going further and getting them to think about a calling. Not so. There are countless examples of young people who have made a significant impact on society because they have developed a calling. For example:

Drisana Levitzke-Gray – Young Australian of the Year in 2015, who has become a powerful advocate for the Deaf. Being born to parents who were both deaf, and being deaf herself, Drisana taught herself Auslan – the sign language used in Australia, which has enabled her to contribute richly to society.

Jacqueline Freney, OAM – Young Australian of the Year in 2014, who is Australia's most successful Paralympian in a single Olympics. She won eight swimming gold medals in the London Paralympics in 2012. Jacqueline is now a powerful advocate for those with a disability. She has shown the world that a person with cerebral palsy need not be prevented from becoming a world champion.

Akram Azimi – Young Australian of the Year in 2013, who came to Australia as a refugee from Afghanistan when he was a small child. Being a refugee, Akram was often harassed and bullied, but he did not let this treatment defeat him. He became head boy of his school and its top student. Thereafter, Akram wanted to contribute to his adopted country and established mentoring programs for Indigenous Australians living in remote communities.

Marita Cheng – Young Australian of the Year in 2012, who founded Robogals Global, an international organisation designed to get girls interested in robotics and engineering.[10] This initiative was in response to concerns Marita had about the disengagement of many girls from this area. She showed the world that through proper teaching, women can achieve in domains traditionally dominated by men.

One does not have to go to the Honour Roll of Australian of the Year to find all the examples of young people advancing a cause. Great examples can be found in nearby schools and those involved in local charity work. Regional newspapers tend to report selfless service rather more frequently than national news outlets. Therefore, local news can sometimes be worth scanning before consigning it to landfill.

FINALLY

Our sons and daughters need a calling. Furthermore, they need a calling that takes them away from a preoccupation with self. It need not necessarily be the sort of calling that sees them rescuing the planet. It can be nursing the cat back to health, rescuing a grandparent's garden, contributing to National Clean Up Australia Day, giving blood or some other relatively simple task.

Developing a calling, an other-person centredness, not only increases leadership credentials, it increases the wellbeing of society.

SUMMARY

- Our children need to know their purpose in life. They need to find out what they have been put on earth to achieve both for themselves and for others.
- When one plans to advantage oneself, it is an ambition. When one plans to advantage others, it is a calling.
- A cause, conviction and calling needs to be developed that takes us away from a preoccupation with self.
- Indifference and ignorance can hinder the hearing of a call.
- A knowledge of, and engagement with world affairs should be encouraged.
- It is important for our sons and daughters to work out where they stand politically and what their convictions are about local, national and international policies.

- Establishing clear goals can help fulfil a call and achieve an ambition.
- The achievement of a large goal can be helped by breaking it down into a number of smaller goals.
- Goal setting is good but goal getting is better. Plans need to be translated into action.
- Having goals does not necessarily guarantee achieving goals.
- Developing a vision for the future can be helped by thinking about one's career options and future employability.
- Not everything that happens in our lives can be planned for.
- Teenagers have the capacity to develop a calling.

LESSON SIX

A skill to have

'Look what I can do, Pappa,' said my three-year-old grandson the other day. He was dressed in his Spiderman outfit, something he's grown quite attached to – even wearing it to a viewing of the film *Frozen* with his elder sister. He was blissfully unconcerned that he was the only Spiderman amid a sea of Elsas and Annas.

'What can you do, Will?' I asked.

He raised a clenched hand clad in a red-and-blue exo-skeleton fist with a Spiderman motif on it, from which he can fire thingummies. 'I can shoot you,' he giggled. And he did.

The projectile was soft enough for me to survive the experience, so I chased him as he fired another missile. Some time later, I found other things had been targeted. The Christmas tree. The toilet. The coffee machine.

LEADERS NEED WEAPONS

Any decent hero and self-respecting heroine needs a skill, a weapon, a power that can turn the tide against a sea of villainy. This chapter is all about finding that skill and learning how to use it.

Not everyone is comfortable about the idea of having a weapon. This is not surprising. Weapons have done more damage than good to society. However, the weapon suggested in this chapter is akin to a skill, a force that can be used for good.

Variety of weapons

If anyone needs an illustration of different weapons, they only have to pick up a comic book, or watch a TV series based on a comic-book character.

I was probably not the first man to fall in love with Wonder Woman – or, more particularly, Lynda Carter, who played Wonder Woman in the 1970s TV series. Wonder Woman's skills included an ability to throw a lasso. However, this was no ordinary lasso. It was a lasso of truth that compelled baddies to spill the beans. This skill, together with her indestructible bracelets and weaponised tiara, meant that goodness prevailed wherever Wonder Woman went.[1]

A FACT TO KNOW

Wonder Woman was the invention of a PhD student from Harvard University, Dr William Moulton Marston. Marston was a psychologist who not only invented characters for DC Comics, he also invented the lie detector, or polygraph. In a manner not dissimilar to the 'lasso of truth', the polygraph is an apparatus that measures systolic blood pressure and is able to tell if anyone tells a fib.[2]

The lasso of truth illustrates that not every weapon needs a keen edge, immense force or humongous firepower. An ability to know the truth can be a very powerful weapon – and all the more so in a society where truth can be difficult to discern.

EVERYONE HAS POWER

As evidenced above, my pre-pubescent days saw me reading comics. One of the things I remember about the comics was the adverts on the back asking me to send USDs (whatever that meant) to a zip code (whatever that meant) in return for which they promised to teach me how to build up my muscles, throw my voice and learn ju-jitsu so no-one would kick sand in my face.

What was suggested on the back of these comics was that I already had the latent ability to do these things – all I needed was to develop the skills and learn how to use them. It is much the same with leadership skills. We already have them, but we need to develop and learn how to use them.

Lest it be thought that the weapons we need should be characterised by muscles, thrown voices and ju-jitsu skills, let me take you back to Wonder Woman. Her mother was Hippolyta, who used ageless beauty as her major weapon.

What this goes to show is that without a gun in sight, a person can still have a weapon and wield power. With the mere flutter of an eyelash, an attractive girl can reduce a strong man to putty. When having to operate without anaesthetic on a wounded soldier in the Middle Ages, the patient could either be held down by six men, or one woman.

Even those without the beauty of Hippolyta have great power. We have the power to grant life. On seeing an insect, we can squash it or let it live. We can also plant seeds, breed mice and feed the cat. We also have the power to control others. By merely raising a middle finger, we can cause someone to have an ordinary moment. Even the young can wield enormous power. Not for nothing do many companies rely on 'pester power' to sell their products. A tantrum or a scowl from a child can reduce an adult to a pleasingly obedient state.

Bullies have long learned that they have power. With a few hurtful words they can cause the most amazing reaction including tears, sleepless nights and depression. This is power. Some people get 'high' on this sort of behaviour, which is why one of the best ways to deal with bullies is to ignore them.

The question is not whether we have power. The question is how we use our power. Is it used for good or for evil? Are our weapons used for self-advancement or for the advancement of others?

Consider the unpopular person, the one on the fringes of the group, the person who lacks the social skills to fit in. The opportunity to impact positively on such a person is enormous. A warm word of greeting, a kind comment, an effort to include them can, quite literally, change their life.

Let no-one say that they have no power when there are those around them whose lives can be changed by just a few words of encouragement.

Everyone is a weapon of mass destruction and a weapon of mass creation. Even the gentlest person has a weapon they can use to advance a cause.

A STORY TO SHARE

SADAKO SASAKI (1943-1955)

Sadako Sasaki was born in Japan during World War II. When Sadako was two, the war concluded after America detonated two atomic bombs. One bomb was dropped on Nagasaki and the other bomb exploded over Hiroshima. Although escaping the initial effects of the Hiroshima atomic bomb, Sadako did not escape the secondary effects. At the age of eleven, Sadako was practising for an athletics race but became dizzy and collapsed. She was diagnosed with leukaemia, a cancer caused by the radioactive black rain that had fallen on her shortly after the atomic blast nine years previously.

Sadako was frightened by her sickness, but was encouraged by a friend who reminded her of a Japanese legend that said if anyone made a thousand paper models of a bird called a crane, they would be granted a wish.

Sadako wished to be well, so, using the ancient art of origami (paper folding), she began to make the cranes. After some time it became clear to Sadako that she would die. Sadako's prayers changed from wanting personal healing to wanting world peace. After folding 644 cranes, Sadako died. It was left to her classmates to make the remaining 356 cranes.

Inspired by the courage of this little girl, her friends built a monument to Sadako that still stands in the Hiroshima Peace Park. Sadako and her 1000 paper cranes have become symbols for world peace. Even today, people fold paper cranes and put them on the Sadako Statue to signal their wish for peace.

One small girl developed an international movement for peace.[3]

Even in the most hopeless of situations, a person has power. It might not be a power that can change their circumstances, but it may be a power that can change the impact of those circumstances.

A CASE TO STUDY

An American soldier, Major James Nesmith, was captured during the Vietnam War and imprisoned. His cell was a cage one-and-a-half metres long and just over a metre high. It was a desperate situation. Nesmith suffered constant abuse, was given minimal food and was left wondering whether each day would be his last. Many would have thought that, in his position, he was totally powerless.

Nesmith may have been powerless in a physical sense because he could do nothing about his imprisonment. However, he was not powerless in a mental sense. What Nesmith decided to do was to cope with his imprisonment by visualising himself playing golf. He would picture himself on the fairway; he would smell the freshly mown grass, listen to the birds, feel the breeze; and within this imaginary setting he would play a game of golf over the same number of hours it would take him to play a real game.

Nesmith was not content to play a game of golf; he wanted to play the game of golf well. In his mind Nesmith would play every shot carefully and correctly. He would concentrate on his grip, his stance, his swing.

Many years later, Major Nesmith was freed and returned to America, where he was able to indulge his passion of playing real golf. The fascinating thing was that, despite Nesmith not having touched a golf club in seven years, he went round the course some twenty shots better than he had done prior to his captivity.

It was clear that the mental discipline Nesmith engaged while in captivity enabled him to improve his golf skills. Even in prison, Nesmith had the power to improve himself.[4]

DEVELOPING A STRENGTH

Although we all have amazing powers, if we don't use them, they will atrophy and die. We must 'use it or lose it'.

Our sons and daughters need a curiosity about their latent powers that compels them to discover what is possible for them to achieve. Leaders become leaders not because they have different gifts; they become leaders by developing the gifts they have and using them as a weapon to enhance their leadership credentials.

Too many minds are switched off to the possibility of achievement. Too many are unwilling to test for excellence. Too many are content to limit themselves to the normal.

It is never too late to develop a 'weapons grade' strength. Such a quest can interrupt the humdrum and make life extraordinary.

An example of someone who never stopped pushing back the boundaries of what he could do was Leonardo da Vinci.

AN EXAMPLE TO SHARE

LEONARDO DA VINCI (1452-1519)

Leonardo da Vinci was the central figure of the Renaissance. His life was an endless search for knowledge. Da Vinci dissected corpses to find out how the body worked. He conducted experiments with model aeroplanes well before aeroplanes were invented. He was also fascinated by water and warfare and how to use the former to help with the latter. Da Vinci was particularly gifted as a painter and as a sculptor, and was assisted in both by countless notebooks in which he wrote all manner of observations. Da Vinci was a man who loved to explore, who loved to experiment, who loved to extend and develop his strengths.

Hundreds of years before da Vinci was born, there was another period in which people enjoyed intellectual pursuit. It was called the Classical period and featured great thinkers such as Archimedes, Plato, Pythagoras, Hippocrates, Sophocles and Homer. The Classical period ended with the fall of Rome to the barbarian hoards. The thirst for knowledge then dried up for several centuries, a barren period known as the Dark Ages began because very little was done to illuminate knowledge or enlighten understanding.

The Renaissance period centred in Italy in the fifteenth and sixteenth centuries, involved a search for knowledge and an appreciation of beauty. Part of this recovery was due to the invention by Johannes Gutenberg of moveable type that allowed the mass production of books and the easier sharing of knowledge. Another reason for the recovery was the discovery of many of the lost works written during the Classical era. Yet another was the preparedness of a great number of artists and scholars - such as Leonardo da Vinci, Michelangelo, Galileo Galilei, Alberti, Brunelleschi and Toscanelli - to push back the boundaries of what was normally done and develop new definitions of beauty and understanding.

The term 'Renaissance' comes from the word *rinascita*, which means rebirth. We need our sons and daughters to institute a renaissance in their own lives, to test for giftedness and a proper understanding of what is possible.[5]

THE CURSE OF MEDIOCRITY

Too many capitulate in their quest for excellence. A morose indifference to excellence, an addiction to the trivial and a preoccupation with short-term pleasure can divert many from identifying their gifts.

The few that do not follow this path stand out – much to the annoyance of the majority. Think of the migrant family that grasps educational opportunities with both hands. The aspirational student from a disadvantaged background who takes the speech-day prize.

The common ingredient of these examples is work. It is the ability to endure the tedium of practice. It is being able to toil towards a deferred reward. It is being prepared to do multiple redrafts and rehearsals until something has moved from being ordinary to being extraordinary.

AN EXAMPLE TO SHARE

SIR JOHN MONASH (1865-1931)

John Monash is generally credited with playing a major part in winning World War I. His heroic leadership at Gallipoli led to him commanding the Australian Corps in France a few years later. Rather than treating his men as 'cannon fodder' and using the outdated military tactics of the British military, Monash adopted new tactics, including the use of tanks to protect the infantry. These tactics won the battles of Amiens, Hamel, Mont Saint-Quentin and Péronne, and turned the tide of the war.

Monash did not have an easy military life. He was despised for being of German descent, for being Jewish, for being an Australian and for not being a regular soldier. Yet Monash prevailed.

The genesis of Monash's success was found in his early years. He did not content himself with doing the same amount of work as most of his peers. He learned German, French and Hebrew on top of his usual school subjects. As a student of Scotch College in Melbourne, he undertook an hour of piano practice before school and then walked several kilometres to school.[6]

There is often a quality of ease within the lives of our young. This is not true of all, but in some there is a laziness that needs to be eroded by industry and by an understanding that:

- Good and worthy goals are seldom achieved without sacrificial effort.
- There is a need to develop habits of excellence now, rather than waiting until later.
- We should not content ourselves with what we can do now.
- We should measure our performance against excellence rather than against normality.
- Our time on earth is limited, therefore we need to use our allotted time well.

THOSE WHO WOULD COMMAND OTHERS MUST FIRST COMMAND THEMSELVES.

To refine one's skills to a level that is useful requires self-discipline and self-control. Burdensome toil is the price exacted for excellence. This might come as something of a surprise in the 'add water and mix' world we inhabit.

Having noted the value of effort, it needs to be acknowledged that even with a massive amount of blood and sweat, tears of disappointment can still be experienced. Despite diligent application, a goal may still prove elusive. However, even in failure, things can be learned — even if it is that some things are not possible. The value of this lesson should not be underestimated. It can cause a refocusing of life's goals onto something that is more realistic.

The value of pain should not be dismissed and neither should the rewards that come from being disciplined to give something a go until it is either achieved, or it is clear that nothing can be gained by pursuing it further.

Even if a skill is developed, it will take effort to maintain. A strength can wither if not honed by ongoing training — just ask the likes of Bruce Lee, Jackie Chan, Chuck Norris, Jean-Claude Van Damme, Steven Seagal and Wesley Snipes. It is unlikely that any of these developed their fighting skills within a few days of sending some USD to a zip code.

THE WEAPONS WE HAVE

No-one is born without something to offer the world. Everyone has some sort of skill that needs to be identified and developed.

What sort of skills can we reasonably expect our sons and daughters to develop?

Fortunately, there are many ways to be skilful, including:

- **Physical skill:** strength, size, speed and fitness.
- **Intellectual skill:** knowledge, understanding and wisdom.
- **Social skill:** interpersonal ability, charisma and a capacity to relate well with others.

MULTIPLE INTELLIGENCES

Hey, airhead. Shit-for-brains. Dork. Idiot. Dumbo. The contemporary lexicon used to put down someone is as large as it is obscene.

Even if someone is deficient in some area, to write them off as a comprehensive failure is inappropriate. Why? Because everyone is good at something.

Their skill may not match the needs of the moment, but they still have a skill – a skill that can emerge to confound and amaze. It is still a weapon they can use; it's just that it is a different weapon. It may be a force-field created by a radiant smile. It could be a sword of rapier wit. It might be the capacity to go on running when most of the world have given up and gone home to nurse sore muscles and blistered feet.

In his 1983 book *Frames of Mind: The Theory of Multiple Intelligences*, Howard Gardner argued that there are lots of different ways to be intelligent. Rather than clapping those with a stellar IQ, Howard maintained that there are many 'intelligences', any one of which deserves to be applauded. In other words, there are many skills a person can have apart from a high IQ, including:[7]

- An ability in music.
- An ability to see things that other people don't see, to notice patterns, to be good at creating computer graphics, reading maps and understanding engineering drawings.
- An ability to speak and write well, and win people over with words.
- An ability with maths, a capacity to crunch the numbers and to work out puzzles.
- An ability to run, dance or move in a way that amazes others.
- An ability to connect with others – to know what they are feeling.
- An ability to feel comfortable in one's own skin.
- An ability to understand nature, to cultivate gardens and/or work well with animals.
- An ability to connect with the spiritual world, to be tuned in to powers that escape the attention of others.

As parents, we might consider some skills rather more useful than others. However, we need to allow our children to choose their skill to develop and to restrict our words to guidance rather than choice.

Musical skill

Some may have difficulty seeing musical ability as a significant leadership skill, but history has shown just how powerful music can be as a force in leadership.

As the 2000 Olympic Games closed in Sydney, Peter Garrett and the other members of Midnight Oil pulled off their outer garments to reveal outfits emblazoned with the word 'sorry'. This was their protest against the Australian government not formally saying sorry for the abuse suffered by the Indigenous people of Australia. Political statements by Midnight Oil have been even more effective in song than in costume. Their *Diesel and Dust* album incorporates the protest song 'Beds are Burning', written to draw attention to the poor treatment of Indigenous Australians. This has not been the only area where Midnight Oil sought to lead popular opinion. Their song 'Blue Sky Mine' complains about mining exploitation.[8]

The Caribbean crusader for human rights Bob Marley (1945–1981) used reggae to speak for the ghetto-dwellers and dispossessed. His music often took on apartheid and a host of other injustices.[9] Bob Dylan (1941–) is another who used his music to protest against 'the system'. Dylan's most famous song, 'Blowin' in the Wind', has been used extensively as a protest song. Other songs are more specific, such as 'Masters of War', which is a musical attack on the arms industry, and 'Ballad of Hollis Brown', a musical portrait of rural poverty. Dylan's song 'A Hard Rain's A-Gonna Fall' was inspired by the Cuban Missile Crisis.

The 1960s was a time of musical protest against the Vietnam War. The following decades were less focused in their musical protests with their causes ranging from the environment, the nuclear debate, abortion, feminist issues, world hunger, poverty, Nicaragua and

South Africa. For example, the Campaign for Nuclear Disarmament (CND) was supported by the Glastonbury Music Festival in Great Britain. There was a series of 'No Nukes' rock shows at Madison Square Garden. A group was formed called MUSE (Musicians United For Safe Energy). Musician Jackson Browne campaigned for a change in US policy towards the Sandinistas in Nicaragua with songs such as 'For America', 'Soldier of Plenty' and 'Lives in the Balance'.

Well-known artist Stevie Wonder was particularly active in the anti-apartheid movement, as reflected in his song 'It's Wrong (Apartheid)', recorded for his 1985 album *In Square Circle*. Wonder also campaigned successfully to establish the third Monday in January as a national holiday to remember the crusading work of Dr Martin Luther King, Jr.

Ireland, that beautiful and tortured country, has given the world a wealth of wonderful music. Much of it is soulful, mournful and politically inspired. The sending of British troops to Northern Ireland in 1969, the introduction of internment in 1971, and the killings on 'Bloody Sunday' in 1972 sparked many musical protests. The group Wolfe Tones was probably the best example of the musical protestors, but others included Paul McCartney, with his 'Give Ireland back to the Irish', and John Lennon's 'The Luck of the Irish'. Subsequently, Van Morrison, the Clash and Bono of U2 also picked up Irish issues in their songs.

Bob Geldof, together with Midge Ure, wrote 'Do They Know It's Christmas?', which raised over £8 million for Live Aid. Ninety thousand people packed JFK Stadium for one of the Live Aid concerts. Another song, 'We are the World', co-written by Lionel Richie and Michael Jackson, was also used to promote Live Aid.

The Wall concert held on the Potsdamer Platz in Berlin on a site that was once in 'no-man's land' was beamed to a television audience of five hundred million. The event took place in 1990 and featured the ritualistic destruction of the Berlin Wall and all things that divide humankind.

As a weapon, musical skill can be powerful – very powerful indeed.

A way with words

The ability to speak well in public constitutes one of the most powerful weapons a person can have as a leader. It can also be one of the scariest to use. Fortunately, it is entirely possible for anyone to be moderately skilled at speaking in public, even if it is not a natural strength.

Examples of two great speeches come from Australia (ask your teenager to find them on YouTube).

The first speech was made by then Australian Prime Minister Julia Gillard on 9 October 2012. She was responding to a motion in parliament supported by then Opposition Leader Tony Abbott, to have the Speaker of the House of Representatives removed because of his sexist comments. Among other things, Gillard said that Abbott was sexist and misogynist. She railed at Abbott and said:

I will not be lectured on sexism and misogyny by this man;
I will not . . .

Clips of the speech went viral with over one million YouTube views in the first week alone. What was even more interesting was that the speech caused the *Macquarie Dictionary* to change its definition of misogyny to include, 'Entrenched prejudices of woman', as well as a hatred of woman.[10]

The second speech was delivered on 4 November 2014 by the Indigenous Australian leader Noel Pearson. It was a eulogy to a past Australian Prime Minister, Gough Whitlam, and was described as one of the finest speeches in Australian history.[11]

The power of words should not be underestimated. Neither should it be overestimated. Research suggests that the impact of a speech is governed less by content and more by appearance and sound.

A botched speech given when there is no time to prepare can be forgiven. A botched speech given when there is time to prepare is more difficult to forgive. This is because the most reluctant and hesitant person can give a thoroughly acceptable speech if they prepare well.

Every speech needs to have a logical sequence to it or some sensible order in presentation. If sequenced correctly, even a simple speech can be thoroughly acceptable.

A sequence that can work well when giving a speech is the 'G Plan'.

The 'G Plan'

A PHOTO TO TAKE

STEPS TO GIVING A SPEECH
THE 'G' PLAN

Get ready: (Deep breath and relax.)

Greet audience: 'Ladies and gentlemen.'

Grab attention: 'Speech Night speakers are expected to be dull.'

Give message: 'Mrs Smith was not dull, in fact she was very interesting.'

Get off: 'So, I ask you to show your appreciation for Mrs Smith.'

Given the importance of speech making as a weapon, a little more detail needs to be added to the composition of the G Plan.

1. Get ready

- Check you have all your equipment (notes, computer, mobile phone, etc).
- Check the equipment is working.
- Check you have a contingency plan in case the equipment does not work.

- Pay particular attention to the microphone. Is it working? How do you switch it on? How close do you need to get to the microphone for the best sound?
- Check the basics – the names of your hosts, the name of the gathering, the reason for the talk and the names of the guests of honour.
- Calm yourself and mentally slow yourself down. The temptation to rush and gabble at the start can be overwhelming.
- Check flies, stockings, straps, buttons, hems, laces, buckles, armpits, hair, dandruff, glasses, nose, make-up and general appearance.
- Take a few deep breaths, and say to yourself, 'I can do this.'

The short stroll to the lectern, stage, podium or other such place of speechifying can be a dangerous one. As soon as you appear, people will make judgements about you:

'Looks scared stiff.'
'Looks awkward.'
'Looks like a stuffed shirt.'
or
'Looks like she's done this before.'
'I'm looking forward to what he has to say.'

In order to elicit the latter comments, the following advice is worth remembering:

- Walk in a measured, confident way.
- Approach the lectern in a state of relaxed alertness.
- Take your time, let the expectation build.

- Arrange your notes carefully (if you've got them).
- Check your microphone but move it only if it needs to be moved. Do not move it because nerves compel you to fiddle.
- Look at the audience – right into their eyes – and wordlessly win them over with an intelligent and engaging gaze.
- Pause, count to five, then start.

REMEMBER, THE MOST IMPORTANT THING TO SAY AT THE START OF A SPEECH IS NOTHING.

Do not:
- Fiddle or tap fingers or feet.
- *Umm* and *err*.
- Smile or laugh at nothing because you are embarrassed.
- Cover your embarrassment by being overly casual.
- Rush.
- Read mechanically without expression or feeling.
- Start apologising for your lack of skill or experience.
- Drink the water unless you need it.

Do:
- Speak clearly.
- Look at the audience every five to 15 seconds when a natural break occurs.
- Create a sense of expectation by pausing at the start.
- Speak to the audience, not to the notes.
- Rehearse.
- Keep within the time limit.
- Speak with meaning, energy and feeling.

2. Greet the audience

Chairman, Mrs Green; Distinguished Guest, Mr Wartleburg;
Members of Yackville Surf Lifesaving Club . . .

These sorts of long greetings can be effective if done well and if no-one significant is omitted. The general convention is to mention the person in charge of the occasion first and then the more distinguished guests in order of importance, followed by the rest of the audience, again in order of importance.

President of the SRC, John May; Guest of Honour, Mrs Jenny
Flame; Principal, Dr Hollyfield; staff and students.

With this complexity and the risk of panic not far off, it can be a good idea to keep things simple. It is very difficult to think of a gathering that is going to be upset by a simple greeting such as:

Ladies and gentlemen
or
Members of the Mt Swanston School Community

Sometimes little or no greeting is needed other than:

Good evening.

3. Grab their attention

There is truth in the saying that you only have one shot at a first impression, so don't mess it up.

All too often speakers declare with their first few words and with frightening accuracy that their speech will be boring and poorly delivered. Too many speeches start badly. There are nervous apologies, admissions of inadequacy, awkward giggles, poor microphone technique, rushed and mechanical utterances, and words blurted mindlessly without any attempt to sense the mood of the audience or the needs of the audience.

Audiences will turn off in droves at a speech that has not attempted to engage them. Engagement occurs when listeners' needs are met – be it giving them useful information, entertaining them or inspiring them. If a speaker is not able to meet the needs of the audience, they should not speak at all.

A great way to grab the attention of an audience is to use humour or anecdote. Humour is even more appreciated if it is linked to the topic of the speech. Telling a joke about a three-legged cow at the opening of a new music department may not be a good idea.

Far better to say something like:

My musical skills lie in my ability to download U2 and Jimmy Hendrix . . .

Humour is not always appropriate. In my experience, having to tell off a school about litter, theft or some other behaviour does not always lend itself to humour, but this does not mean that some sort of impact is not possible at the opening of a speech.

It's not always Houston that has a problem. We've got one right now . . .

The humour may not be there, but some effort is made to form a connection with the audience, even when having to tell them something unpleasant.

4. Give the message

To give a message one must have a message. If a speaker does not have a message, the greatest contribution they can make is to not speak.

Some of the best speakers break their message into three parts:

- **First**, tell them what you are going to tell them.
- **Second**, tell them.
- **Third**, tell them what you have told them.

Slightly overstated perhaps, but the principle is clear. Reinforce the message several times in a speech, otherwise it runs the risk of being lost.

Another way of reinforcing the message is to use well-positioned phrases such as:

- *The key point of my talk is . . .*
- *If there is one thing I want you to remember, it is this . . .*
- *So, what is the point of this speech? It is this . . .*

Speeches that have a logical sequence are appreciated more than those that don't.

If there is a slight hesitation in sharing this fact, it is because a sequence disturbed in a deliberate fashion can also have a good effect. For example:

- *Jill is brilliant as an academic . . .*
- *Jill is brilliant as a friend . . .*
- *Jill is appalling as a dumb blonde, for although she is blonde, she is not dumb. In fact, she is very intelligent.*

The sequence can be as simple as three key points:

- *A good quality found in this proposal is . . .*
- *A better quality found in this initiative is . . .*
- *The best quality found in this idea is . . .*

There are many other ways to provide a sequence to a talk. For example:

- North of us lies the danger of irrelevance . . .
- East of us lies the danger of financial ruin . . .
- South of us lies the danger of breaking the law . . .
- West of us lies the danger of losing political support.

- The most important second of my life was when . . .
- The most important minute of my life was when . . .
- The most important hour of my life was when . . .
- The most important day of my life was when . . .
- The most important year of my life was when . . .

Sometimes, it can be useful to build in interruptions. The regular rhythms of a read speech can set an audience nodding. The drone can leave people uninterested and distracted. This is why interruption is important. Stop the speech. Pause. Look at the audience, then deliver a comment without any notes.

- Ladies and gentlemen, what I am really trying to say is this . . .
- I want you to understand that this is important to me because . . .
- Speaking personally, I think the best quality about this proposal is . . .

AN EXAMPLE TO SHARE

The following eighteenth-birthday speech shows how humour and serious comment can be used side by side.

My sister was born without an expensive dress on, in the year of our Lord only knows. The event so surprised her she was speechless for a year.

Given the light-hearted start it is now probably best to include a sincere observation about the fun had in growing up together. This done, time for some more amusement.

> *As teenagers we were alike in many disrespects. We were in that*
> *awkward stage between being too young and being too old. Bev*
> *was between pigtails and cocktails.*

Now for a change in pace, a telling of a true story that reveals something of the sister's more noble and admirable qualities.

It might then be appropriate to comment on the three qualities you have most appreciated in your sister.

Then conclude with a touch of humour in the cutting of the cake:

> *Another candle on Bev's cake.*
> *Another cause to cheer and shout.*
> *But let's give thanks, for heaven's sake,*
> *She has the wind to blow them out.*

The illustration above is by no means suggested as a model in terms of content, but it is a model in terms of style. This may be summarised as a speech having engagement.

5. Get off

If people start to sleep during your talk, it is not a good sign. If you fall asleep in your own speech, it is a worse sign.

The solution to these problems is simple: stop talking. This is not easy for some. Great speakers have generally learned to:

> *Say less in order to be heard more.*

This needs to be written at the top of every speech in the land.

An audience will often be more likely to be won by fewer words than more. Gifted communicators wrestle for hours to make a speech better by shortening it. Poor communicators wrestle for hours to make a speech better by lengthening it.

Arguably one of the best speeches ever was Abraham Lincoln's Gettysburg Address. It lasted only a few minutes.

Leaving an audience on a high is important. A closing story or a powerful punchline delivered with passion can be used to good effect. At the very least, make sure the audience is left with a clear conclusion. For this reason it is worth highlighting the one phrase you really want the audience to remember. Use this one phrase in your concluding comment.

The exit should be done in style. Do not apologise for what you have said or how you have said it. Speakers have enough critics without adding themselves to the number. Far better to restate the main argument in simple terms, give a memorable quote or illustration that reinforces the argument, and then say something like:

Ladies and gentlemen, thank you for your attention.

If applause is given, this needs to be received graciously by looking at the audience and giving some form of acknowledgment. A small bow often works well.

A STORY TO SHARE

ROSA PARKS (1913-2005)

On Thursday, 1 December 1955, after a day of ironing and stitching shirts at the Montgomery Fair department store, Rosa Parks boarded a bus to go home. She sat in the rear of the bus sectioned off for black people. Soon the white section of the bus filled up, resulting in a white man having to stand. The law said that black people had to give up their seats if a white person had no seat. Accordingly, the bus driver, James Blake, called upon Rosa Parks to stand up and let the white man take her seat.

Rosa Parks's speech in response was limited. What she said, more or less, was, 'No'. There was little by way of eloquence in her response yet her words sparked a revolution and a change in racial law. After saying she was not going to move, Rosa was arrested, jailed and fined. The response by the black community of Montgomery was to organise a boycott of the buses.

The protest against racism was taken up by others, including Dr Martin Luther King, Jr. A non-violent policy of demonstration resulted, including an assembly in Washington on 28 August 1963. During this demonstration, Martin Luther King gave his famous 'I have a dream' speech, which was delivered to over 200 000 people in front of the Lincoln Memorial.

This is the speech that is remembered. These are the great words of rhetoric that have become famous. Yet it can be argued it was the few words of defiance spoken by a black woman on a bus that had the greater impact on the nation.[12]

Leadership is not always about the capacity to deliver the lofty and well-structured speech. Assertive words can be powerful. Just a few can change a nation.

ASSERTIVENESS

Assertiveness does not always enjoy the greatest of reputations. This is because there is a thin line between being assertive and being aggressive.

Assertiveness is important because it provides leaders with their voice. It recognises their right to an opinion and it gives conviction to their cause.

Leaders need to be assertive, to be able to develop an opinion and be prepared to defend it. This should not translate into bloody mindedness or an *I-have-made-up-my-mind*, *do-not-confuse-me-with-the-facts* sort of attitude.

If a leader is going to be assertive, it is important that they be assertive about the right things. It can be very damaging if our sons and daughters choose to be assertive over things that:

- Have not been carefully thought through.
- Are inaccurate.
- Are motivated by self-interest.
- Are distorted by prejudice.

Assertiveness should be seen as being in the middle of a continuum from 'pushover' to 'aggressive'.

Pushover
- Rarely disagrees with others for fear of losing friends.
- Puts others first at their own expense.
- Feels guilty saying no.
- Has difficulty giving or receiving criticism.
- Reluctant to ask others for help.
- Easily intimidated and bossed around.

ASSERTIVE

Aggressive
- Can be explosive, particularly when challenged or criticised.
- Tends to put themselves first at the expense of others.
- Demanding and uncompromising.
- Forceful personality that can intimidate others.

A, B, C
Being assertive requires learning the ABC.
A = Attitude
B = Behaviour
C = Communication

Attitude

- Be positive.
- Know that you have unique gifts, knowledge and insights.
- Know that you have a right to your opinion.
- See opposition as an opportunity not a problem.

Behaviour

- Avoid aggressive or weak body language.
- Use good body language, such as squared shoulders and good eye contact.
- Use your voice well. Do not mumble or whine. Do not snarl or shout.
- Be polite.
- Learn how to say:
  I think there is another point of view to be considered.
  I'm not comfortable with what you are saying.
  I disagree.
- When angry, do not 'lose it'; stay in control. Avoid inflaming the situation with accusations. Send 'I' messages rather than 'you' messages. For example:

  I have a problem with what you are saying.

Rather than:

  You always talk a lot of garbage.

Communication

- Be a good listener. Use body language to confirm you are listening.
- Summarise what has been said to give confirmation you have heard the person. For example: *What I hear you saying is . . .*
- Speak clearly, confidently and concisely.

- Be able to receive a compliment by saying, *Thank you.*
- Learn to give praise and encouragement but make sure it is sincere and deserved.
- Choose the right time and place. For example: *Jill, may I have a brief word with you in private?*

AN EXAMPLE TO STUDY

JOHN F KENNEDY (1917-1963)

PRESIDENT OF THE UNITED STATES

John F Kennedy was part of a leadership dynasty in the United States that was to influence American political life for decades. His father was a multi-millionaire businessman who also served for a time as the American Ambassador to Great Britain.

After graduating from Harvard University, John F Kennedy joined the US Navy. In 1943 when on duty in the Pacific, his motor torpedo boat PT-109 was rammed by a Japanese destroyer and sank just off the Solomon Islands. Kennedy survived the incident and was involved in the heroic rescue of many of his crew.

After the war, Kennedy entered politics and obtained a seat in the US House of Representatives. In 1952 he won a seat in the Senate and in 1960 defeated Richard Nixon to win the Presidency. During his time in office, Kennedy established the US Peace Corps, an organisation that sent thousands of Americans to help those in developing countries.

However, it was the assertiveness shown by Kennedy during the 1962 Cuban Missile Crisis that was to immortalise him as a leader.

The Soviet Union did not have the capacity to hit the United States with land-based nuclear weapons. On the other hand, the United States could, in theory, hit Russia using nuclear missiles deployed in Turkey, which is only 240 kilometres from Russia. Understandably, the Russians wanted to even things up a bit, so they established nuclear-missile bases on the island of Cuba, just 140 kilometres off the American coast.

The Cuban leader, Fidel Castro, was happy to allow the Russians to put their nuclear missiles on his island, for they would serve to deter the Americans from invading his country. This was not an unreasonable fear because in the previous year the Americans had backed an invasion of Cuba by Cuban exiles. Unfortunately for the Americans, the Bay of Pigs invasion was a disaster. It also strengthened Castro's resolve to forge closer links with Russia.

The timeline of events relating to the 1962 Cuban Missile Crisis is a great lesson in assertiveness.

- Monday 15 October: U-2 spy plane pilot Richard Heyser confirms Russian SS-4 nuclear missiles in Cuba.
- Tuesday 16 October: Kennedy's team of twelve military advisors known as EX-COMM propose an air strike and invasion of Cuba. Kennedy resists this advice.
- Wednesday 17 October to Saturday 20 October: American U-2 spy planes discover Russian SS-5 missiles on Cuba. These missiles are capable of reaching most parts of the United States. The Soviets deny they have offensive nuclear weapons in Cuba.
- Sunday 21 October: Kennedy is advised that destroying the Cuban missile sites will kill between 10 000 and 20 000 people. He decides to blockade Cuba instead.
- Monday 22 October: Kennedy informs the American public of the nuclear missile crisis. The US military is put on full alert. Castro mobilises Cuba's military forces.
- Tuesday 23 October: Further aerial photographs are taken to confirm the missile sites. The US Navy prepares to destroy any ship taking missiles or military equipment into Cuba.
- Wednesday 24 to Thursday 25 October: Soviet ships bringing goods into Cuba are stopped by the US Navy. The threat of nuclear war becomes extreme. Kennedy prepares for an immediate nuclear attack.

- Friday 26 October: Russian leader Nikita Khrushchev writes to Kennedy promising to remove his missiles if the United States promises never to invade Cuba.
- Saturday 27 October: US spy planes are shot down over Russia and Cuba. Khrushchev writes again demanding America remove its missiles from Turkey. Kennedy refuses this demand.
- Sunday 28 October: Khrushchev announces that Russia will dismantle its nuclear missile sites in Cuba.[13]

Kennedy's assertiveness against Russia paid off and advanced his reputation as a strong and assertive leader.

TAKE AN INVENTORY OF YOUR ARMOURY

A great way for our sons and daughters to reflect on their skills is to get them to write their CV. Although often a task associated with the adult world, this task would be appropriate for most children over the age of fifteen.

A reflection on their strengths can be an affirming and encouraging exercise. A reflection on their weaknesses is also useful because it can give our budding heroes and heroines a wake-up call and cause them to engage in initiatives that might enrich their CVs.

Before a CV is prepared, it is useful to have some sort of an idea of what sort of job you want the CV to obtain. If you are looking for a practical, hands-on type of job, then the CV needs to be slightly different from one used to apply for a place at university. For this reason, one of the first tasks is to consider the sort of strengths the person receiving the CV is looking for. Without straying into fiction, the CV should then be slanted in such a way that these desired characteristics are prominent.

Most organisations receive hundreds of CVs. Most are scanned rather than read. Our sons and daughters need to assume that their

CV will be looked at by a critical and cranky person who will be seriously annoyed by poor layout, angered by 'speling misteaks' and put off by pages of irrelevant personal details.

The covering letter

Encourage your child to ensure they have a 'wow' factor at the start of their CV by writing a good covering letter. This letter needs to grab the reader and get them excited at the prospect of reading the accompanying CV.

The covering letter needs to have the right balance between:

- Bragging and humility.
- Respect for the organisation, yet a sense of how you might contribute to making it even better.
- Brevity and comprehensiveness.

A covering letter should also:

- Never be more than a page long.
- Be easy to read, with short, sharp paragraphs.
- Make good use of summary techniques such as dot points.
- Not be addressed to 'Dear Sir or Madam'.

Here is an example of a poorly constructed covering letter.

From
J Smith
153 Somewhere Lane
Fictitiousville
To
Acme Fish Exporting Company
Pretend Lane
Makebelieve Place

Dear Sir/Madam,

I would like to work for you. I have a great deal that I can do that you will find makes it well worth your while to employ me as I am hard working, reliable, honest, and teachable. I am particularly interested in working for Acme Fish Exporting Company as I like computers. I am unemployed and so I can start work at any time. I am looking for a job that will pay me well and not treat me unfairly which is why I had to leave my last jobs. I really want to work for a company that does not take me for granted and understands and wants to keep onside its workforce and a company that is prepared to pay me what I am really worth. I am able to do general things. I am used to doing almost anything that does not need training. I left school quite young and so have been doing lots of practical things in the real world rather than in theory. This makes me a really useful employee for I have been schooled by life and not by books. I can be contacted on email on Johnehopeful@dreaming.org.

Yours sincerely,

J Smith

Contrast the covering letter above with the letter below.

153 Somewhere Lane
Fictitiousville
21 July 2018
Mrs Eloise Employer
Personnel Manager
Fiction and Sons Electronics
Made Up Avenue
Someplace

Dear Mrs Employer,

I would like to apply for a job with Fiction and Sons Computers *as a sales technician.*

I have been a fan of Fiction and Sons Computers *to the extent that I have bought both my laptop and tablet from your shop.*

My CV will indicate that I am able to offer you:

- *Giftedness in working with computers.*
- *Creativity in solving problems.*
- *An understanding of the youth market for computers.*
- *An ability to work well individually as well as a member of a team.*
- *Reliability and integrity.*

I am available for interview at any time after Friday 28 July 2018. My contact details are:

e-mail: jksmith@everhopeful.com.zwy.abc

Telephone: (123) 4567 8901 or mobile (978) 6543 2109

Yours sincerely,

John Smith

As can be seen, the second letter is easier to read, it highlights the applicant's strengths, it has provided up-to-date contact details, it is addressed to a person rather than 'Dear Sir/Madam', it is suitably modest but still advances the applicant's credentials, and it does not hint at past employment failures.

The CV

There are no hard and fast rules. A good CV is one that gets you the job. The people who read CVs differ so much in what they like and do not like that it is difficult to give firm guidelines as to how to write a winning CV. It should also be remembered that there are different styles of CV needed for different types of jobs. Having noted the above, the following guidelines might be useful to share.

- The CV should be no longer than four pages.
- Ensure that the CV is easy to read, does not look cramped, has well-spaced text and uses short paragraphs.
- Use techniques such as dot points to summarise a lot of information in an economical fashion.
- Use good-quality white or cream paper. It can have a subtle fleck in it but nothing too bizarre. Avoid using brightly coloured paper.
- Print the CV so it is easy to read. Do not handwrite the CV. The covering letter may be handwritten if the handwriting is neat and legible.
- Number the pages and put a footer or header that states something like: 'Page 2 of 4 Curriculum Vitae for John E Hopeful'.
- Avoid using flowery fonts. Use a font that is either 12 point or 14 point in size and is easy to read such as:
  - A 'serif' style where the letters have 'little feet' at the bottom of each letter, such as Times New Roman.
  - A 'sans serif' style where there are no 'little feet' at the bottom of each letter, such as Helvetica
- Limit underlining. Use bold instead.
- Justify against the left margin. Justifying against both left and right margins is also acceptable.
- Use A4 paper and staple it. If other binding techniques are used, choose a method that allows the pages to be turned easily.
- When listing employment history, education and so on, do so in reverse chronological order – i.e. with your most recent activity or achievement listed first.
- Have a slightly bigger margin at the bottom of the page than the top of the page, particularly if you are using a 'footer'.
- Avoid long lists. They are difficult to read.
- Be economical with words, and what words you do use should be chosen for their accuracy.

When you have checked your CV for errors, do it again. When you have double-checked, give the CV to a capable person who can also check it.

There are no absolute rules about the order of presenting material in a CV. However, an order that might work well for a school leaver is:

1. Name, address and contact details.
2. A brief personal overview that is designed to capture the interest of the reader.
3. Educational history and record of educational achievements.
4. Personal interests and achievements.
5. Other relevant personal details.
6. References.

When writing a CV it is best to write in the past tense and use active verbs. Do not use verbs that are low-impact or passive. For example:

- 'I'm a helper at social events' sounds a bit lame when you can write, 'Negotiated with suppliers to ensure school dances made a profit'.
- 'I'm helping a group of junior students' is weak when it is just as accurate to write, 'Counselled a Year 7 tutor group and advised them on pastoral matters'.
- 'I set up a canteen group' can be put as, 'Initiated a product advisory committee for the school's canteen'.

Starting each point with a powerful verb such as *negotiated*, *counselled* and *initiated* can make a CV more effective.

Using the past tense gives the indication that something has been achieved. It results in a stronger statement than using other tenses.

NOTE

It is vital that whatever is written is the absolute truth and nothing but the truth. Improving the presentation is one thing; improving the facts is an entirely different thing. There is nothing wrong with the former but if the latter is engaged in, then it is wrong. DON'T DO IT.

Without straying from the bounds of factual accuracy, it is entirely possible to take a lame CV and make it more interesting. For example:

'I like watching TV' could be accurate but it is probably a real turn-off for the reader who could be tempted to condemn you as a couch potato with little energy, imagination or wit to do anything other than sit in front of a TV. It would be much better to say, 'I enjoy British television comedies of the 1980s.'

'I like reading' is very tame when you can write, 'I am interested in maritime novels set in the eighteenth and nineteenth centuries.'

Even the listing of subjects studied at school can be enriched. 'Geography' could be changed to 'Geography with a particular emphasis on Economic Geography and the retail habits of Sydney shoppers'.

Having noted this advice, it is all very well selling the 'sizzle as well as the steak' but do not become too long-winded or put in irrelevant information. Steak ceases to have much sizzle if the reader is a vegetarian. Not all readers will have an interest in the retail habits of Sydney shoppers. Then again, someone running a store in which you want a holiday job may be very interested.

The extent to which a CV details strengths and achievements needs to be handled with care. Too much egocentricity should be avoided. Hype and self-praise do not go down well. There needs to be enough 'wow factor' to turn a reader on, but not so much that it turns a reader off.

For example, the following is a little too strong:

I am incredible at seeing through people and am able to sense what is troubling them. I am able to mix in fantastically well with others and lead them socially, for I am particularly skilled in sensing how others are feeling. People always tell me that they want me as their friend because I am so caring. This means I am wonderful at customer relations, and have the extraordinary ability to make others feel good.

This might be more appropriate:

My particular strengths are in working with people. I have demonstrated that I have the interpersonal skills necessary to be an effective counsellor. Volunteer work with the school's help-line has extended my abilities in this area.

Whether a CV is actually used is not important. The very act of writing a CV can be an encouraging reminder of the attributes and strengths a person has. If the exercise is not an encouraging reminder, there may be added motivation to acquire the skills and experiences necessary to turn a pedestrian CV into a good one.

FINALLY

A leader needs a reputation for being good at something. It need not always be something ooh-la-la like administering a lasso of truth. Neither must it always be something that can readily be identified as an awesome and persuasive strength. The weapon a person might have to advance their credentials as a leader could be a strength at gaming, a tremendous ability at Manga art, skateboarding, cooking or the capacity to sense the needs of other people.

This strength needs to be identified and developed. Honing a skill to the extent that it becomes a weapons-grade strength will take time and effort. There are very few shortcuts to this process. Discipline and perseverance are needed to arrive at excellence.

SUMMARY

- Leaders need skills or 'weapons', something that gives them the capacity to have an impact on others.
- These skills need to be discovered, developed and deployed not just to the advantage of the leader but for the benefit of the broader community.
- There is a latent power in all of us that we can use to advance our leadership credentials.
- There are many ways to be strong and powerful. People can be gifted in the use of very different skills.
- A skill loses its usefulness if a person does not know how to use it. A skill will characteristically require time and effort to develop.
- Leaders need to recognise that their skills should be used responsibly. They must use the power they have for the benefit of all.
- The strengths that define a leader vary, but a useful skill is the ability to speak well in public.
- Skills confer power. Power can corrupt and power can create. A balance is needed between being aggressive and being a pushover. The middle ground of being assertive needs to be learned.
- A good way to reflect on one's personal armoury of skills is to write a CV.
- Developing a skill takes discipline, perseverance and time.

A team to assist

Most heroes and heroines, both real and fictional, work in teams. In the 1960s TV series *The Avengers*, the suave John Steed (played by Patrick Macnee) relied heavily on Emma Peel (played by Diana Rigg) and a variety of other partners to overcome all manner of evil. Likewise the Teenage Mutant Ninja Turtles, Leonardo, Michelangelo, Raphael and Donatello, relied on each other to combat the black arts of various baddies.

These are just two of countless fictional teams whose capacity to work together was sufficient to clean up most of the villains on this planet. There have been many real-life teams who have been pretty successful at doing much the same thing.

THE TEAM OF FRIENDS

Our sons and daughters will find themselves in all manner of teams. Some will be formal teams (debating, sports, etc.). Some will be informal teams, a loose assemblage of friends who swirl and float together, sometimes on their own, sometimes coalescing as they flow through life.

The choice of who our children raft up with on life's journey is important. That is because we tend to absorb the qualities of those around us. For this reason, deciding who to team up with needs careful thought.

A PHOTO TO TAKE

Show me your friends and I'll tell you your future.

(Source unknown)

Good friends can be the making of our sons and daughters. Bad friends can be their ruin.

Children typically have three major social influences on them as they go through life: parents, peers and partners.

The peer influence is probably its greatest in the teen years when a child is seeking their independence and their freedom from parental control. It is important that the 'team' of friends used in the quest for identity is one that enriches.

Given that the focus of this book is on the teen, the majority of this chapter will focus on teams made up of peers – i.e. teen teams. Such teams are not controlled by a Japanese mutant rat, as is the case with the Teenage Mutant Ninja Turtles; they are controlled by a mobile phone.

THE ELECTRONIC TEAM

The mobile phone is not just a means of communication for our teens. It holds within its casing the people who are part and parcel of a young person's life. It is the resource they use when they need entertainment, friendship or help. Their phone is the team.

Parents will have their own opinion as to whether the phone is a good team or a bad team. If the phone is full of good people saying good things about good topics, then it can reasonably be thought to be an asset. However, it may cease to be an asset if it has too high a profile in a child's life.

Contemporary technology is only partly understood by many parents, which can result in them feeling marginalised in the cyber world. With teenage phone and screen time accounting for several hours of their day and conversation time with parents being measured in just a few minutes a day, it is reasonable to suggest that many teens are being reared by phones rather than by parents. On the other hand, some parents see the mobile phone as an asset and use social networking and mobile phones to engage with their children.

MANAGING MOBILE PHONES

The team in the mobile phone can be invaluable, but it can also become unwieldy and even counterproductive, particularly if it becomes too big and cannot be controlled. Therefore, promiscuous online friending needs to be discouraged. The practice of syncing electronic phonebooks can also be problematic, because it can result in an electronic team that is not well known, whose allegiance cannot be guaranteed and whose integrity cannot be trusted.

The British anthropologist Robin Dunbar gave his name to a number. The Dunbar number is 150 – this being the number of people with whom a person can have a meaningful relationship at the same time. If this thesis is accepted, it suggests that a lot of pruning of a lot of friends on a lot of phones might be necessary.[1]

Knowing how to use the mobile phone properly is important because of its ubiquitous nature and the capacity for our children to become enslaved to it. The ever-increasing power of the mobile phone may be exciting, but it is also frightening. With increasing power the phone is no longer the servant of its master, it *is* the master.

For those in doubt, look at the queues outside the technology shops when a new gizmo is launched. Some are bought with little thought as to their utility. For example, an app that tells you how far away your Facebook friends are might be the 'must-have' thing, but it can be purchased without much consideration of privacy. Is it always in our best interests for others to know exactly where we are?

TAKING CONTROL

Our sons and daughters need to manage their support teams — both real and virtual. Too many are surrendering their lives to contemporary technology. The mobile phone is a resource that needs to be well managed.

The following is the sort of advice parents might share with their children on this matter.

- Remind them that a mobile phone is expensive. It needs to be looked after. Get them to record their 15-digit International Mobile Equipment Identity (IMEI) number in case the phone is lost or stolen. If it is stolen, they must notify the police and insurance company immediately. It can also be helpful to go to sites such as www.lost.amta.org.au and follow the advice as to what to do to deactivate the stolen phone or to recover it.
- Insist that they protect their privacy. Get them to check their settings so that they are not sharing personal files with inappropriate people. Remind them never to tell anyone their password and get them to change their password at least three or four times a year. When choosing a password, don't make it an obvious password.
- Tell them why they are not going to get a phone that allows them unfettered access to the internet. This would be like allowing them to download anything they wanted — the R-rated as well as the supportive stuff for an essay on Shakespeare.

- Explain that a mobile phone comes with some parental controls. For example, Optus has a Mobile Security App. Telstra has Mobile Controls. Vodafone also has resources for parents that limit access to inappropriate sites. There is a range of apps that can set controls on the use of mobile phones and monitors their use. For example, Vodafone has a Guardian App, which limits the time of day the phone can be used and what it can be used for. The app can also be used to bar calls and block certain types of messages. Mobile phones are adult technology and must be adapted if they are going to be used by our children.
- Explain when mobile phones are not allowed to be used. For example, mealtimes and homework times should be phone free except for emergencies. When travelling in the car, why not use that time to talk, rather than using the phone? With meaningful interaction between parents and children being just a few minutes a day, it might be good to use travel time and mealtimes to talk.
- Tell them no, then tell them why. They have to be aged over thirteen to have a Facebook account, and you do not want to be a party to breaking the law.
- As a family, agree on a social-networking policy. For example, 'We're going to talk about the virtue of not "friending" everyone and the value of being choosy.' It's also worth talking about the dangers of scams and rip-offs.
- Explain why you want to 'Facebook friend' your own children. It's because you love them and want to stay connected with them. Whether you also confess to seeing it as a means to monitor what they are doing is up to you.
- Share your concern that mobile phones and other forms of modern technology have been implicated in robbing children of sleep. This is why all electrical devices should be switched off and/or removed from bedrooms at night. Teenagers need at least eight hours' sleep a night. Pre-teens need more.

- If things go turnip shaped and self-control remains an issue with a son or daughter, inform them that they have given you the right to fix things. There are several apps out there that can help. For example, there is a SelfControl App. SelfControl is a free Mac application that can block specific websites for up to twenty-four hours. Another anti-distraction app is Freedom, which prevents users from connecting to the internet during specified times. Others include BreakFree, AppDetox, StayOnTask and Moment.
- If a child is constantly bombarded by distractions because of notifications, tell them they should turn off their notifications when they want to remain undisturbed. A good way to do this is to activate the 'airplane mode'.
- Encourage your sons and daughters to cull their social contacts. Experience shows that 80 per cent of social contacts are of no relevance. Anyone who is of marginal significance, whose input is not helpful or whose values are questionable should be removed, as should those whose online presence is asinine, egocentric or boring.
- Get your children to demonstrate they can control their technology. The moment they are unable to prove they can stay in control, explain that they may lose the right to use that technology.
- Remind your child that whatever is put on social networking sites or the internet can remain there forever. People can capture information that may only be on a screen for a few seconds. Material, once put into the cyber world, can return in the future to embarrass them.
- Inform them that the power of the mobile phone needs to be used wisely. Cyber bullying is an ugly feature of the contemporary age. Discuss what they should do if they experience cyber bullying. Make sure your child knows the

dangers associated with sexting. It is all too easy to be charged with distributing paedophilic material.

- Advise that mobile phones lend themselves to impulsive behaviour. Mobile phones have no safety catch; with a push of a button, lethal damage can result.
- Alert them to the dangers of peer-to-peer (P2P) file sharing. Warn them not to breach copyright and to be careful not to introduce viruses.
- Talk to your child about their phone holding the secrets about a person's true character. What sites do they look at? What language do they use? What values do they betray? If someone was to take a forensic look at their phone, what would they find?
- Encourage your teen not to become a sucker for irrelevancy. Mobile phones and similar devices can be time thieves. If this is a matter of concern, it can be helpful to get them to review what they did every thirty minutes before and after school, and on weekends. Then, ask if they are happy with this time allocation. If not, they should be encouraged to do something about it. This can be particularly helpful for the child addicted to online gaming.
- Get them to disinfect their phone often. Mobile phones are frequent carriers of germs and faecal matter.
- If of an appropriate age, remind them that texting when driving is extremely dangerous. It is also illegal.
- Advise them to be sensitive when using the mobile phone. Conversations on the mobile phone can be inappropriate in restaurants, public transport or in designated 'quiet' areas.
- Remind your children that you will not necessarily bail them out financially if they run up huge phone bills, lose their phone or don't check how much things cost when they buy online. Likewise, remind them of the significant fees that can be incurred if they travel overseas without turning 'data roaming' off.

- If your teen resists your advice, explain that because a significant amount of online activity is devoted to porn, gambling, gaming and rip-offs, you have a right, as a loving parent, to set guidelines.
- Make sure your children know that people are not always who they say they are in the cyber world. There are good people out there and there are creeps. Tell children never to trust the credentials of anyone they don't know.
- Advise them that if you detect that the phone is becoming too big a crutch in their life, it will be removed. FOMO (Fear of Missing Out) and nomophobia (no mobile phone phobia) need to be managed.[2]

Our sons and daughters practise teamwork via social networking sites, phone calls, text messages and emails. They will use these electronic means to collect friends and contacts to build their 'team'. They will use electronic means to connect with their team, coordinate with their team and calibrate against their team. They will also use electronic means to find out how they are measuring up against others.

This cyber team can be powerful. It can teach good things and bad things. It can take over the task of raising our children if we let it. It will become the confidant if we fail to be effective in that role. It is able to set our children off on missions that save the world and ruin the world. It is the modern-day 'squawk box' that directs our heroes and heroines.

THE ELEMENTS OF A GOOD TEAM

Whether virtual or real, whether online or flesh-and-blood, some teams are good and some teams are bad.

So – what is a good team?

There are many elements to a good team. One element is that the members of the team develop a sense of belonging. This sort of membership is secured by ceremonies, companionship and communion.

If this journey should entail hardship, then the resultant bonds are likely to be even greater.

Strong teams can be formed through a shared adventure, a shared risk and a shared experience. This is captured beautifully by William Shakespeare in *Henry V.* In the play, the young King Henry of England finds himself confronting a much larger French army at Agincourt. It is Saint Crispin's Day, 1415, and the Duke of Westmoreland wishes aloud that he had more soldiers. King Henry gently rebukes him:

Oh, do not wish one more!
Rather proclaim it, Westmoreland . . .
That he which has no stomach to this fight,
Let him depart; his passport shall be made
And crowns for convoy put into his purse.
We would not die in that man's company
That fears his fellowship to die with us.
This day is call'd the feast of Crispian.
He that outlives this day, and comes safe home,
Will stand a tiptoe when this day is named,
And rouse him at the name of Crispian.
He that shall live this day, and see old age,
Will yearly on the vigil feast his neighbours,
And say, 'Tomorrow is Saint Crispian.'
Then will he strip his sleeve and show his scars,
And say 'These wounds I had on Crispin's day.'
Old men forget, yet all shall be forgot,
But he'll remember with advantages
What feats he did that day . . .
And Crispin Crispian shall ne'er go by
From this day to the ending of the world,

But we in it shall be remembered,
We few, we happy few, we band of brothers.
For he today that sheds his blood with me
Shall be my brother; be he ne'er so vile,
This day shall gentle his condition;
And gentlemen in England now a-bed
Shall think themselves accursed they were not here,
And hold their manhoods cheap whiles any speaks
That fought with us upon Saint Crispin's day.

To some, all this might be seen as rousing stuff. Others might dismiss King Henry's speech as being overly sentimental. However, to those facing a battle, these words can inspire. And that's the point: shared danger can unite like nothing else can.

GOOD TEAMS HAVE SYNERGY

A term often associated with teamwork is synergy. Synergy relates to the collective energy of a group. A good team is one in which members not only contribute their own energy, they also stimulate others to contribute more than they otherwise would.

For example, when geese fly in a V formation, less effort is needed to fly because the geese in front create an uplift of air to help the geese behind. Over 70 per cent greater flying range is achieved. This is synergy.

GOOD TEAMS ALLOW DIFFERENCES

The effectiveness of a team is improved when each member is allowed to use their unique strengths for the benefit of the whole team. Not everyone in the team needs to have identical skills. Identical purpose – yes, but not identical skills. It would be a very ordinary football team if all players only had the skills of a goal-keeper.

Leaders need to build a team that is loyal and has common purpose, but not a team that is sycophantic and mono-skilled. It can often be useful to have someone in the team whose role is to challenge assumptions. This can have the effect of sharpening an argument and exposing weak spots in an intended course of action.

Our sons and daughters need to understand that their most faithful friend will tell them that what they're wearing makes them look like a sack of potatoes, or that they'd be a bloody idiot if they were to drive in that condition. A good team will protect its own – even if the action is unpopular at the time.

Good teams are not always unified in agreement, but they are unified in purpose. A friendship group that is going to collapse because of disagreement does not have the features of a strong team. Intelligent people can still disagree with each other. If this cannot happen without it degenerating into a personal attack, then it is not a friendship group worth keeping.

Having noted the above, there are tricks that allow different opinions to be expressed while protecting group unity. For example, everyone can be encouraged to discuss the pros of one point of view and then the cons of that point of view. Only after all have voiced the positives and negatives of each option is individual preference then invited to be shared.

What this approach suggests is that it is okay to disagree on a matter and still remain a team. It is okay to tell a friend off at times. It is okay to dislike what someone is thinking but still like them as a person. Teamwork can be enriched by differences of opinion.

GOOD TEAMS HAVE A LIMBIC ATTRACTOR

Limbic attractor! What the . . .?

Yes – it's a term likely to leave most people nonplussed. The term 'limbic attractor' was coined by Daniel Goleman[3] to describe a person who has the capacity to draw people to them and influence their moods and attitudes.

Interestingly, the limbic attractor is not always the formally recognised leader of a group. It can be the junior member of staff rather than the manager. It doesn't have to be the school prefect. There can be a problem when the limbic attractor is not the official leader. If the attitude of the limbic attractor is not aligned with that of the official leader, then the official leader can be in trouble. It is far better for the official leader to be the limbic attractor.

Finally, a limbic attractor is not a good asset if they promote values that are inappropriate. The value of a limbic attractor is determined by their alignment and attitude.

A PHOTO TO TAKE

RANGATIRA

The word 'rangatira' comes from New Zealand and has many meanings. One meaning is 'weaver of people'. Rangatira describes a person who is able to gather people and weave them together as friends or as a team. It suggests a person who is creative, who has influence, who is a leader.

If our sons and daughters need a little more encouragement to strengthen their skills as a limbic attractor, the following advice might help.

- Be a little more confident in sharing your views with others, but do not be domineering or manipulative.
- When appropriate, be more open in showing your feelings.
- Reinforce your words with complementary body language. Appropriate posture and expression can greatly increase the impact of leadership.
- Be attractive as a personality. By being kind and empathetic, people will want to identify with you.
- Be empathetic. Understand the moods and feelings of others.

Companies can have their bosses, schools their prefects and communities their mayor, but the real leader, the person to whom others are drawn is the limbic attractor ... and they may be pushing the tea trolley.

GOOD TEAMS WORK TOGETHER

In a team, no-one should be allowed to be a passenger. Nowhere is this illustrated better than in a rowing VIII. As a headmaster of a rowing school, I was often in awe of the disciplined coordination of my rowers. Everyone had to, quite literally, pull their weight.

This is why rowers often remain friends for life. They have shared pain, shared tasks and shared experiences that have moulded them into a team.

They have a collective memory that is similar and much of that memory is about working in unison with others in a boat. Try shaking their hands – it is like gripping a brick wrapped in sandpaper! These callouses unite like nothing else can.

Early in the morning, buses would carry my rowers to dark rivers where they would train for fluvial conflict. The intensity of their combat drills was at odds with the serenity of their setting. Gently rising steam would ghost the air above the water. Into this calm would come the war boats, splintering their mirrored reflections with the wash of their urgent strokes. When the rest of the world awakened to wonder at them, they would put away their craft and blend into normal life.

What my rowers showed me was the reason they were mates. It was the sacrificial commitment. It was the shared experiences. It was the pain.

Some feel they are making a strong contribution when they really are 'passengers', carried along by the momentum of others rather than putting in the power strokes necessary to win. Teamwork involves making a sacrifice for the benefit of others.

There is a definition of commitment that goes beyond that which many, in this frivolous age, are not prepared to accept. Some of our children need to be reminded that commitment to a team, either as leader or as follower, needs to be total if that team is to be effective. To illustrate this fact, the following illustration can be helpful.

> *One day, a chicken and a pig were walking into town to find work. They came across a restaurant with a sign that said it served 'bacon and eggs'.*
>
> *'Let's go in there,' said the chicken. 'If we form a team, we could get great jobs.'*
>
> *'No way,' said the pig, 'For you it is only cooperation but for me it is total commitment.'*

A better example is watching a successful partnership. The partners glide around each other in the kitchen, stirring this, washing that and mixing the other. It's like a dance. There is unconscious coordination and mutual support. A hand is put out: wordlessly, the required item is placed in it. When a phone interrupts, one leaves and the other takes over. It's seamless. It's efficient. It's awesome. The two have become one.

POLITICAL TEAMS

Examples of teamwork, both good and bad, can be found in politics.

The impact of politics has a way of making itself felt in so many ways. It controls how much tax we pay, our schools, defence initiatives, hospitals – the list is considerable.

We should engage with the political world for many reasons, but not least because it provides many examples of good and bad leadership. The Julia Gillard versus Kevin Rudd wars between 2007 and 2013 over the leadership of the Australian Labor Party serve as an example of how toxic a political team can become when it doesn't work properly.

However, there are many examples of politicians who have been successful in team building.

AN IDENTITY TO SOLVE

Who am I?

In terms of honours and awards, I have been presented with:

- The Order of Merit of the Italian Republic.
- The Presidential Medal of Freedom from the United States.
- The Order of the Sun of Peru.
- The Order of Abdulaziz Al Saud from Saudi Arabia.
- The Indira Gandhi Peace Prize.
- The President's Medal from Israel.
- The Order of Prince Henry from Portugal.

I have won the hearts of people in many nations. I have even been awarded a 'Vision for Europe Award' for my all-embracing thinking on a grand scale.

Similar to the former British Prime Minister Margaret Thatcher, I have a degree in Science.

Who am I?

ANGELA DOROTHEA MERKEL (1954–)

As the above list of awards indicates, Merkel knows how to build political teams. Her teamwork with other nations is legendary and has resulted in her being elected President of the European Council and Chair of the G8, as well as the de facto leader of the European Union. However, her influence has extended beyond Europe. In 2006, Merkel pursued Indo-German partnerships with the Indian Prime Minister, Manmohan Singh. In 2007, she pursued transatlantic partnerships with the United States by helping to establish the Transatlantic Economic Council.

This is someone who knows how to build teams. Hardly surprising: Merkel's domestic politics is a story of alliances and teamwork.

After the fall of the Berlin Wall in 1990, Merkel joined a new party called Democratic Awakening. This name hinted at the inclusiveness that was to propel Merkel to the title of the most powerful woman in the world.

Following the reunification of Germany, Merkel was elected to the Bundestag and became the Federal Minister for Women and Youth in 1991. Other ministerial posts followed before her party, the Christian Democratic Union (CDU), lost office in 1998.

The German federal election would have seen Merkel stay out of office had it not been for her willingness to team up with the Christian Social Union (CSU) and the Social Democratic Party of Germany (SPD). Her Centrist Protestant politics found favour in the 2013 federal election but, again, she had to form a team that was made up of CDU, CSU and SPD politicians.

Angela Merkel would have never have held her country's highest office had it not been for her willingness to work with others.[4]

TEAM BUILDERS

One doesn't need to be the leader of Germany to get involved with team building. Our sons and daughters will be put into many teams throughout their lives. Sometimes they will have no say about what team they are put into. At other times, they will. Sometimes, they will be a team leader. At other times, they will be a team member. Sometimes the team will already be in existence. At other times they will be required to form a new team. Therefore, it can be useful to know a little about how to build a team.

GOOD TEAMS ARE BUILT WITH CARE

Quite what is needed to build a good team will vary depending on the purpose of the team. That said, some general principles can be shared.

Establish core values

There must be something that binds the team together, a value or goal that is shared by all. Each member of the team must know the purpose of the team. Collectively working out the mission of the group, its values and its aims can be a useful starting point.

Foster unity

The motto of Indonesia is 'Unity in diversity'. This is a good motto for all teams. They must have the unity of a common goal, but they must also bring to the team different strengths, different perspectives and different skills. Differences should be allowed, but not disunity. There are enough dangers outside the team without having to face dangers within.

Be collegial but take responsibility

Better decisions are made if an idea is tested against a number of informed and intelligent people. A collegial approach to decision making also increases a sense of ownership. However, there should be limits to consultation. It is possible to suffer paralysis by analysis if too many people are involved. It is also important to realise that, in the end, it is the leader who will be held responsible, so it is the leader who has the right to make the final call.

Be fair

Having favourites is fine. Demonstrating favouritism is not fine. There should be fairness and equity when dealing with team members. As far as possible, a leader should ensure that like King Arthur, the table they sit at is round. Encourage inclusiveness and equity where no-one is condemned to a place of insignificance.

Maintain good communication

Good communication is vital. Team members need to know what is going on and feel as though they are trusted with this knowledge.

Obviously, some confidentiality is sometimes required. It is entirely possible to share too much information so that knowledge of what is going on is lost in a sea of *blah*. Get the right balance between too little information and too much information.

Celebrate rituals

A good team will develop its own customs and traditions, its own humour, its own identity. This needs to be encouraged, because it reinforces a sense of belonging.

Theodore Roosevelt once said that the best leaders have the sense to pick good people to do what has to be done, and the self-restraint to stop meddling while they do it.

TWO STORIES TO TELL

ROBERT SCOTT (1868-1912)

Two of Britain's greatest Antarctic explorers, Robert Scott and Ernest Shackleton (who we met in Lesson Three), were team builders. However, they liked to build their own teams because they disliked each other intensely. This dislike was fuelled by contrasting personalities. Scott was a brooding, introverted Englishman. Shackleton was an optimistic, extrovert Irishman. The animosity was heightened by a similar objective: both wanted to get to the South Pole first.

Shackleton had once been a part of Scott's team and had joined Scott's first expedition to the South Pole in 1901-1903. They had sailed in the *Discovery*, established a base at Hut Point on Ross Island in Antarctica and engaged in an ill-prepared but heroic push to the South Pole. Scurvy, exhaustion and lack of food forced the party back. Shackleton collapsed and Scott used this as an excuse to send Shackleton back to England while the rest of the party stayed on for another year.

Wanting to redeem himself, Shackleton launched his own expedition to the South Pole a few years later. In 1907 he set sail in the *Nimrod*. Scott was furious, because he regarded it as his right to be the first to reach the South Pole. At only 150 kilometres from the South Pole, exhaustion, dysentery and frostbite forced Shackleton back. He was philosophical about the failure, suggesting that it was better to be 'a live donkey than a dead lion'.

Like Scott's attempt, Shackleton's expedition was compromised by an over-reliance on brawn over brain, on ponies rather than dogs, and on walking rather than skiing. These failings were to cost one of these men the prize of reaching the South Pole and the other his life.

Scott launched another expedition to the South Pole in 1910, but this time his adversary was not Shackleton: it was a Norwegian called Roald Amundsen (see Lesson Five, p. 118). The Norwegian planned his assault on the South Pole in secret at the same time as Scott was planning his expedition in public. Amundsen sailed with a team that expected him to go north to the Arctic, but when they reached Madeira, Amundsen confessed his true destination. Scott learned of Amundsen's plans in a telegram he picked up in Melbourne, which read, 'Am going south. Amundsen.' The race was on.

Chasing after Amundsen, Scott sailed on the *Terra Nova* and established a base at Cape Evans, McMurdo Sound. He then started laying supply depots along his proposed route to the South Pole. When the push to the Pole began, Scott's party made slow progress. The horses proved inadequate, the mechanised sledges broke down, the blizzards raged.

Meanwhile the Norwegians set off from a base closer to the South Pole and, using skis and dogs, they made good progress and travelled at more than twice the speed of Scott's team. When Amundsen was slowed down by the troublesome Trans-Antarctic Mountains, he had no qualms about shooting twenty-four of his forty-two dogs for food. With fewer supplies to pull, fewer dogs were needed. On 14 December 1911, Amundsen's team reached the South Pole, took photos, raised the Norwegian flag, left some supplies and a note for Scott, then set off for their home base. Having spent fewer than 100 days on the entire journey, the Norwegians arrived back to their base from which they then set sail for Europe.

A little over a month after Amundsen's team reached the South Pole, Scott's team arrived to find the Norwegian flag flying, Amundsen's tent pitched and their dreams shattered. It was a dispirited team that began the return journey. Scott's party battled fearful weather, inadequate food, frostbite and injury; Edgar Evans collapsed first, then Lawrence Oates. Conscious that he was endangering the chances of survival of the party due to his injuries, Oates quietly stepped out of the tent to walk into the blizzard and die. His last words were, 'I am just going outside and may be some time.'

Unfortunately, the sacrifice made by Oates was to no avail. Scott, Bowers and Wilson froze to death in their tent just 18 kilometres from one of their supply depots. Scott's diary read:

> *Had we lived, I should have a tale to tell of hardihood, endurance and courage of my companions which would have stirred the heart of every Englishman.*

Their bodies were found by a search party seven and a half months after Scott's lines were written.[5]

ERNEST SHACKLETON (1874–1922)

With the prize of being the first to reach the South Pole achieved by Amundsen, Shackleton had to think of another reason to mount an expedition. He decided to be the first to walk across Antarctica. A sceptical public suggested the South Pole had already been discovered, and asked, 'Why go there again?' Others argued that the party would be better employed fighting in Europe's new war rather than sailing on some expensive expedition. Nonetheless, Shackleton and his party set off in the sailing ship *Endurance* on 8 August 1914.

Not long after the *Endurance* sailed into the Antarctic region it became trapped in pack ice, where it remained bound through endless winter months. The following summer did not see the ice loosen its embrace. The grip tightened to a death-hug, which crushed and sank the ship.

A bold plan was then engaged in to walk 480 kilometres across the pack ice towards land. Shackleton's team packed their supplies into wooden life-boats, put the life-boats on sledges and began dragging them toward the northwest. However, exhaustion forced the party to stop and reconsider. Shackleton then set up 'Ocean Camp' on an ice floe. Summer arrived and melted the ice, thus forcing the party to move to a new patch of ice and set up 'Patience Camp'. There they drifted until they spotted land.

The twenty-eight men got into their life-boats and headed for the land. After seven days of gales and contrary currents, they finally set foot on solid ground. However, they soon found that Elephant Island was a barren, windswept place. Even more of a problem was the fact that no-one would think to search for the party on the island. Therefore, it was up to Shackleton and his men to rescue themselves.

A scheme was hatched whereby six of the party would sail the 7-metre lifeboat *James Caird* 1200 kilometres to South Georgia in South America. This was no small challenge. Ahead of them lay some of the most dangerous seas in the world.

The journey was a catalogue of hardship. Skin was rubbed raw, bones were chilled and the men were exhausted by the constant requirement to chip away at the ice that threatened to sink them. Two weeks into the voyage Shackleton saw what he thought was a break in the clouds. It wasn't. It was the crest of the most enormous wave he'd ever seen. They were swamped but survived. After sixteen days at sea, the *James Caird* finally reached a rocky inlet called King Haakon Bay in South Georgia.

However, they were still not safe. Haakon Bay was uninhabited. Help was still 32 kilometres away at the Stromness whaling station.

In between lay several large mountain ranges. With rotting shoes, Shackleton and two of his companions had to scale a succession of icy mountain ridges. They descended one ridge in two minutes by forming a human toboggan and sliding down 1000 metres.

The settlers at Stromness were shocked to see the dishevelled party stagger in. After resting and recovering, Shackleton rescued his three colleagues left at Haakon Bay and made plans to recover the remaining twenty-two men on Elephant Island. A series of attempts to rescue the men failed because of thick pack ice, but finally the Chilean steamer *Yelco* arrived off Elephant Island in a blanket of fog. As the fog lifted to reveal the ship to those marooned on the island, there was great excitement. This excitement was matched on board the *Yelco* as Shackleton counted his men through the binoculars and realised that all had survived.

TEAM BUILDING

Although both Scott and Shackleton were blighted by failure, there is much that can be learned about teamwork from these heroes of the ice. Our sons and daughters can be encouraged to undertake the following activities to show leadership and foster teamwork.

- **Inspire others with charisma, energy and vision**.
  To equip both the *Nimrod* and *Endurance* expeditions, many millions of dollars, in today's terms, were needed in sponsorship. Despite sponsorship being difficult, Shackleton was successful in raising this money. He did this using his personal charisma and passion.
- **Undertake proper research**. Shackleton was a voracious reader and researched matters carefully. He was not afraid to take advice from his team and from experts. The Burberry boots issued to his crew were based on a design used by the man who had beaten him to the South Pole, Roald Amundsen.

- **Establish yourself as leader**. Shackleton was called 'The Boss' by his team. At all times, Shackleton's men were never in any doubt as to who the leader was, and whose responsibility it was to make the final decision.
- **Set challenging goals for your team but if they become impossible, revise them.** Shackleton's goal was to be the first to reach the South Pole. When he was beaten in this endeavour, he was not afraid to change his goal to being the first to walk across Antarctica. When adrift in lifeboats after the sinking of the *Endurance*, Shackleton gave up trying to reach King George Island to the west, or Hope Bay to the southwest. He sailed to Elephant Island from which he masterminded a dramatic rescue.
- **Build a balanced team**. In choosing the crew for the *Endurance* expedition, Shackleton selected a balanced team of experienced polar veterans and new members. Shackleton also rotated assignments in order to be fair and remove any sense of hierarchy.
- **Appoint a good second in command**. In Frank Wild, Shackleton had a fine deputy, one on whom he relied a great deal. Wild had to run the camp on Elephant Island for many months while waiting to be rescued.
- **Isolate and control potential troublemakers**. When the *Endurance* sank and the party had to live in tents, Shackleton ensured that the more difficult members of the party were placed with him. This included the rather egocentric but brilliant photographer Frank Hurley. When sailing in the lifeboats, Shackleton was careful to place the two more pessimistic team members, John Vincent and Henry McNish, with him.
- **Remain accessible and connected to your team**. Shackleton remained close to his men and gave each member of his team easy access to him. His cabin on the *Endurance* became a conference and counselling centre for the entire crew.

- **Lead by example**. Shackleton never gave a task to others that he was not prepared to do himself. This included cleaning the wardroom on the *Endurance*, pulling sledges and going on watch at night. His rations were the same as his men, and when there was a dangerous task to do, as often as not he would do it himself.

- **Be self-sacrificing**. On the *Nimrod* expedition, a half-starved Shackleton threatened to bury his biscuit in the snow if Wild did not take it and eat it. On the *Endurance* expedition, when Hurley lost his gloves in the freezing seas, Shackleton insisted that Hurley wear his own gloves.

- **Maintain high morale in the team**. Shackleton was a natural wit. His humour, love of singing hymns, enjoyment of birthdays and special occasions helped raise the spirits of his men. The long days and nights on the *Endurance* were punctuated with slide shows, special dinners and music evenings.

- **Be solid in a crisis**. When abandoning the *Endurance*, Shackleton made an inspirational speech that gave hope to his men.

- **Establish routines and discipline**. When the *Endurance* sailed to the South Pole, discipline was not strong. It was only when Shackleton joined the ship at Buenos Aires that good discipline – including regular work details, physical exercises and proper standards – was established.

- **Weather setbacks**. When Shackleton was sent back from the South Pole by Scott on the *Discovery* expedition in 1903, he was bitterly disappointed. However, Shackleton did not give up. He went back to Great Britain and organised another expedition to the South Pole using the *Nimrod*.

- **Remain optimistic**. With his ship crushed by ice, his men marooned on a freezing lump of rock and a perilous journey over several mountain ranges ahead of him, it would have been easy for Shackleton to give up. He didn't.

- **Have a moral base**. Shackleton's life was not without fault, yet he was deeply moral and frequently called upon his religious convictions to help him through life.[6]

As evidenced by the Antarctic explorers, it is important for a team leader to have an ability to do the following:

- Win the trust and confidence of their team.
- Ensure the team has ownership of the goals.
- Communicate well and keep the team informed.
- Take a personal interest in each team member and make them feel important.
- Give praise and encouragement.
- Work collaboratively but accept responsibility.
- Use individual strengths.
- Set an example.
- Make good decisions.
- Care for the team.
- Train their team well.
- Share the success.

Heroic example is all well and good, but most of our sons and daughters will not be trudging the frozen wastes of Antarctica. They will be at school – so let's look at teamwork in schools.

TEAMWORK IN SCHOOLS

In truth, schools are not always good at encouraging teamwork. Some teamwork occurs both in and out of the classroom, but for much of their time students are required to work individually. Worse than that, they are often in competition with each other. Academic rankings and scholastic league tables can kill off teamwork and cause students to hunch over their work and share with no-one.

TEAMING UP WITH STUDENTS

Some schools try to develop teamwork by insisting on group-work in class. This is done in many ways, not least by setting group assignments. In reality, this approach does not always work, because some students do a great deal of the work, while others are passengers. This results in grumbles because everyone is given the same mark.

A CONUNDRUM TO SOLVE

The above scenario is a good one to discuss with your teenager. Is it fair to give the same mark to everyone for a group assignment when the lazy and weak have been carried by the industrious and able?

Is there a way to overcome this problem? Should the assignment be broken up into sections and each part marked on its individual merit? On the other hand, perhaps the same mark should be given to everyone, recognising that it is the task of the whole group to motivate, direct and encourage the underachieving member. Is this not what leadership is about?

Although teams choreographed by teachers don't always work, teams put together by students usually do. Those who take the initiative to find 'study buddies' and form groups that are prepared to share notes, evaluate essays and help with learning tasks do themselves a great favour. Groups such as this can be the salvation of a student.

TEAMING UP WITH TEACHERS

It is also important to team up with teachers. Why? Because so much of leadership depends upon using the skill of others.

Fortunately, the awesome gap between teacher and student in the early years of school typically begins to close in the later years. Although there must always remain some professional distance between student and teacher, the final years of schooling can often see a closer relationship between the two.

Those students who insist on preserving the 'us and them' mentality are denying themselves a source of great enrichment. Those who work with their teachers and see the teacher as an ally rather than an enemy are usually the ones who flourish at school.

A STORY TO SHARE

ANNE MANSFIELD SULLIVAN (1866–1936)

An example of a great student-teacher relationship is provided by Anne Mansfield Sullivan, who not only became Helen Keller's teacher but also her friend.

Anne arrived at the Kellers' home in Alabama having journeyed there from the Perkins Institution for the Blind in Boston. She was met by an angry deaf-mute called Helen who wanted to have nothing to do with her new teacher. In her book, *The Story of My Life*, Helen described herself as being in a dense fog, a white darkness. This was not surprising, because Helen was blind.

However, Anne Sullivan persisted with her teaching and Helen's attitude changed. Anne helped Helen understand that everything had a name. Within three years, Helen had learned to read and write in Braille. Later, Helen went on to school and university. Thereafter, she had a distinguished career as a pioneer in helping the deaf and blind.

Helen and Anne remained friends until Anne died in 1936.[7]

'Yes,' I hear your teen say, 'but I haven't got Anne Sullivan as my teacher. I've got Mr X. He drones on in class, has no sense of humour, and has a dandruff issue. Then there is Ms Y. She's a loser and hates everyone – especially me.'

If this sort of response is heard, then the challenge to give our smouldering critic is to make the relationship work anyway.

You don't always have to like your teacher, but you have to respect them. If a teacher is difficult to get on with, then make it a game and try to win the teacher over. Don't add to the problem of having a poor teacher by allowing it to wreck your school grades. Make the situation work for you. Life is not always going to present you with wonderful people to work with. Get used to it!

There are all manner of ways to win over a teacher. Start with a smile. Ask the occasional question in class. Get them to help you with your assignment. Work it. Work it. Work it!

It *is* possible to get teachers to operate as a member of a student's 'team'.

WHEN TEAMWORK IS NOT HELPFUL

There are times when teamwork is not a good idea. Others can hold you back.

It has been suggested that, 'There is no "I" in team'. This aphorism is trotted out to encourage devotion to the team rather than to self. While the sentiment is good at one level, it is extremely dangerous at another.

No-one should ever surrender their complete identity. Just because others are doing something does not abrogate the responsibility to think through whether you should do it. *I was led astray* is the confession of a weak person. Our sons and daughters need to be reminded of the importance of taking ownership of their lives.

Just as eating some foods accelerates and improves mental functioning (think fruit and vegetables) and some foods slow mental activity (think fries and other forms of junk food), some teams can accelerate personal development while other teams can slow it.

More than one teenager has been led into alcohol and drug use, abusive sexual relationships and high-risk behaviours that have blighted leadership opportunities. More than one young person has been accelerated into significant achievement by a team that has inspired, equipped and encouraged them.

There is an 'I' in team. This is important to remember because there are good teams and there are bad teams. Complicating things is when a team is both good and bad. It might be good to give total allegiance to a team on the footy field. However, it may not be good to give total allegiance to that team in the pub.

LEADERSHIP IN MEETINGS

A common situation where leadership is expressed is in meetings.

There are all sorts of meetings our children will attend in life. Many of these will be informal gatherings. Because of the huge range of variables associated with such meetings, it is difficult to give specific advice about informal meetings other than to seek to understand more than be understood, to listen more than speak and to act with wisdom.

With formal meetings, rather more specific advice can be given. A resigned gloom often tends to settle on people when they are asked to attend a meeting. This is probably a product of two main things: a frantic life in which little time is available to attend meetings, and previous experience of meetings that were long and unproductive.

A GOOD MEETING IS MADE UP OF TWELVE PEOPLE, OF WHOM ELEVEN ARE ABSENT.

It is possible to show leadership and run a good meeting, but the meeting must be prepared for.

One of the essential prerequisites of a good meeting is that it be necessary, and that matters need to be discussed and issues decided upon. If a meeting is being held merely to give information, then other options exist such as sending emails, faxes and bulletins.

Therefore, before calling any meeting, check whether the meeting is really necessary or whether there is another method of dealing with the issues.

If a formal meeting is necessary, then the following advice might be helpful:

- Have a clear purpose for the meeting.
- Be careful to have the right people at the meeting. All those eligible should be informed and invited, but it can be useful to ensure those with the capacity to contribute meaningfully to the meeting are given particular encouragement to attend.
- Make sure discussion is not dominated by a few.
- Ensure the meeting is orderly, collegial and businesslike.
- Keep the meeting focused on the relevant issues.
- Ensure a proper record is kept of the meeting.
- Discuss matters in a balanced way with all contributing to the pros and cons of a proposal. If possible, avoid factions.
- Insist on proper procedure.
- Action points need to be decided, duties given and timelines attached.
- Avoid having a meeting that fails to maintain good traction on issues.

Meetings need not be boring and unproductive. If well run, meetings can be useful in advancing the cause of an organisation. Further details on how to run a more formal meeting can be found on the internet. The roles of the Convenor, Chair, Secretary and Treasurer need to be well understood by those whose leadership duties will involve attending such meetings.

DELEGATION

The happy news for the budding leader is that a leader doesn't have to do everything.

Some leaders feel it is necessary to be worn to a frazzle, and they use their exhaustion as a testimony to their dedication. It is often praised as 'setting the example' and of asking more from themselves than their followers. However, the non-delegating workaholic can be a liability. They may be a revealing a distrust of others and an over-inflated opinion of their own abilities. Our sons and daughters need to learn that delegation can be a strength, not a weakness.

More than once I have read descriptions of a head's role in a school. Typically, it involves a depressingly long list of tasks. It is then that I find myself tempted to retire.

A PHOTO TO TAKE

> Leadership is not about the capacity to do things.
> It is about the capacity to get them done.

It is worth remembering that it is one thing to delegate and it is altogether another thing to delegate effectively.

To delegate effectively means:

- Taking time to select trustworthy people.
- Taking time to train them.
- Taking time to define their tasks properly.

DELEGATION SHOULD NOT BE CONFUSED WITH DERELICTION.

When a job is delegated, it is the duty of the team leader to monitor those who have been given tasks, to check there is progress and that those who have been given the tasks feel supported.

Do not delegate when:
- You can do the job better than the person delegated to do it.
- The issues are so important they should not be decided by anyone other than the leader.

- The issues are difficult, and could overwhelm the person delegated.
- The opposition is strong and could overwhelm the person delegated.
- You do not have complete faith that your delegates share your views, will keep you informed and will check major decisions with you.

Do delegate when:
- Your delegates can do the job better than you could.
- You have delegates who are strong.
- You have delegates who are loyal.
- You have delegates who are competent.
- You have delegates who understand the limits of their authority.

All for one, and one for all.
Alexandre Dumas, *The Three Musketeers*

LOYALTY

Leaders have no right to expect loyalty if they are not prepared to give loyalty.

More than one executive has moaned about lack of loyalty without realising they have never modelled loyalty themselves. One hears of workers who, after labouring a lifetime for a company, are retrenched without warning because shareholder dividends must increase and executive bonuses protected. Despite calling it 'downsizing' or 'restructuring', people's lives are shattered and, with it, any right to loyalty from those remaining.

Loyalty can be described as the allegiance of one to another. It hints at commitment, solidarity, dedication, constancy and devotion. If leaders devote themselves to their followers, their followers will devote themselves to their leaders.

DESERVED LEADERSHIP

In some organisations, senior executives are so self-absorbed that they are unable to identify with, or even appreciate, their junior workers. This results in the junior workers failing to identify with or appreciate their senior executives. As a result, an 'us and them' mentality flourishes and any prospect of teamwork vanishes.

Teamwork will also vanish if it is felt that leaders are seeking to advantage themselves rather than the organisation.

That said, beware the green-eyed monster of jealousy. The bigger paycheque and bigger office given to an executive is not always inappropriate. They are usually the ones who must bear the burden of responsibility.

'ENVY IMPERILS LOYALTY'

FINALLY

No-one should think themselves unable to draw a team around them. Even if it is a loose assembly of friends and loved ones, it is a team. All teams, whether formal or informal, need to be valued and nurtured.

Some of our sons and daughters will be privileged to lead teams both at school and later on in life. They need to be prepared for this role. The best preparation is to learn to be a good team member.

SUMMARY

- Everyone needs a support base, even if it is an informal team of friends and family.
- Informal teams, such as friendship groups, can have an enormous influence.
- Many teens treat their mobile phone as their team. It is a source of friendship and support, but like any team, the mobile phone needs to be managed carefully.

- Effective teams have a number of common features including a sense of belonging, pride, common purpose, commitment, synergy and loyalty. They also have similar core values, collegial thinking, equity and good communication.
- Team leaders can be more effective if they are a 'limbic attractor'.
- Teams should accommodate differences of opinion but not differences of purpose.
- Good teams need a diversity of skills.
- Teamwork can be encouraged at school between students and other students, and between students and teachers.
- Sometimes teamwork can stifle individual creativity.
- There are certain protocols to running a formal meeting that can be useful to know.
- Effective delegation is an essential skill for a team leader. It is not necessary for team leaders to be able to do things, but they must be able to get them done.
- Leaders deserve the teams they get. Good leaders create good teams.
- You cannot be a good team leader if you haven't learned to become a good team member.

A strategy to adopt

Leadership is improved when a leader plans – and even more so when a leader plans strategically.

By strategically, I mean the deliberate deployment of ideas and stratagems in order to achieve one's objectives. Planning involves deciding where you want to get to, plus some consideration of how you are going to get there. Strategic planning is more. It involves a deeper analysis and it takes within the orbit of its consideration a careful evaluation of the variables that may affect the outcome of the plan. Furthermore, it institutes a response that ensures these variables are dealt with.

Knowing where you want to get to is often seen as the key challenge. This is not true. Our sons and daughters usually have no problem dreaming of untold wealth, unending fun and unspoiled ease. Having a plan to achieve this end is also seen as an essential task, which is good. However, having a *strategic* plan is better.

ENTHUSIASM IS NO SUBSTITUTE FOR THINKING.

GUNNERS

There are some who don't even get as far as planning. They are 'gunners'. They are gunner do this and they are gunner do that, but they never get around to doing anything. Whether it is an organisational issue or because they are so distracted with the present they do not plan for the future, some people are unable to get themselves started. Inertia steals such opportunities that exist to transform a dream into a reality. That, and procrastination.

Some do have a goal, but the strategy they use to attain it is hopeless. They have learned that if they want something, all they have to do is whinge, moan and carry on like a wet week and someone will come along and give it to them – often a parent. In the early years, it is ice-cream. In the middle years it is the mobile phone and Facebook account. In the later years, it is the money, the car, the room, the . . .

However, outside of the home, this strategy tends not to work. The famous British physicist Ernest Rutherford once said: 'We haven't got the money, so we've got to think.'

Strategic thinking becomes even more important when the problems are significant.

STRATEGIC THINKING

Strategic thinking needs a mindfulness of the variables that have an impact on the situation. It requires an understanding of what is important and what is not. It involves an analysis of strengths, weaknesses, opportunities and threats. It demands higher-order thinking skills.

Strategic thinking is the mental process engaged in to achieve a goal. It is often linking to strategic planning, which involves putting a plan in place to achieve a goal.

The forming and implementing of a strategic plan is generally made more effective if it has benefitted from left-brain logical thinking and right-brain creative thinking. Common sense and the use of tried-and-tested lessons from the past can also be helpful. However, room should also be made for 'out-of-the-box' thinking, left-field solutions and totally new approaches.

For this reason, strategic thinking is often enriched by a team made up of different thinkers. That said, it can also be good for the leaders to spend some time alone, in order to bring to bear their own thoughts without the clamouring distraction of others.

STRATEGIC PLANNING

A plan is generally thought strategic if it works. For a plan to be successful, it requires a thorough understanding of what will make it work. One of the main things that will make a plan work is whether it is successful in meeting the needs of the main stakeholders.

For example, it is strategically silly for a student to petition a school for a student car park if it means knocking down the staffroom and principal's office. For a strategy to be successful, the key stakeholders need to support it.

A useful way to check stakeholder support is to use the mnemonic CATWALK:

C   Clarify exactly what the goal is. Check that it is a realistic venture to embark upon.

A   Assess the whole picture. Who are the permission givers and what are the obstacles?

T   Tease out the relationships between the venture and the key people involved.

W   Work out what the stakeholders want.

A   Align what the stakeholders want with what you want.

L   Leverage the support of a few to gain general acceptance.

K   Know how to reward those who have supported you.

In the end, strategy needs the support of people to make it work. Therefore, it is not enough to have a plan. It must be a good plan.

The VUCA world

The term VUCA derives from the US military. It describes a world characterised by:

Volatility   Change is rapid and its direction uncertain.

Uncertainty   It is increasingly difficult to predict the future.

Complexity   The interrelationship between multiple variables can be chaotic.

Ambiguity   Reality, morality and meaning are less clear.

These characteristics of the modern world can overwhelm the young. *Where should I start when sorting out my career? How should I react to my best friend coming out? Will my parents' divorce mean I see less of them?*

How can the young cope with the VUCA world?

There are no magical solutions, but the following mnemonic is not a bad antidote to VUCA:

C   Clarify what is important.

A   Analyse the facts.

L   Let the emotion out.

M   Make an informed decision.

Any decision that is made needs to be:

Morally right. *The guy selling dope at the train station needs to be reported.*

Strategically clever. *Let's turn the graffitied toilet block into a place for quality graffiti art.*

Generative. *We shouldn't just tell the principal there's a problem, let's suggest a solution.*

Decisive. *We're going to hold the fundraiser on 8 August on the sports field at 11 a.m.*

The military world can be a useful resource when searching for examples of effective strategy. Although not all military strategy relates well to a teenager's life, some principles can be drawn from good military leaders.

The general must know how to get his men their rations and every other kind of stores needed for war. He must have imagination to originate plans, practical sense, and energy to carry them through. He must be observant, untiring, shrewd, kindly and cruel, simple and crafty; a watchman and soldier; lavish and miserly; generous yet tight-fisted; both rash and conservative. All these and other qualities, natural and acquired, he must have. He should also, as a matter of course, know his tactics; for a disorderly mob is no more an army than a heap of building materials is a house.

Socrates

> The father of western military strategy was the eighteenth-century Prussian Carl von Clausewitz. The father of eastern military strategy was the Chinese General Sun Tzu, who lived around 500 BC.

STRATEGIC MILITARY LEADERSHIP

Military history gives examples of strategy being used well and used badly. Among those generally considered good strategic thinkers are the following:

Arthur Wellesley (1769–1852) Duke of Wellington
The 'Iron Duke' and victor over Napoleon often limited his casualties by using the 'reverse-slope' tactic. This involved keeping his forces behind the brow of a hill so that they were effectively screened from artillery fire.[1]

Shaka (c. 1773–1828) Founder of the Zulu Empire

The military tactic used by Shaka was to arm his warriors with a short stabbing spear called the *assegai*. This forced the opposition into close combat at which the Zulus excelled. Shaka would resist the enemy using a strong 'chest' and then use two 'horns', which would encircle the enemy. A reserve unit, known as the 'loins', would back up the assault. This reserve unit would sit facing away from the fight lest they get too excited and join the battle prematurely.

Horatio Nelson (1758–1805) British Admiral

Nelson was one of the great British maritime commanders. His tactics varied, but they generally were characterised by originality and daring. Nelson would sometimes come alongside enemy ships and, trusting in his sailors' ability to fire three broadsides to the enemy's two broadsides, battle it out with the odds on his side. At other times Nelson would cut through the enemy line and fire into the two weakest spots: the stern and the bow of their ships.[2]

Marina Raskova (1912–1943) Russian Airforce Pioneer

In World War II, Marina Raskova was instrumental in establishing three all-female flying units to take on the Nazis. The 46th Taman Guards Bomber Aviation Regiment was given outdated Polikarpov Po-2 biplanes to use. However, by using these bombers at night, they proved to be very effective, to the extent the Germans called them 'The Night Witches'.[3]

CONTEMPORARY MILITARY TACTICS

When thinking about what is strategic, it is important to consider context. For example, Nelson's advantage of well-built ships and superior firepower may have guaranteed victory in the eighteenth century but not necessarily in the twenty-first century.

The contemporary age is witnessing the tactical use of 'asymmetric warfare': military confrontations in which a powerful nation, such as Britain, Russia or the United States, fights a much less powerful group such as Al-Qaeda or ISIS.

What stops the confrontation from becoming a short-lived, one-sided affair is the employment of tactics that neutralise superior fire-power.

These tactics are painfully well known to the west. Melting into the local community. Operating in small groups. Instilling terror through barbarity. Gaining converts by indoctrination. Promising religious rewards. Using women and children. Attacking soft targets. Using social-networking sites.

Another term that has made an appearance in contemporary times is 'netwar'. This is a war against a force that is scattered. It is a war fought by a loose connection of individual units committed to the same general ideal. It has no centralised command-and-control system that can be neutralised by a well-aimed bomb. It is hydra-headed: cutting off one branch merely sees another grow elsewhere.[4]

TACTICAL WISDOM

Advice parents give their teens needs to be finessed with a little tactical wisdom. The 'In my day' speech may not be as effective as it once was.

Having noted this, some advice is timeless.

A PHOTO TO TAKE

The lion cub said, 'Mum, let's rush on down there and grab one of those goats.'

The lioness replied, 'No son, let's sneak on down there and grab both of the goats.'

The lion cub was planning. The lioness was planning strategically.

A feature of strategic action is that the consequences related to each option are carefully thought through. A plan might be strong, forceful and brave, but it can also be stupid. Check out what happened at the Charge of the Light Brigade on 25 October 1854 during the Crimean War. It was courageous, but it was also stupid.[5] The charge of the British light cavalry against Russian forces during the Battle of Balaclava pitted 670 mounted troopers against 50 artillery pieces. Two hundred and seventy-eight troopers were killed or wounded. Many others were taken prisoner and 335 horses were killed. No military gains were made as a result of the heroic obedience to suicidal orders.

Our sons and daughters need to understand that for an action to be strategic, all possible options need to be considered. Often, diplomacy is better than confrontation. Often, handing the problem over to the proper authorities is better than trying to solve it yourself. Often, a goal will only be achieved if a number of intermediate steps are taken.

WHERE DO WE WANT TO GET TO?

This book cannot give advice on how to reach all the goals our sons and daughters may have. However, a number of general guidelines can be given.

Achieving a goal requires planning – strategic planning, which means finding out:

- Where am I now?
- Where do I want to get to?
- How am I going to get there?

Where am I now?

We all need a firm base from which to launch any initiative. Part of this base is a solid understanding of our current position. If incorrect assumptions are made at this early stage, we will be building plans on shaky ground rather than on a solid foundation of accurate knowledge.

GALILEO

The Christian leaders in the early seventeenth century thought they knew where they were: they were at the very centre of God's universe. To say otherwise was to risk expulsion from the Church, torture and death.

Galileo Galilei, an Italian astronomer and physicist, was born in Pisa in 1564. After inventing the telescope, making a number of other important discoveries and moving to Florence, he published his *Dialogue Concerning the Two Chief World Systems* in 1624. Within the book, he suggested that the earth was not at the centre of the universe, but rather revolved around the sun.

The Church was appalled at this suggestion and forced Galileo to apologise and withdraw his theory. Furthermore, he was required to live the remainder of his life under house arrest. Science and theology combine today to suggest that the Church was wrong and that Galileo was right. The Church thought it knew where it was, but it did not. As a result, it stifled one of the greatest intellects of the age.[6]

It is important to test assumptions and check the validity of other ideas.

Where do I want to get to?

Some people are content with where they are and don't want to go anywhere else. This can be fine in some circumstances. There will be times when staying where we are is the best option.

However, for most, life is a journey. To stop journeying is to stop progressing, and to stop progressing is to stop living life to the fullest.

Deciding where you want to get to means having an objective. The best objectives are practical, achievable and measurable. At least, this is the sort of thing many management gurus suggest. But are they right? Not everything in the world can be measured in neat, quantifiable terms. We mustn't fall into the trap of measuring only those things that can be measured. What about love? What about service? What about contentment?

Some goals are difficult to measure but this does not necessarily make them any less valuable. Other goals may be considered difficult to achieve but this should not prevent you trying to achieve them. Finally, some of the best things that have ever been done have not been all that practical. Pyramids. Easter Island Statues. The Statue of Liberty. Much of the world's art and music – one could go on. Therefore, we need to be careful accepting what some management gurus say about the sort of goals we need to set.

Having noted the above, it is good if our sons and daughters know what they want to achieve in life. If not, they should think through various options.

Seneca once said: *'If a person does not know what harbour they seek, then any wind is the right wind.'*

How are you going to get there?

SWOT

A useful approach to solving the question of how you are going to achieve a goal is to undertake a SWOT analysis. This method of strategic thinking has been around for some time and has proved effective in helping many to decide the best way to improve a situation.

SWOT is an acronym for:

- **S**trengths
- **W**eaknesses
- **O**pportunities
- **T**hreats

An analysis of strengths and weaknesses typically involves an analysis of internal factors, i.e. factors to do with you.

An analysis of opportunities and threats typically involves an analysis of external factors – that is, factors to do with the environment.

A PHOTO TO TAKE

Some steps to find out what you should do in the future:
1. Think through what your strengths are.
2. Think through what your weaknesses are.
3. Think through what your opportunities are.
4. Think through what your threats are.

Becoming a leader at school

It is not unknown for some teens to be quite chuffed at being selected for a student leadership position at school. Others couldn't care less. Nonetheless for the purposes of illustrating a SWOT analysis, we'll assume a scenario in which a son or daughter is hoping to become a school prefect.

A good way to start this quest is to get a job description of a school prefect. If no such job description exists, don't worry. You don't have to be clairvoyant to know the job description would probably go along the lines of that which is described on page 62.

Having done this, get your aspiring leader to assess themselves on each element of the job description. This will allow them to work out their strengths and discover the areas of weakness they may profitably work on.

Thereafter, look at the opportunities and threats. The threats are pretty clear. They may not get selected. Others may get chosen instead. They might have a bad behaviour record. They may not get on well with those who do the selection.

Whatever the threats, there are opportunities available to neutralise most of them. For example:

- Signalling interest in a leadership position to the people who matter.
- Getting advice from the selectors as to how to improve selection chances.
- If necessary, making a full apology for behaviours of the past and promising reform.
- Taking opportunities to become involved and to demonstrate initiative, such as running a fundraising event or charity function.
- Start behaving like the person in the job description.

If prefect selection is determined by a student ballot, then adjust the advice above to make it more student friendly. Remember that popularity is not as helpful as respect. Being known as a 'good' person is better than being known as a 'good time' person.

The issue of school leadership is not big in the minds of all our sons and daughters. So – what is?

Answer: Sex. Love. Friendship.

Even in this delicate area, elements of the SWOT approach can be employed.

Finding romance

At times, no strategy is needed to find a girlfriend or a boyfriend. Often, Cupid fires an arrow and – kapow! – it just happens.

At other times, the process of finding a girlfriend or boyfriend can be painfully difficult. The days of clubbing the desired partner over the head and dragging them into your cave are gone. A rather more nuanced approach is needed.

We'll not spend long on the 'strengths' and 'weaknesses' element of this exercise other than to say that a good and realistic understanding of one's own personal strengths is vital – but not to the extent it breeds arrogance or vanity. Our sons and daughters need to know what they have to offer in a relationship.

They also need to be aware of what they cannot offer – of the weaknesses they have as a person. It may be a difficulty with words. It can be a tendency to be moody. It might be a frantic lifestyle that leaves little time for intimacy. If some honest reflection reveals a few areas that need to be worked on, then good – they have something to work on to improve their chances of adding romance to their life.

When it's the weekend, the music's pumping, the drink is flowing, the hour is late and the hormones are running, it is unlikely that a SWOT analysis centred on some gorgeous creature on the dance floor is going to take place. It won't. So – let's talk Monday morning.

When the time for sober reflection arrives on how a relationship might be advanced, a number of options exist, including:

- Getting their phone number and 'friending' them on Facebook.
- 'Liking' their photos on Instagram.
- Showing an online interest in them.
- Hanging out with them.
- Paying conscious attention to personal grooming.

- Listening. Asking questions. Employing humour.
- Sharing in an interest or hobby. Watching them play sport, etc.
- Inviting them to join your friends on group outings to the shops, cinema, beach, etc.
- Saying nice things about them to friends (this usually filters back).
- Soliciting mutual friends to check out how they are feeling about you.
- Dancing with them at the next party.
- Inviting them round to watch a movie.
- Ensuring that texts and emails confirm ongoing interest.
- Giving a little gift when the opportunity comes. For example, a chocolate egg at Easter, a Valentine's Day card, a birthday or Christmas card, a souvenir from a holiday.
- Giving them opportunities to help – be it fixing a loose chain on a bike, assistance with an English essay or sympathy when you've had a row with parents.
- Looking for opportunities to be kind to them – be it giving them a lift in the car (if legal to do so) or minding their goldfish when they've been whisked away on a family holiday.
- Connecting with what they're interested in. Make them a cupcake in the colours of their football team, share their interest in online gaming and so on.
- Carefully and sensitively disconnecting from any existing romance.

The list could go on, but enough has been shared to illustrate that for a goal to be achieved, it requires a person to get off their backside and do something. It's no good moping around and doing the sobbing and sighing thing because the love of your life is not yet found or is not returning affection. Take the initiative. Within the bounds of decency and good taste, think of ways to become more attractive. Be nice.

Even if all the initiatives listed above fail, options still exist to find romance. For example, go to venues frequented by people you like. Put yourself out there!

DIFFERING STRATAGEMS FOR DIFFERENT TIMES

Our sons and daughters need to be adaptable. They must be able to adjust their leadership style to suit a situation. Sometimes it will be appropriate for a leader to act alone. At other times, it will be more appropriate for a leader to use a team. There will be times when a leader must be forceful. There will also be times when a more conciliatory approach is better.

Leaders must be flexible in their choice of strategy. They need to recognise that different occasions require a different leadership style.

SEASONS OF LEADERSHIP

The concept behind 'leadership seasons' is that different leadership styles are needed at different times.

Summer

Summer is about warmth, T-shirts and relaxed banter over barbecues. It is a time of holidays. It is a time for sunny smiles and fun. There are some leaders who are summer leaders. They operate in a relaxed and informal manner.

At times it is important for a leader to be a summer leader, but it should only be for a season. Over-familiarity with followers can trivialise the role of a leader. Productivity can be compromised by an overly relaxed working environment.

In any organisation, there will be moments when a leader needs to be a summer leader. For example, at the office party, the executive team-building weekend, the lunchtime banter and the moments when one celebrates success within an organisation.

Potential strengths of the summer leader: approachability, warmth and a relaxed leadership style.

Potential weaknesses of the summer leader: a lack of authority, which can lead to reduced productivity and a decline in respect.

Winter

Winter is the season of closed doors and double glazing. It is about coats, scarfs and hunched backs against the cold. It is storms and chills. There are those who operate in a cold fashion, who are aloof and separated from others.

It is important for leaders to be able to be winter leaders, but only for a season. To be cool towards others, to be shut away behind private thoughts, can help protect the mystery of leadership. However, expressed too often, the winter leader can become too aloof and unapproachable, and people can become disconnected from their influence.

There will be moments when a leader must be a winter leader, when they cause storms and bring the chill winds of reprimand and discipline. There is also some truth in the saying, 'More often seen, less often wondered at'.

Potential strengths of a winter leader: clinical efficiency, short-term productivity, a strong feeling of accountability and a certain mystique.

Potential weaknesses of a winter leader: alienation from others, a cold method of operation, which may distance a leader from their followers.

Spring

Spring is the season to clean, to clear out the old and to make room for the new. It is a time of awakening, of new growth and the birth of lambs, flower bulbs and ideas. A hitherto bleak landscape takes on a new promise. Fragile new colours emerge, tender growth is seen. There is the promise of bounty.

It is important for a leader to be a spring leader at times, but only for a season. To create new things, to be innovative, to awaken others from dormancy is good, as is generating a feeling of hope and promise. Any organisation needs creativity and updating.

Potential strengths of the spring leader: creativity, the generation of new ideas, innovation and the ability to accommodate different ways of doing things.

Potential weaknesses of the spring leader: too much that is new can destabilise the old and risk unsettling an organisation. Spring leaders can have an energy that others may find threatening.

Autumn

Autumn is a time to consolidate, to prepare for the winter ahead. It is a conservative season, a time to drop off the leaves and sink the roots down into a safe zone beyond the frosts. Autumn is a time for mature reflection and to plan for the uncertainties of tomorrow.

It is important for a leader to be an autumn leader, but only for a season. There is wisdom in regrouping. It is important to plan for tomorrow, to be prudent, wise and careful. There must be times to remember past winters and the risk such winters can bring.

Potential strengths of an autumn leader: prudence, forward planning, an ability to work towards a deferred reward, long-term thinking and wisdom.

Potential weaknesses of an autumn leader: autumn leaders can be conservative and so busy worrying about the future they forget to enjoy the present. Autumn leaders are often not open to new ideas.

Our sons and daughters need the ability to lead in every season. At times they will be called upon to innovate and take risks. At other times, they will need to be much more careful and conservative. Those who are able to adjust their leadership style so that it is appropriate for each occasion are the leaders society wants.

However, being able to lead in every season is not easy. This is because all our children have a predisposition, a certain character that will mean they prefer certain seasons to others. This needs to be acknowledged but should not serve as an excuse to remain inflexible in leadership style.

It is also important to note the make-up of the whole leadership team. It might be entirely acceptable for a leader to stay 'wintry' for much of the time, providing there is balance in the leadership team with someone else of a more summery disposition.

These caveats noted, it does not weaken the claim that gifted leaders need to be able to change according to their circumstances. They need to become a seasoned leader.

A PHOTO TO TAKE

LEADERSHIP 'SEASONS'

SUMMER: warmth, casual wear, holidays, fun, open doors.
AUTUMN: rugging up, preparing for winter, conserving, consolidating.
WINTER: cold, isolated, insulated and weathering storms.
SPRING: new life, creativity, emerging possibilities, growth, awakening.

LEADERS NEED TO BE ABLE TO OPERATE IN ALL SEASONS

LOOKING FORWARD AND LOOKING BACK

Being able to adjust strategy so that it is relevant to the time and to the occasion is an important skill for a leader to learn. It can be helpful for a leader to look at the past in order to decide what to do in the present. For example, if the past has shown that an opposition cricket team is unable to play spin bowling well, it might be appropriate to use a lot of spin against them in future matches.

Looking at the past

The past is useful to study because there are lessons associated with the past that can be of relevance to the present.

That said, it is important not to be bound by the past too much. When young, captive elephants are tethered with a rope to a stake in the ground. Being small, they cannot pull the stake out. When older and much stronger, the same small stake is used to tether the elephant. Despite being able to pull the stake out of the ground with ease, the elephant will not do so because it has been conditioned to believe it cannot. A small stake can pin down a big elephant for life.

Looking at the future

It can also be useful to look at the future, to identify trends and try to respond appropriately. For example, if all internet, television and similar services in the future could be run through already existing electricity lines, the strategic thinker might buy shares in companies that own the electricity lines. Or, if the average age of retirees is rising, the strategic thinker might decide to build some retirement homes.

Probing the future and seeing the implications for the present is strategic. Even more strategic is creating the future – doing something entirely new. If this is thought to be out of the question for a teenager, think again. More than one teen has become financially comfortable because of an app they invented, or because their internet game has become a raging success.

Creativity is not reserved for adults. The young are often less inhibited and more in touch with contemporary thinking than those who are older. When only fourteen years old, Sean Belnick created an internet retailing business called BizChair.com. By 2010, the company had sales greater than $58 million.[7] In 2012, Brooke Martin of Spokane, Washington, invented a hugely successful app called iCPooch, which enabled her to stay in touch with her dog.[8]

Let no-one say that strategic thinking – really effective strategic thinking – cannot be engaged in by teenagers.

NO MAGIC CURE

Having noted the above, we must recognise that no strategy, however ingenious, can guarantee a desired outcome. With the best will in the world, a disappointment can result and painful compromises may be necessary. The best strategic plan will sometimes fail. This is because we do not control all the variables.

HOW TO SOLVE A PROBLEM

Part and parcel of strategic thinking is the ability to solve problems. We all face problems. Sometimes it is just trying to finish the crossword without looking up the answers or the chess game without your king falling over. At other times the problems are rather more serious. Whatever the scale of the problem, there are a range of problem-solving techniques that can help, including the following:

- Break the problem into parts and seek to solve each part in isolation.
- Try a different approach.
- Use trial and error.
- Draw about you a team of helpers and brainstorm the problem with them.
- Check all the assumptions.
- Seek to enrich your team with expert help.
- Look at the problem from a totally different perspective.
- Leave it for a while and then tackle it again, refreshed and having rested yourself from the issue.
- Narrow down the possible solutions by trialling various options.
- Note what you learned from the experience and move on.
- Know when to let go.

A great film about problem solving is 2014's *The Imitation Game* starring Benedict Cumberbatch as the World War II code-breaker Alan Turing. It tells of the efforts of the British to break the Enigma Coding system used by the Germans in the war. Breaking the ciphers required not only mathematical brilliance, it required creative thinking. It was only after realising that the last phrase of the intercepted German messages always contained the phrase 'Heil Hitler' that the Enigma code was able to be broken. What this story reminds us is that creative thinking is a vital part of problem solving.

SLOW DOWN

It is not always easy to control the adolescent desire to solve problems quickly and to achieve life goals at an early age. This energy and optimism can be refreshing, but not if it results in a sense of unrealistic entitlement. Some children want what their parents took a lifetime to achieve. *If Mum and Dad can get a house, car and a big TV, then sure as hell I should be able to*, is their thinking. They may need to be reminded that acquiring these sorts of assets is often only possible after many years of hard work. Things of value are rarely achieved easily.

A STORY TO SHARE

An American was visiting a stately home in England and was hugely impressed with the quality of its lawns. Approaching one of the gardeners, the American said, 'Hi. Great lawns. How can I get a lawn like this back in the States?'

The gardener thought a bit then replied, 'Well - get some liquid cow manure and spread it over the lawn in early spring.'

'No worries,' the American replied. 'We've lots of bullshit at home. I'll use it.'

'I'm not finished yet,' said the gardener. 'Throughout summer, you've got to water the lawn so it gets a soaking at least once a week.'

'Still no worries,' said the American. 'I'll suck up some bore water and drench my lawn when I get back.'

Then the gardener looked at the American and said, 'Sure you can - but you've got to do it for 400 years.'

FINALLY

Our sons and daughters are often experts at virtual thinking but are relatively unskilled in real-world thinking. Their online gaming activities can exercise strategic thinking a great deal, as does the game of chess with Grandpa. But the transfer of these skills into real-world challenges, such as obtaining a job, is often fraught with difficulty.

For this reason it can be useful to encourage our sons and daughters not only to set leadership goals, but to tease out the steps that need to be taken to reach that goal. Get them to convert game theory into life theory. Let them see that solving a real-world problem can be an absorbing game.

SUMMARY

- There is a difference between planning and strategic planning.
- If something important is wanted, it usually needs a well-worked plan to get it.
- Worthy goals are seldom achieved without considerable effort.
- Operating strategically can be encouraged by working out where you are now, where you want to get to, and thinking of ways to get there.
- Undertaking a SWOT analysis can be useful in helping to cope with a diverse range of challenges, such as securing a leadership position at school. Its principles can even be used in sensitive areas such as romance.
- Different strategies are needed at different times. Wisdom comes from knowing when to use what and when.

- Determining a good strategy includes looking at what worked well in the past and what opportunities exist in the future.
- Difficult objectives can be realised using a few simple tricks.
- Realising objectives can take time.

A costume to wear

Convincing people of one's leadership credentials requires a person to have something tangible and positive that they can offer. Leaders who are without substance are soon exposed as not being real leaders. That said, leadership credentials can be assisted by a touch of theatre. If a person takes the trouble to wear a leadership costume, people will more readily believe they are a leader. If you look great, people will think you're great. If you look like a loser, people will think you're a loser.

Yes – I know, 'You mustn't judge a book by its cover.' Perhaps we shouldn't, but we do. Trust me, I'm an author and more than a little attention is paid to the cover of a book!

It's no different with our sons and daughters. By looking at what they wear, people will make judgements about them. This represents a massive liability. It also represents a huge opportunity. By neglecting our appearance, we can put people off. By being careful about our appearance, we can be attractive.

What we wear, how we look and what we do, says something. At times this is completely unintentional: egg on the shirt and dandruff in the hair may be shouting a different message from the one that is intended. Sometimes, what is suggested by our appearance is completely intentional: more than one bloke has decided to wear black, put on Ray-Bans and get some tattoos in order to look thoroughly cool, and more than one girl has shortened the distance between hemline and neckline to look 'sexy'.

Most teens are very aware of what they are wearing and what they look like. Their preen time can be significant; the queue outside the bathroom bears testimony to this truth.

However, paying attention to appearance is one thing, paying the *right* attention to appearance is an entirely different thing. The search for a solution to good appearance is complicated because each generation has its own definition of 'good'.

Does this mean parental advice in this area must necessarily be muted? The answer is: yes. However, there is virtue in reminding our sons and daughters of three things:

1. What they adorn themselves with on the outside will cause people to make judgements about what they are like on the inside.
2. Appearance is made up of more than clothes. Body, bearing and behaviour also play a part.
3. If you dress to please yourself, you will please yourself. If you dress to please your peers, you will please your peers. If you dress to please the workplace, you will please the workplace. In other words, it is as well to know how your dress and bearing will have an impact on different groups of people.

The right costume has to be worn at the right time.

'A costume to wear?' What does this imply? It suggests there are things we can wear that can help us be more convincing in a part. There are ways to look that can help us to portray a character. Morticia is dressed to belong to the Addams Family. Freddy Krueger (*Nightmare on Elm Street*) is dressed to scare the living daylights out of us. Miley Cyrus and Madonna dress to entertain and sell songs.

In a manner not greatly different, we need to choose our costume. More than one costume may be needed because actors can be called on to play more than one part on the stage of life.

The chinos and casual shirt suggests contemporary, smart casual. The 'G–t f–ck–d. Do you need to buy a vowel?' T-shirt and ripped jeans suggests something else. The trouser suit suggests executive power.

Surely, we know all this – but do we? Even prime ministers and presidents get it wrong. If any proof were needed, the habit of the former Australian Prime Minister Tony Abbott wearing red Speedos, and the Russian President Vladimir Putin shedding his shirt, has caused more mirth than either would have liked.

As well as wearing the costume, we need to act the part. There needs to be a congruency between bearing, behaviour and apparel if we want to be persuasive in our performance as a leader. Power dressing is more than a little undermined by stooped shoulders and snivelling voice.

What part do our sons and daughters want to play in life and how will they dress for it? Of course, the parts they play will vary. Sometimes they will want to be convincing as a saint. At other times, they will want to be a sinner.

Given that this is a book about leadership, we'll concentrate on what it takes to dress like a leader. This is not easy given that leaders wear different costumes at different times. That said, there are some general guidelines that can be shared.

The first guideline is to 'get it'. Some people have 'got it', others have not. Some have a sense of presence, a style that sets them apart. This is not a pretentious air, a conceited foppery or a precocious affectation. It is an elegance, a refinement that gives an indefinable aura of style and, with it, enhanced leadership credentials.

POWER DRESSING

Power dressing is not a new concept.

LOUIS XIV

Louis XIV was King of France between 1643 and 1715. He was known as *Le Roi Soleil* (The Sun King) because all power and brilliance was said to radiate from the King. His court at Versailles set the fashion of the day. Whatever the King deemed to be fashionable became fashionable.

When the King got up in the morning, more than a hundred courtiers would watch the King dress. The simple task of the King getting dressed developed a huge formality and became known as the *Grand Levée* because it set the fashion of the day.[1]

NAPOLEON BONAPARTE

The nineteenth-century French Emperor Napoleon (1769–1821) could not be described, even by the most generous, as being particularly handsome. Yet he dressed with propriety and with a courtly appearance that left no-one in doubt of his power. Smart jackets bearing Napoleon's multiple insignia of office were worn over a fashionable shirt that was tucked into high-quality breeches, which in turn were tucked into immaculately polished boots.

CLEOPATRA

The Egyptian pharaoh Cleopatra (69–30 BC) knew about the importance of appearance. She was a master of theatrical embellishment.

The Egyptian ruler was, in fact, Greek. Cleopatra was born to a lineage that extended back to one of Alexander the Great's generals. In earlier times this general had seized Egypt and proclaimed himself pharaoh. On her father's death, Cleopatra successfully battled for the throne of Egypt against her younger brother. In 48 BC, she met Julius Caesar. Legend has it that she was smuggled into Caesar's presence by rolling herself up in a carpet.

In the following spring Cleopatra organised a boating holiday along the Nile for Caesar and herself. To further her relationship with Caesar she used a houseboat that was lavishly supplied with every creature comfort. No fewer than 400 other boats were in attendance.

Not surprisingly, Caesar and Cleopatra became lovers and she bore him a son called Caesarion. Cleopatra was not only a reputed beauty, she spoke six languages, was an excellent strategist and a wonderful organiser. When Caesar brought Cleopatra back to Rome, she reformed the Roman mint, reorganised the Roman calendar and reinforced Caesar's tax program.

When Caesar was murdered on the Ides of March, Cleopatra returned to Egypt. Caesar's eventual successor, Mark Antony, demanded that Cleopatra meet him at Tarsus in Asia Minor. Cleopatra sailed for Tarsus but did not go to see Mark Antony. Instead, she stayed at anchor and enticed Antony to come to her. She added to the enticement by using purple sails, and having the oars of her ship coated in silver. Cleopatra dressed herself as the Roman Goddess Venus and lay under a gold awning. About her wafted incense and she was attended by beautiful slaves dressed as sea nymphs and cupids. Mark Antony couldn't resist and went to visit her.

Cleopatra bore him twins and four years later they married. As his wife, Cleopatra extracted from Mark Antony the gift of huge tracts of land and massive wealth. It all started with dressing up a little.[2]

Given that purple sails and silver oars are in short supply and Venus outfits are usually restricted to themed parties, what can we reasonably expect our sons and daughters to look like in order to establish leadership credentials?

In answering this question, we need to look at three things: costume, appearance and behaviour.

THE COSTUME

There are many outfits a leader must wear. Our politicians know this. When they go on 'walkabout', sometimes it is the fluoro safety vest and hard hat, sometimes it is the business suit and sometimes it is the 'farmer Joe' look.

This brings us to a key point: dressing for the part is one thing, dressing convincingly for the part is another.

Most of our sons and daughters will know what is appropriate to wear on most occasions. Where a few can get unstuck is when they have to dress for a more formal occasion. Even if these formal occasions are not frequent, they need to possess the knowledge of how to look right when wearing faded jeans is not appropriate.

Guidelines for formal dressing

For the purposes of this exercise, the definition of 'formal' will be taken to mean executive-business attire, guest-at-a-wedding attire and wanting-to-impress-the-judge attire.'[3]

- Dress to highlight your best features but do so with due modesty and with good taste.
- Experiment to see if you look better in tight- or loose-fitting garments.
- Find out what colours best suit your skin colour.
- Do not mix patterns. A checked shirt with striped pants would not be advisable.
- Limit colours to two or three that go well with each other.
- Add the third 'thing'. Jeans and a jumper make you look casual. Jeans, jumper and scarf add the pizzazz. Do not overdo this by seeking to add the fourth or fifth thing.
- If you are short in stature and wish to appear taller, wearing clothing that changes at the waist may not be wise. Long dresses can make a shorter person look taller.

- A person with short legs should avoid trousers with turn-ups.
- Horizontal stripes can be less flattering on shorter figures.
- Hairstyle should complement body shape, skin and character. If in doubt, keep it simple and natural.
- The tie should just touch the belt.
- Double-breasted jackets should not be left unbuttoned.
- Do not combine a patterned shirt with a patterned jacket and patterned tie. Two patterned items with one solid colour is fine, but the two patterned items must not 'compete' with each other.
- Colour contrast is fine but contrasting style is not.
- Wear lightweight and lighter-coloured suits when it is warmer, and darker, heavier suits when it is cooler. Darker suits should be worn at more formal occasions and at events such as funerals.
- Trousers should have a gentle break just above the shoes. Socks should not show.
- A handkerchief in the jacket pocket can be a little over the top unless it is tastefully done. A handkerchief that matches the tie can work well.
- A clean handkerchief is a good idea. It is amazing how often a clean handkerchief is needed at functions.
- Do not overdo the jewellery. Reducing, or temporarily removing, some of the more arresting piercings can also be appropriate.
- Dark shoes should generally be worn with dark suits.
- Shoes should be polished and in good repair. Remember that people see shoes from a different angle. The split in the back of the shoe may not be noticed by you but is almost certain to be noticed by others.
- Aftershave and perfume are no substitute for good hygiene. Having noted this, deodorant is useful especially if prone to sweating.

For those more formal occasions such as 'black tie' events:

- 'Black tie' for her provides several options including a long gown or a shorter cocktail dress.
- Shoes with heels are often a feature, as is fashionable jewellery.
- A clutch bag or small evening bag on a long chain are frequently seen on more formal occasions.
- Bling and sparkle are also allowed but they should be tasteful.
- 'Black tie' for him means formal evening wear including black dinner jacket and trousers, white dinner shirt with cufflinks and/or studs. Do not make the mistake of buying an evening shirt that is too fancy. They can make a person look cheap.
- Cummerbunds, white scarves and so on may be added at 'black tie' events but it is as well not to be overdressed. The cummerbund should either be black to match the black jacket or the same colour as the bow tie.
- White tie or evening dress is just about obsolete and is only worn for very grand occasions. It involves fur, ball gowns, gloves, tail coats, waistcoats and winged collars. Let's move on.

Finally, it's worth checking how you look from different angles. Is there an unsightly underwear line? Are there tears in your stockings? Is the trouser seat baggy? Are the flies done up?

Guidelines for complimenting your son or daughter

There is a plethora of advice parents can share on how to look good. Mind you, intergenerational agreement on these matters is not renowned, so try the artful use of the following:

'You look great, darling.' (Then a long and admiring look that slowly translates into a more thoughtful pose.)

'What? What?'

'Wellll . . . something that might make you even more stunning is . . .'

Or words along those lines.

Work it!

Leaders of fashion

Some people do not follow accepted fashion; they lead it. This is important to note because what is now classed as acceptable, even at formal occasions, is changing rapidly. 'Casual Friday' for executives has now become an all-week affair. Chinos, sockless loafers and a stylish jacket can now be worn by him at just about any event, and anything lovely can be worn by her!

The famous fashion designer Coco Chanel (1883–1971) did not become famous by being a follower of convention. Not for her the restrictive, uncomfortable and unflattering fashions of the day. She moved away from the long shirts and corsets, and introduced the trouser suit, short skirts, elegant turtlenecks and flat-heeled shoes – things that had sensible elegance.[4]

It is worth remembering that the rebellious teenager who refuses to wear what is expected could be the trendsetter of fashion in the future.

With that caveat noted, it is still appropriate for our sons and daughters to know what current convention requires, even if it is only to rebel against it.

A few years ago, a group of young men in my school formed a friendship group.

They called themselves 'The League of Gentlemen'. It was a quaint and slightly worrying title but they were saved from being a pretentious group by engaging in great acts of charity. Their peers judged them as just having a bit of fun – which was entirely correct.

While most students were shovelling lunchtime food from tray to mouth as quickly as they could, the League would set their refectory table formally. Trays were banned. Over their meal, they would enter into spirited discussion about the virtues of different food when staff were about, and drink when they were not. They developed the skill of tying a bow tie and wore them whenever they could. All things worthy and of noble taste were discussed.

They were seriously 'over the top' and different, but this is precisely what made it fun for them and others who watched them. Now they have left school but they still meet from time to time and they still enjoy dressing well.

THE APPEARANCE

You can't always do much about the body you were born into. We can colour the hair and buy the make-up, but we can't do much about the height thing other than wear platform shoes. What we can do is care for the body we were given and ensure that its appearance does not compromise what we want to achieve in life.

Keeping in shape

While we can't make ourselves any taller, there are masses of things that can be done to control the shape of our body and maintain a healthy weight. For expert advice, the input of a trained professional is essential. It is also important to recognise that some conditions, such as thyroid malfunction and hormonal misbehaviour, can mean that the normal ways of controlling body shape – diet and exercise – need to be augmented by proper medical intervention. If in doubt, seek expert advice.

In terms of physical appearance, the most common desire in teens is to gain weight or lose weight. There are other goals, such as an unblemished face, larger breasts, bigger penis, hair that behaves itself and better muscle tone. However, the weight issue is probably a constant in the lives of most teens – largely because weight tends to influence body shape more than anything else.

Getting rid of the 'muffin top' is a common goal for both boys and girls. The bulge over the tummy can be tackled by taking on board fewer calories (eating less) or by burning up more calories (exercising more).

The body typically needs about 2400 calories a day, but this will vary according to age, sex, activity and other variables. To gain a kilogram, about 7500 calories needs to be added to a diet; likewise to lose a kilogram, 7500 calories need to be shed. So, our sons and daughters need to do the maths. For example:

- A packet of chips is 250 calories. If you cut out the chips each day, in 7500 divided by 250 calories, you will lose a kilogram in 30 days.
- A 60 gram chocolate bar is 300 calories. If you cut out the chocolate each day, in 7500 divided by 300 calories, you will lose a kilogram in 25 days.

These are not exact calculations and there are other variables to consider, such as the amount of exercise engaged in, but the general point can be made that by cutting out a treat, the muffin top can disappear.

Others need to add weight. Chips and chocolate are not recommended! It is entirely possible to put on weight in the wrong places. The body functions better and looks better when weight is in muscle rather than fat. A protein-rich diet with plenty of fresh meat, eggs, fruit and vegetables, together with some exercise, can see the gain of a kilo or so in a fortnight. There is a large range of protein supplements available to help in this regard, but care is needed. Expert advice should be sought before any bulking-up powders are bought on the internet, or from anywhere else for that matter. Some supplements can be dangerous. Be careful.

There are various ways to control weight and gain fitness. Whatever way is chosen will vary according to whether the goal is to build up fitness, strength, flexibility, stress resistance, muscle bulk or to lose weight. Many options are expensive. Personal trainers and gym memberships are usually not cheap – but alternatives exist. You can buy a bike. Get a treadmill on eBay. I have a personal trainer – it's a dog!

The simple initiative of cycling to school instead of being driven, of doing a newspaper round, of going for an early morning swim, can achieve as much as an expensive gym program.[5]

That said, exercising with others can be a great way to foster friendships. It can encourage a commitment that may not be there if you were not disappointing someone by failing to turn up for a communal workout.

Some apps to consider

There are many impressive apps around to help with fitness and weight issues. A browse on the internet will reap rewards for those wanting more information, as will a visit to sites such as: www.bodyandsoul.com.au

Your online search will also bring you to an amazing array of walking gadgets such as wrist pedometers that can be obtained from electronics stores and websites. The options are considerable and include:

- Jawbone UP
- Nike+ Fuel Band
- Polar Loop
- Misfit Shine
- Fitbit Flex and Fitbit Force.

These gizmos look tolerably attractive as wristbands. They will not only tell you how far you have walked each day; they can be programmed to reward you with a happy trill and a celebratory burst of lights when you have reached your goal. These devices can also monitor sleep pattern, calories consumed and, and, and . . .

Other health-promoting devices and wellbeing programs are out there, such as smartphone fitness apps. Care needs to be taken to ensure they are compatible with whatever it is your teen owns, be it an iPhone, Android or Blackberry. Available titles betray their function. For example:

- Build Muscle
- 101 Yoga Poses
- Water Your Body.

In relation to weight control and fitness, several options exist. For example:

- 'Calorie Counter' by FatSecret
- 'Google Fit' by Google Inc
- 'Workout Trainer' by Skimble Inc
- 'Lose It!' by FitNow Inc.

Most apps have their strengths.

- The 'Nike+ Training Club' iPhone app is free and gives suggested workouts complete with visual demos and audio guidance.
- 'adidas miCoach' can track performance over time. It offers a range of activities designed to suit particular needs such as running, getting fit, staying fit and so on.
- 'Calorie Counter – MyFitnessPal' probably doesn't need much more explanation.
- 'Pocket Yoga' sounds a bit worrying but it provides poses and breathing challenges you can do any time.

Other great fitness apps to consider include:

- 'Twenty Chinups' by Software, which offers a six-week strength-building program.

- 'Couch to 5k' by Felt Tip promises to move a teen from the couch to the footpath if obedience to its dictates are adhered to.
- 'ifitness' by Medical Productions not only gives more than 300 exercises; it allows you to track body changes such as waist circumference and Body Mass Index (BMI).
- 'Runkeeper' by FitnessKeeper uses the iPhone's GPS tracking ability to help monitor where you have been and how fast you were going at various stages of your walk or run. It will also chat to you and give you audio feedback on how you're going. A nice extra feature is the ability to take happy snaps of where you are running and upload them to www.runkeeper.com.

Eating disorders

There are a range of body issues that owe their genesis to under-eating rather than over-eating. These eating disorders are not just about under-eating, they can be about eating the wrong things.

Most people have heard of anorexia nervosa – usually evidenced by a person skipping meals and severely limiting their food intake while exercising a lot because their self-worth is tied up with looking thin – and bulimia nervosa – generally expressed through a person purging themselves, i.e. vomiting, or taking laxatives, after meals. However, there is a range of other eating disorders out there.

'Drunkorexia' is where a person forgoes the calories in food in order to enjoy the calories in booze. There is also 'anorexia athletica', which is when there is an obsessive use of the gym, or equivalent, to burn off calories. To this list of eating disorders can be added binge eating and binge drinking, both entered into as a form of self-medication and often associated with conditions such as depression and bipolar disorder.

All eating disorders need to be taken seriously, and immediate medical advice should be sought by any who are concerned in any way.[6]

Narcissism

Caring for our body is one thing. Cossetting our body is another.

Becoming a narcissist is not a good thing. It is possible to spend too much time looking after yourself and thinking about yourself.

A LEGEND TO KNOW

According to Greek legend, Narcissus was a beautiful youth who held himself in such high esteem that he fell in love with himself. Narcissus also had a cruel streak – which can often happen in people who like themselves too much. No-one else is worth caring for.

A beautiful nymph called Echo had been cursed by Juno to only repeat what was said to her. Juno put this curse on Echo because Echo always wanted the last word. Echo fell in love with the handsome Narcissus, but when they met, Narcissus rejected Echo and said he would rather die than be with her. The heartbroken Echo pined away. Her flesh melted and her bones became rocks from which, according to legend, she still speaks and has the last word.

Narcissus went on to treat other maidens with similar cruelty. However, an avenging goddess heard their distress and put a spell on Narcissus that caused him to fall in love with his reflection in a pool of water. Whenever Narcissus reached into the water to touch his beloved, the reflection would disappear. It was now Narcissus' turn to pine away and die. His body turned into a flower still known today as Narcissus.[7]

Taking care of the soul

Speaking of bodies, do we care for our spiritual body?

This is not the book to engage in weighty discussion about spiritual matters. However, it is good to be reminded that wellbeing is predicated not just on health, diet and fitness, but on psychological wellbeing, emotional and social resilience and on an untroubled soul.

By *soul*, what is meant is not so much a religious awareness but rather that seat of conscience, character, morality and meaning; that place where nature and nurture forge the deep you; that place where imagination and reality meet; that place where consciousness and unconsciousness convene.

The soul is responsible for making good people glow *goodness* and bad people *badness*.

Thomas Moore, in his book *Care of the Soul*, suggests that one of the great problems of the twenty-first century is our neglect of the soul. This is revealed in shallowness, loss of meaning and a failure to recognise the sacredness of ordinary things. We need to care for the soul with deeds and thoughts that enrich our inner being.

It is significant that many of the Amazon tribes are not so much afraid of the white man's world but, rather, they are horrified by its effect on their souls. Perhaps we should all be horrified, and seek to counter the soullessness within. This is why sunsets should be watched, meditation practised and the mind fed with those things that edify and enrich. We need our sons and daughters to engage in *soulwatch*, and to check frequently on their soul's health.

Tattoos

'Inking' is in.

What we are talking about is tattooing. The interest of the young in getting a tattoo is increasing. Many of their heroes and heroines have 'tatts' and they want one too.

Tattoos have been around for a long time. Captain Cook brought the term back to Europe after his 1771 voyage to Tahiti. As a rite of passage, punishment, sexual statement, religious reason or as punishment, tattooing has been going on for several millennia. In Roman times, slaves would sometimes have 'Stop me. I'm a runaway' tattooed on their head.

There are laws related to tattooing. For example, in Australia, you are not allowed to give a tattoo to anyone under the age of sixteen, and if they are under eighteen, parental permission is required.

Speaking of permission, piercings can only be done with parental permission if under the age of sixteen. Piercings in private places such as the genitals or nipples are not able to be given, even if permission is granted, until the age of sixteen. Other countries have different laws.

Piercings are removable. Tattoos are not . . . unless a fair amount of pain, time and expense is invested in dermabrasion, cryosurgery, excision or some form of laser treatment. With research indicating that a quarter of those getting a tattoo regret it within a month, parents have every right to apply the brakes to an offspring's desire to get a tattoo – at least until they are of an age to make a mature decision. Even then, many get it wrong and find themselves writhing under lasers.

If pestering continues, allow them to have a henna or some other form of temporary tatt instead.

Even when of an age to make their own decision, there is wisdom in making sure your teen is thoroughly convinced they will love the tattoo in sixty years' time.

If our teenager is still intent on going ahead with a tattoo, encourage them to start small and start with patterns, pictures or words that are of ageless appeal. Remember, the average number of infatuations and declared loves they will have in life will typically be more than one. If each love of their life is inked on their arm, then the latest love may not feel all that permanent.

Going for the whole bodysuit tattoo is not a good idea as a first adventure into the art-form. Likewise, holding off the tatt on the *mons pubis* or *glans penis* might also be wise.

Some tattoos are attractive. Others are not. A few tattoos are designed to intimidate and frighten. Bikers and prisoners often engage in tattooing to intimidate, to look macho, to signal an allegiance to an anti-establishment culture. The teen who wants to go down this track needs to be reminded that whereas the tatt may give prestige among the gang, it might scare the living daylights out of children and aged aunts.

The health risks associated with getting a tattoo also need to be understood. A cheap tatt done in the back streets of a Balinese village may be good for the wallet but not so for the health. Encourage your son or daughter to go to a reputable place that uses equipment certified by the Therapeutic Goods Administration, or equivalent. Blood-borne pathogens exist. Hepatitis, herpes, HIV, staph, tetanus and tuberculosis have not been unknown in tattoo parlours.[8]

Looking sexy

An even more common area of concern for parents is having children dress in a sexually provocative way. This is an ageless battleground that has caused parents, particularly parents of teenage daughters, to lose a lot of sleep.

The premature sexualisation of our young is rampant, with the result that childhood is lost and adult adventures are engaged in at an ever-younger age. Advertisers use sex to sell, the pornography industry runs virtually unchecked and that which was taboo a decade or two ago has now been granted mainstream acceptance.

The fact that sexual maturity occurs several years earlier in daughters than it did five decades ago doesn't help much either. Pre-teens can now have babies. Talks about birds and bees need to be moved from the secondary school into the primary school.

When parents discuss this topic with their children, it is important not to scare them. Sex is great. However, premature sexualisation is not. We need to allow our young a few precious years of childhood before their sexual innocence is lost.

Unwittingly, we can be complicit in rushing our children through childhood. 'Big boys don't cry.' 'You're looking so grown-up.' We say these things, then wonder why our daughter dresses provocatively and causes her parents to look up websites on monastic boarding schools.

There can be benefit in having a frank discussion about the mixed messages a 'costume' can give. It is not always, 'I'm beautiful'. It can be misinterpreted as, 'I'm available.'

It might be useful to remind our daughters that a dress can be more attractive if it intrigues rather than reveals. A dress that preserves the mystery of a woman can be enchanting.

Likewise with sons. Overly coiffured and fussily dressed can come across as vain and narcissistic, and too much dark macho can signal faux manliness.

Looking the part is not always about wearing the right clothes. The bearing of a leader can give dignity to someone wearing little more than a loincloth. Look at the Zulus. A balanced stride, square shoulders, level eyes and a gracious poise can be just as important as clothes when conveying a sense of presence. We need to look not just at what is worn but how it is worn. We need to look not just at the quality of the costume but also at the quality of the acting.

A costume can be rendered useless if the person wearing it does not act in a way that is appropriate to the costume. A person in a leadership 'costume' who behaves like an idiot will not be remembered as a leader. They will be remembered as an idiot.

Therefore, it is necessary that attention be paid not just to costume and appearance. Attention must also be paid to the acting – to ensure that leaders behave like leaders.

THE BEHAVIOUR

The boys' uniform at The King's School, Parramatta, makes them look like the lost remnant of Napoleon's army. I know this because I have been its headmaster for the best part of two decades. With its grey jacket, red cuffs and blue pants with red stripe, it is a distinctive uniform – very distinctive. The upside is that the boys are different and easy to see in a crowd. The downside is that if a boy misbehaves, I can never ask, 'Are you sure it was a Kingsman?'

The behaviour of our sons and daughters needs to be in keeping with their costume. Someone in a military uniform looks awful if they are scruffy and unkempt. Given that The King's School uniform is the oldest military uniform still worn in Australia, this is something I have told my boys more than once!

The Spice Girls knew how to reinforce character with dress. They each developed a persona to go with their names – Posh, Scary, Baby, Ginger and Sporty. If actions are out of kilter with the costume, the credibility of the performance is compromised. Our sons and daughters need to pay as much attention to how they wear their costumes as to what they wear.

What spills out?

Leaders are often defined by what spills out of them when people bump into them.

- If you are wandering along holding a mineral water and someone bumps into you, what spills out? The answer is: mineral water. Duh!
- If you are wandering along holding a mug of hot chocolate and someone bumps into you, what spills out? The answer is chocolate.

If you are wandering along and someone bumps into you, what spills out? Is it:

Hi Jenny, great to see you. How's your dad? I heard he just got back from overseas?

Or is it:

Watch what you're fucking well doing! I've already had a shite day.

We have all had our moments when we are not good to be with, but some make a habit of it. When they 'bump' into people, what spills out are moans and groans.

- When a heart is full of anger and bitterness, that's what spills out.
- When a heart is full of anxiety and fear, that's what spills out.
- When a heart is full of peace and contentment, that's what spills out.

When you crack an egg, you get to see what is inside. It's the same with people.

So – what are our sons and daughters like on the inside?

If we, or they, don't like what we see on the inside, get them to change what they say and do. Much of life is an act. If they're not nice when someone bumps into them, encourage them to change. The best way for parents to make this happen is to model this niceness.

The mantle of power

Leaders are also defined by how well they use their power. If they use their power well, they will be considered a good leader. If they use their power badly, they will be considered a poor leader.

Not everyone handles power well. Some use their power:

- Apologetically, and find it embarrassing to be given a leadership role. This can lead to power not being exercised for fear it will alienate from peers.

- To entertain. For much the same reason as above, there is a wish to identify with peers. This is achieved by being a joker rather than a leader.
- To dominate. They are keen to demonstrate their power. This can result in bossiness and even bullying.
- Well when exercising power over others, but poorly when exercising power over themselves. The leader may be good at leading others but may be a disaster in their private life.
- Well when exercising power over themselves but poorly when exercising power over others. However good their grades and reliable their habits, they just haven't got what it takes to inspire others.

Others use their power:

- To enrich the lives of others by using their influence to meet the needs of the broader community.
- Fearlessly to tackle an evil and bring about justice.
- To create things that bring wonder, joy and entertainment.
- To give people leadership and direction.

A PHOTO TO TAKE

There are two types of people:
those who give energy, and those who take energy.

In order to give a powerful performance as a leader, it is not necessary to shout your lines. Strong words softly spoken can have an awesome effect.

Having noted this, any lines uttered by a leader should be spoken with confidence – otherwise the 'audience' will not hear them.

A STORY TO SHARE

MUHAMMAD ALI (1942–)

Someone not lacking in confidence was Muhammad Ali.

He is regarded by many as one of the greatest heavyweight boxers of all time. He was born in 1942 in Louisville, Kentucky and because of his self-promoting banter, Cassius Clay, as he was originally known, was given the name 'The Louisville Lip'.

At a time when only the boxers' managers would speak to the media, Clay did his own talking and would even predict the round his opponent would be knocked out.

'He might be great but he'll fall in eight.'

He was no shrinking violet. Cassius Clay bordered on the narcissistic. 'I am the greatest.' 'I float like a butterfly and sting like a bee.' However, unlike most others, Cassius Clay *was* the best, winning the heavyweight boxing gold medal in the 1960 Rome Olympics and becoming Heavyweight Champion of the World after defeating Sonny Liston in 1964.

That same year, Cassius Clay converted to Islam and changed his name to Muhammad Ali. Because of his religious beliefs, Ali refused to serve in the armed services when he was drafted. This resulted in Ali being stripped of his championship title. When the conviction was overturned in 1971, Ali regained the heavyweight championship title by defeating George Foreman in the 'Rumble in the Jungle' held in Zaire in 1974. After losing the Heavyweight Title some time later, Ali regained it a third time by defeating Leon Spinks in 1978.

Throughout his boxing career, Ali's showmanship was extraordinary. The extent to which his self-promotion was a reflection of an egocentric character, or whether it was a reflection of great publicity, is a matter for debate. What is less a matter for debate was the ability of this remarkable boxer.[9]

Manners

If someone is 'putting on an act', their behaviour is often thought shallow and insincere. Some may even have thought this of Muhammad Ali. However, putting on an act is an important skill for a leader to learn. They may feel tired, but they should not show it. They may feel worried, but they should not reveal it. They may feel powerless, but they should not confess it.

An important act for a leader to 'put on' is to behave well even if they do not feel like doing so. Being well mannered is an important element in behaving well. If a leader is aware of the social conventions necessary to make them more agreeable, they will have more chance of being accepted as a leader. These social conventions are called manners. Another term for them is etiquette.

It has been suggested that 'Manners maketh the man'. Some may think this a touch grand, but there is a fair amount of truth in it. People are drawn to those who behave well. Our sons and daughters need to be as at ease at an eighteenth birthday party complete with technicolour yawns and people falling into rose bushes, as at a black-tie dinner at the clubhouse to celebrate a premiership win.

I stunned my students a few years ago when I said to them, 'I don't mind you eating like pigs.' (Long pause.) 'But I need you to know that you are eating like pigs and have the capacity not to eat like pigs when the occasion demands it.'

I think this is realistic.

Let's have a look at some of the key etiquette issues a teen should know.

When dining in a formal setting, our sons and daughters need to know:

- How to set the table properly.
- What glasses to use for what drinks.

- What the seating etiquette is.
- How to use the napkin properly.
- How to be a good conversationalist.
- How to dress appropriately.
- What cutlery to use and when.
- How to attend to the dining needs of others – drink, butter, salt and pepper, etc.
- How to serve and clear away properly.
- How to send an invitation to dinner, say grace and/or give a toast at the dinner and say thank you after the dinner.

A TEST TO TAKE

Here's a little test.

Would your teen know about the following?

1. To tip a soup bowl away from you, not towards you.
2. How to break bread and cut toast.
3. How to avoid the baby grip - or any other inappropriate grip - on cutlery.
4. How to leave your plate when finished and when you are not finished.
5. How to use things like a butter knife and a salt spoon.
6. To not slurp, burp or fart.
7. To bring the food to your mouth, not your mouth to the food.
8. To pace your eating to match the speed of others.
9. Which fork to use and when.
10. How, when and where to put salt and pepper and any other condiments.

If the score out of ten is unimpressive, there may be added reason to teach our sons and daughters a little more about table manners.[10]

There are myriad other things to learn in relation to fine dining, but even a list of this length can be a reminder that there is value in knowing how to behave when eating in a formal setting. More than one job opportunity has escaped because of poor manners. More than one relationship has failed because of poor manners. More than one leadership opportunity has been lost because of poor manners.

AN IDEA TO CONSIDER

Every fortnight or so, why not make the evening meal a formal dining occasion? Announce the dress code as 'smart casual'. Get the whole family involved in preparing dinner and cleaning up afterwards. Use it as a time of family bonding and to teach the arts of fine dining.

Any whinging might be reduced by having something popular for dessert - and main course too, for that matter!

ACTING WITH WISDOM AND INTEGRITY

Staying with behaviour, there is no shortage of acting tips one can give to an aspiring leader. One is to act with wisdom and integrity.

To act with wisdom

> *By three methods we may learn wisdom:*
> *First by reflection, which is the noblest;*
> *Second by imitation, which is the easiest;*
> *And third, by experience, which is the bitterest.*
> Confucius

Wisdom is more than rat cunning or being politically savvy. Wisdom requires a heart for the truth and a mind that understands. Wisdom may be described as the ability to see connections and think clearly.

TWO STORIES TO SHARE

ALEXANDER THE GREAT

Alexander the Great was King of Macedon from 336 to 323 BC. During a hugely successful reign, he ruled over the Greek states, and conquered Persia, Syria, Egypt and much of India. A story is told of Alexander's father, King Philip, being offered a beautiful horse called Bucephalus. However, the horse was wild and unrideable. Alexander stepped forth and turned the horse to face the sun. He realised that what was terrifying the horse and making it unmanageable was fear of its own shadow. King Philip applauded his son Alexander and advised him to seek a bigger kingdom because Macedonia was too small and unworthy a prize for him.

When Alexander conquered Gordium in Phrygia, Asia Minor, he came across a chariot that was fastened by a rope made from the bark of a cornel tree. The knot was tied so none of its ends were visible. A legend had grown up that the person who untied the knot would go on to rule the world. Alexander had the wisdom to recognise that the problem could be solved another way. He cut the knot with his sword.[11]

CONFUCIUS

Confucius's Chinese name was K'ung Fu-tzu, which means 'Kung, the Philosopher'. Confucius lived from 551 to 479 BC and became revered as a wise man to the extent that some within the world's most populous nation began to think of him as a god.

Confucius never set out to be a spiritual leader but did concern himself with giving his people a moral code to live by. After being born in poverty, Confucius served as a government official but resigned from his posts. This enabled him to travel around the Chinese countryside as an itinerant teacher. Such was the impact of this secular philosopher that he became a spiritual leader. This was not his intention. Indeed, he advised his followers to respect the gods but to have as little as possible to do with them.[12]

Confucius spoke not so much about god but about goodness. The most important virtues for Confucius were *jen* and *li*. The former means love and concern for one's fellow being, and the latter means good manners, etiquette and proper customs. An example of the moral code spread by Confucius was his saying: *'What you do not want done to yourself, do not do to others.'*

To act with integrity

In matters of style swim with the current.
In matters of principle stand like a rock.
Thomas Jefferson

Leaders need to perform with integrity. What is implied is an ethical stance that refuses to compromise on matters of truth. It also implies wholeness or completeness.

Sometimes, our sons and daughters can get confused between integrity and ethics.

- Integrity involves living ethically.
- Ethics involves a system of moral principles by which we live.

Is it reasonable to expect integrity all of the time in a leader?

Leadership is often associated with political expediency, where a good conscience is seen as a liability. Ruthlessness, cutting corners and self-promotion are often seen as essential. 'Kill or be killed' is the sort of sentiment expressed by several contemporary leaders.

Walking close to the edge of what is morally acceptable is where the advantage can be found. However, going close to the edge can be dangerous, because you can go too far and fall.

HISTORY GENERALLY SHOWS THAT A LACK OF INTEGRITY MAY BRING SHORT-TERM ADVANCEMENT, BUT NOT LONG-TERM SUCCESS.

A STORY TO SHARE

AGRIPPINA THE YOUNGER

The Roman Empress Agrippina the Younger (15–59 AD) had a number of partners both in and out of wedlock. Her third marriage was to her uncle, Emperor Claudius, but she was so consumed by an ambition to place her son Nero on the imperial throne that she poisoned Claudius. It was probably not surprising that after witnessing this behaviour Nero adopted a similar habit and soon felt it necessary to murder his mother. This proved a little more difficult than anticipated. According to Suetonius, Nero tried to poison Agrippina three times but she avoided death by taking an antidote. Her bedroom ceiling was tampered with so that it would fall on her, but she was tipped off and escaped injury. Nero then tried to drown his mother, but this failed because she swam to safety.

However, her luck finally ran out. Agrippina was eventually killed by a centurion sent by Nero. Legend has it that she bared her breasts and said, 'Strike these for they have nurtured the great monster Nero.' She was entirely correct. However, Nero fared no better. He took his own life when faced with capture.[13]

We need to raise our sons and daughters to hear the whispered voice of conscience. They need to be uncomfortable if they, or others, are doing things that are not right.

If the right lines are not said on the stage of life, or if the right actions are not taken to support the script, it doesn't matter how impressive the costume is: people will not believe you.

A PHOTO TO TAKE

Watch your thoughts, they become words.
Watch your words, they become actions.
Watch your actions, they become habits.
Watch your habits, they become character.
Watch your character, it becomes your destiny.

(Source unknown)

FINALLY

Leaders need a costume that is worthy of them – a heroic costume. It need not necessarily be a blue body suit and red cloak with a big 'S' on the chest, but they need an outfit that suggests they can lead.

Some people will not even put on a costume but prefer to sit in the audience and watch. They are content to dream their dreams rather than live their dreams, and wait for things to happen instead of making things happen.

We need to encourage our sons and daughters to select an appropriate 'costume' and, having selected it, to get out on the world stage and give a performance that is remarkable.

That said, it is good to remember that what is on the inside is more important than what is on the outside. Substance is more important than form.

SUMMARY

- We judge more than books by their cover – we judge people.
- What we look like on the outside gives clues as to what we are like on the inside.
- Appearance is governed by more than clothes. Bearing and behaviour also play a part.
- Our sons and daughters need to be able to wear the appropriate costume at the appropriate time.
- A costume needs to be worn in a way that reinforces what the actor wants to say.

- Diet and exercise can have an impact on health.
- The inner soul also needs to be nurtured.
- The decision to mark a body with a tattoo needs careful consideration.
- There is danger in choosing a costume that advances premature sexualisation.
- A combination of the right costume, the right body and the right behaviour is needed to put on a convincing act.
- How we perform on the stage of life defines whether we are convincing in the role of leader.
- A leader must not only wear their costume well, they must act their role well.
- How we act when under pressure often defines whether or not we are a leader.
- To be convincing, a leader must act as a leader and understand what behaviours, such as good manners and etiquette, reinforce leadership credentials.
- Acting with wisdom and integrity is also important for a leader.
- The right leadership costume needs to be selected and, once selected, it needs to be worn well.

An ending to have

And *they all lived happily ever after.*

Most of us like happy endings – and all the more when the happy ending is about ourselves rather than some fictional princess finding her fictional prince or some fictional warrior their Valhalla.

Small wonder. We tend to be defined by how we finish rather than how we start. We tend to be remembered by what we were like the last time. We tend to be as popular as our most recent decision.

Not many leaders end well. History is full of leaders losing their crown and often their head with it. When politicians lose an election and their seat of office, they often lose a good deal of their reputation too.

All this goes to show that finishing well is not easy for a leader. A Sudden Insignificance Syndrome (SIS) can develop. Life without a title, without a role, without the perks of office, can be a hard transition to make. I remember one school principal asking to have her computer looked at because it had broken the day she retired. It hadn't. She was simply no longer getting the emails she was used to.

A REFERENCE TO WRITE

When a student ends their school career, many schools furnish them with a reference. These references are not easy to write when the student concerned has done little that is laudable.

So - let our sons and daughters have a crack at writing a reference for themselves. Undertaking such a task might give some a touch more sympathy for those inflicted with the task of having to write a real reference for them. Following are some tips to help them.[1]

1. State the name for whom the reference is written:

    Julia Samantha Smith (centralised and at the top of the reference).

2. Use the appropriate greeting. A personalised reference is best, but, failing that, a more generic greeting can be used such as:

    To whom it may concern.

3. Establish the credentials of the person writing the reference. (Here, our teen needs to imagine who would be writing the reference on them in real life.)

    I have known Julia Smith for the six years during which she was a student of mine at Westfield Secondary College.

4. Give a general and encouraging introduction:

    Julia is a delightful student who has enriched the lives of both her teachers and her friends here at Westfield Secondary College . . .

5. Comment on academic ability:

Academically, Julia's strengths lie in . . .

She can be trusted to work well both as an individual and as a member of a team . . .

Possessed of an active and enquiring mind, Julia can be relied upon to produce work that is . . .

Julia is particularly strong in the arts. Her writing skills are advanced and she is able to communicate well both verbally and in written form . . .

6. Comment on co-curricular activities:

In co-curricular life, Julia has contributed positively to the school by . . .

Sport plays an important part of life at Westfield Secondary College and Julia has involved herself in . . .

Outside of school, Julia has developed a real interest in the retail industry and has worked part time as a . . .

7. Comment on specific areas of responsibilities or achievements:

During her final year at Westfield Secondary College, Julia took on the responsibility for . . .

In addition, her leadership skills were exercised in . . .

8. Comment on general character:

Julia relates well to both peers and adults and is very good company . . .

Because she enjoys being challenged, Julia is able to adjust quickly to any new situation and . . .

In terms of integrity and reliability, Julia is . . .

9. Summary comment:

In closing, I have no hesitation in commending Julia to you as a person who ...

If your teen has some difficulty in writing a reference that is compelling, they may be given cause to engage in activities that could solve this problem. Enough said.

Speaking of writing a reference ... the final days at school can be marked by celebration and mischief. This may be fun for the departing students but it can leave a sour taste in the mouths of the teachers who are writing references for those flinging the water bombs and skylarking because they have finished school.

If the 'leaving season' at school is at hand, why not challenge our restless offspring to leave well. It is possible to celebrate leaving school without trashing the place.

A PHOTO TO TAKE

It has been said that:
You only have one shot at a first impression.

To this should be added:
You only have one shot at a last impression.

When the time comes for our children to celebrate the end of their school days, by all means encourage them to do so. However, amid the excitement, encourage them to leave a good last impression. A way of doing this is to write notes of appreciation. As a teacher, I can tell you that these letters are treasured more than the gold watch.

Life brings many conclusions. For example, the end of each year gives an opportunity to reflect on how we're going. So does the end of each period of employment. Exit interviews are often undertaken at such times. This feedback can be invaluable. However, there is also value in asking how *we* can lift our game. The sorts of questions that a departing Year 12 student can ask of themselves include:

- If I had my school days again, what would I do differently?
- What lessons can I take from my school days?

The third thing that we can encourage school leavers to do is to be someone's champion. Get them to select one or two junior students and become their mentor. Revision and course notes can be handed down, as can textbooks and some good advice on how to cope with life at school.

PROTÉGÉS AND MENTORS

A protégé is someone who enjoys the support of someone who is more senior. They are often in receipt of instruction and training from their mentor, often with a view to them taking over the tasks done by the mentor. The term protégé comes from a French word meaning to be protected.

Unfortunately, some school leavers are so threatened by the thought of a new generation taking over, they actively hinder it. A failure to mentor successors can result in a generation of school leavers being farewelled with rather too much enthusiasm!

It is important to realise that a protégé is not some lackey who acts as a mere cupbearer to the king. The only skill such a person is likely to develop is that of carrying cups. For a protégé to develop the skills necessary to take over the student leadership of a school, they must be allowed to exercise their leadership skills. In this sense, a protégé is more of a companion, more of a partner.

If one is going to train a successor, it is important the training is appropriate and done well. There is truth in the old saying: '*We reproduce fruit after our own kind.*'

A mentor must remain mindful of the privilege there is in serving in this role. They need to share wisdom, knowledge and skills. Mentors can also serve as confidants, giving help and direction as required. The term 'mentor' comes from Homer's tale *The Odyssey* in which Odysseus, before venturing on his epic journeys, entrusts the education of his son to a wise old counsellor called Mentor.

A STORY TO SHARE

ARISTOTLE (384–322 BC)

An example of a faithful mentor is Aristotle.

On 26 July 356 BC, in an area of central Greece called Macedon, a son was born to Philip II, King of Macedonia. It was a great day for the King. His horses had won the most prestigious horse race at the Panhellenic games. This was like winning the 100 metres at the Olympics, to which these games were a forerunner. In addition, Philip's generals had won great victories in Serbia and Albania. The day was very special. When Philip led his troops into Pella, he was greeted with wild cheers. In the torchlight, he held baby Alexander up to the crowds and prayed to Zeus that his son might be an even better man than his father.

Given that the father was one of the most successful kings of his time, the prayer was a bold one. However, the gods must have been listening, for the baby was to grow up to be one of the great empire builders of all time, Alexander the Great.

In order to prepare his son for the responsibility of leadership, Philip sought a teacher who would act as a mentor in Alexander's formative years. According to Plutarch, the person chosen by King Philip was required to provide: *'The rudder's guidance and the curb's restraint.'*

The person selected was Aristotle.

Aristotle had studied under Plato. When called by the King, Aristotle was living a relatively unproductive life on the island of Lesbos. Philip enticed him to be a teacher by building a beautiful school just outside Pella in the attractive village of Mieza. With views across the distant sea and surrounded by botanical gardens, Mieza lent itself to learning.

Philip built the school to train future leaders for Macedonia. It was designed to be a hothouse of military, cultural and philosophical learning. Thus it was that Aristotle became a mentor to the emerging leaders of Greece. He would wander in the gardens and speak to the gaggle of students about him. This teaching by walking around was known as peripatetic education. Students were drawn into the life and thinking of their teacher, who posed problems and gave them insights into his own thoughts.

Aristotle demanded that his students exercise their minds in Socratic dialogue – and be able to argue a position from both sides. He led them in arduous debate and problem solving. He required them to make decisions that involved moral choice. He exercised his students mentally, physically and morally. Seemingly simple problems turned into highly complex tasks as unforeseen variables were added. Warfare, governance, public policy and justice were tackled. The Greek literary works of Homer's *Iliad* and *Odyssey* were read. The great playwright such as Euripides, Sophocles and Aristophanes were also studied.

Aristotle did not instruct in just one subject, he instructed in many. He was a polymath, a person who was knowledgeable in many areas. This meant his students were offered an all-round education. As a result, Alexander was influenced by Aristotle in many areas of his life. His battles, which would win him most of Asia Minor, Egypt and India, were exercises in strategy, logic and problem solving. Many of these skills were learned from his teacher, Aristotle.

Some have disputed whether Alexander was actually taught by Aristotle. He may have been instructed by other teachers at Mieza. It matters little. What is indisputable is that Alexander did have teachers who taught in the style ordained by Aristotle and this instruction was to inspire and guide him throughout his life.[2]

By training a successor, a leader is able to ensure they never die. They will continue to live through those they have mentored. Lasting impact is afforded to the leader who works not only with the current generation but also the next.

DEALING WITH FAILURE

A protégé can learn from witnessing failure in their mentor as well as success. One of the most important lessons a leader can give to their followers is how to deal with failure.

Most famous people have had to endure failure, including the most successful. For example:

- Noël Coward once pitied a man because he had been totally unspoiled by failure.
- Mary Pickford claimed that it was not the falling down that was unacceptable, it was the staying down.
- Henry Ford thought failure an opportunity to start again with rather greater intelligence.

A STORY TO TELL

ABRAHAM LINCOLN (1809-1865)

One leader who experienced a great deal of failure was Abraham Lincoln. His life did not start well. When he was nine years old Lincoln had to help his illiterate father make a coffin for his mother. Education was difficult because the school was five miles from the Lincolns' cabin and the subjects taught were limited to the most basic. Lincoln only went to school for one year because he was required to work with his father as a farmhand and log-splitter.

Lincoln then set himself up as a trader and village postmaster in New Salem, but in 1833 he failed in this venture. It took him fifteen years to repay his debts. Three years later he had a nervous breakdown. Having trained as a lawyer, the world of politics beckoned. Lincoln was a gifted orator but this did not prevent him being defeated when he ran for the job of Speaker in Parliament in 1838.

Lincoln's private life was also afflicted with disappointment. His wife, Mary Todd, had a reputation for being very demanding. When asked why Mary Todd spelled her surname with two 'd's, Lincoln said that one 'd' may have been good enough for God but not good enough for the Todds! Lincoln also suffered from depression and once said to a friend that he feared to carry a penknife lest he use it on himself.

Further disappointments were to characterise Lincoln's life. In 1848, he lost re-nomination to Congress and the following year he was rejected for the post of Land Officer. In 1854 Lincoln was defeated when he ran for the Senate. A few years later, Lincoln lost a series of seven great debates with a rival Republican candidate, Stephen Douglas, who won the nomination in 1858.

When Lincoln finally succeeded in 1860 and became the President of the United States, he had to cope with the dissolution of his government the following year. The country was then plunged into civil war. The pro-slavery states in the south wanted to separate from the anti-slavery states in the north.

The war was bitter and wasteful. It wasn't until April 1865 that the Southern Confederate leader, General Lee, surrendered to Ulysses S Grant and the war ended. However, Lincoln was not able to enjoy the fruits of victory for long. He was shot dead by John Wilkes Booth just a few days after the end of the Civil War.

Despite his failures, Abraham Lincoln is now remembered as one of the most significant figures in shaping the destiny of his nation. Failure may have been a part of Lincoln's life, but he never let it defeat him.[3]

If our children should fail, it might be helpful to remind them that they are in good company. Everyone has failed in some way or other. Failure is valuable if we learn from it. Through trial and error we can grow in knowledge and understanding. Through disappointment we can acquire humility. Through rejection we can learn grace.

IT'S NOT SO MUCH FAILURE THAT CRIPPLES PEOPLE BUT, RATHER, IT'S THE FEAR OF FAILURE.

Being able to handle failure can assist us to do well, as can the ability to handle success.

Success needs to be celebrated and acknowledged, but not to the extent that it suggests immunity from failure. Without failure, we would be unable to define success.

Being able to cope with disappointment requires many things, not least persistence, resilience and courage.

A PHOTO TO TAKE

Nothing in this world can take the place of persistence.
Talent will not; nothing is more common than
unsuccessful people with talent.
Genius will not; unrewarded genius is almost a proverb.
Education will not; the world is full of educated derelicts.
Persistence and determination alone are omnipotent.

Calvin Coolidge

Persistence

Very few leaders have reached their positions of influence without significant setbacks. Most have had to deal with failure and rejection. However, they have ventured on. Abraham Lincoln once stated: *'My great concern is not whether you have failed, but whether you are content with your failure.'*

SOME STORIES TO TELL

NELSON MANDELA (1918–2013)

From 1994 to 1999, Nelson Mandela served South Africa as its first black president. He was given this leadership role after leading his anti-colonial party, the African National Congress (ANC), to a landslide victory. The 1994 elections were the first fully democratic elections held by South Africa. Mandela went on to become an international statesman and philanthropist.

However, Mandela's role as one of the world's most recognised anti-apartheid leaders was only granted after he had suffered significant failure and relative obscurity as a prisoner.

Nelson Mandela spent almost twenty-seven years in South African prisons, much of them in a two-metre-wide cell on a prison island off the coast of South Africa. At the age of forty-six, Mandela was sent to Robben Island to complete a life sentence for his role in a sabotage campaign to overthrow the state. It was very nearly a life sentence, for Mandela arrived at Robben Island in 1964 and was not released until February 1990. However, Mandela never gave up on his goal to end apartheid and have his country governed by democratically elected representatives.[4]

THOMAS EDISON (1847–1931)

One of Thomas Edison's greatest gifts was the ability to learn from failure. He used failure to ensure success. Another of Edison's talents lay in taking other people's ideas, improving them and marketing them. During his lifetime, Edison amassed more than 1000 patents on inventions, many of which were refinements to other people's work.

Edison defined success as requiring 99 per cent perspiration and 1 per cent inspiration. His most significant invention was the first commercial light bulb, which was an exercise in endurance. JW Starr from Cincinnati had invented the first electric light bulb but it was not efficient. Edison, using a team of people, failed 14000 times before he, in conjunction with an Englishman called Joseph Swan, succeeded and established the Edison and Swan United Electric Company to produce the first successful light bulb.

WINSTON CHURCHILL (1874–1965)

The life of the British statesman Winston Churchill seems as though it was like a game of Snakes and Ladders. Snakes and Ladders is a game of chance. If you are lucky enough to land on a square where there is a ladder, elevation towards the top of the game board occurs. It you land on a square where there is a snake, then you slither down the board to the tail of the snake.

Winston Churchill's progress up the Snakes and Ladders board was erratic. At times he was politically popular and at other times unpopular. The outbreak of World War I was predicted with uncanny accuracy by Churchill, but his warnings were rejected by the military as 'amateur' and 'silly'. Nonetheless, a good throw of the dice gave Churchill the position of First Lord of the Admiralty and in that position, with scant political support, he readied the British Navy for war.

However, it was not long before Churchill suffered a poisonous bite. His plan to bring the war to an early end by use of a naval force in the Dardanelles was blown out of the water because the expeditionary force ran into a minefield and its land forces ran into well-fortified Turkish positions along the coast. The campaign was a disaster. The British suffered 205 000 casualties. Churchill was removed from his position as First Lord of the Admiralty and voted out of Parliament.

Churchill's recovery up the game-board was slow. However, step by step, he made progress. Churchill was re-elected to Parliament and on 3 September 1939 British warships signalled to each other *Winston is back*, and he was, as First Lord of the Admiralty.

Further elevation up the Snakes and Ladders board was to be punctuated by near-fatal bites. In Britain's darkest hour, Churchill was elected Prime Minister and promised nothing but *blood, sweat and tears*. He kept his promise. The British Forces were driven out of

Europe and suffered an ignominious retreat from Europe via Dunkirk. However, victories were to follow: The Battle of Britain, the Americans abandoning their neutrality, and the D-Day landings.

In 1945, there was the joy of a ladder right up to the top row ... victory in Europe, and in the Pacific. World War II was won. The nation was in raptures. Churchill wept before a standing ovation in Parliament. The game was nearly over. But, there was still one more snake. On the very next square, a roll of the dice determined that after only two months of winning the war in Europe, Churchill was voted out of office as Prime Minister.

A revival of fortunes in October 1951 saw Churchill re-elected as Prime Minister, but he was tired and quit politics a few years later.[5]

Some people experience more than their fair share of disappointment in life and believe their game to be one of *snakes and adders*. However, the ladders are there. No-one must think their life so bleak that they stop playing. Leaders must keep rolling the dice.

Perseverance, however, is easier said than done. This is particularly true when a problem arises at the very end and victory is snatched away.

A STORY TO SHARE

THE HILLARY STEP

In 1953, the British mountaineer John Hunt led an expedition to the Himalayas in the hope of putting the first person on the summit of Mount Everest and have them return safely. It was a massive logistical exercise involving 350 Nepalese porters ferrying equipment to nine campsites at ever-increasing altitudes. Within Hunt's international party were the two who would become the first to reach the summit of Mount Everest. They were the Nepali Sherpa, Tenzing Norgay, and a New Zealand beekeeper, Edmund Hillary.

The process of ferrying equipment meant that, in effect, Tenzing and Hillary climbed Mount Everest three times. It took many weeks to get themselves, and their equipment, to Camp IX, from which they would launch their final push to the summit. Camp IX was at 8200 metres; the summit was at 8850 metres. Although this does not sound a great distance, Tenzing and Hillary were living in what is known as the 'Death Zone', where the body takes in only 30 per cent of the oxygen enjoyed at sea level. The heart pounds even at rest, hallucinations are common, and the risks of hypothermia, exhaustion, cerebral and pulmonary edema are very real. There were also risks associated with blizzards, unstable ice and the ever-present danger of falling.

Tenzing and Hillary were exhausted as they approached the summit. Then, when the summit was just a hundred metres above them, they were confronted with a 12-metre wall of rock and ice. It seemed impossible to climb. This wall is now known as the 'Hillary Step' and represents the last significant obstacle when climbing Mount Everest.

Tenzing and Hillary studied the wall and saw within it not only an impassable obstacle but the threat of death, for there was a threatening crack in the ice that signalled an imminent ice fall. However, they recognised that the crack also suggested a way up the vertical barrier. There was just enough space in it for hands and feet. Using the crack, they continued to make their way upwards. At 11.30 a.m. on 29 May 1953, the two mountaineers reached the summit and became the first in the world to stand on top of Mount Everest.[6]

Everyone has their mountain to climb. It may not be an actual mountain: it can be overcoming a health or learning problem; it can be trying to get a job or a great exam result. Whatever the mountain, there is a strong likelihood that there will be a Hillary Step, a frustrating last–minute obstacle that threatens success.

It is said, 'When the going gets tough, the tough get going', and this is what Tenzing and Hillary did. Despite the risk of plunging

3000 metres onto the Kangshung Glacier and despite the crack in the ice that suggested it could fall at any time, they pressed on and even used the ominous crack in the ice to help them reach the top of Mount Everest.

THE PRAYER OF SIR FRANCIS DRAKE

... when you give to your servants to endeavour in any great matter, grant us to know that it is not the beginning but the continuing of the same unto the end until it be thoroughly finished, which yields the true glory.

When the going gets tough for your teen, share the following tips:

- Watch your body language – no sighs, no slumped shoulders. Maintain a high degree of creative energy.
- Watch your language – words spoken often have self-fulfilling power. 'We're stuffed . . . we can't do this,' will often result in you being stuffed. 'We can fix this and make it better,' will often result in things getting better.
- Individually, or with a team of creative thinkers, brainstorm ways the problem might be solved. Harvest ideas.
- If the problem remains, brainstorm ways the damage can be reduced.
  1. Look at solving the problem in a totally different way. Do not become fixated. As the saying goes, 'There is more than one way to skin a cat.' The early explorers had great difficulty crossing the Blue Mountains in New South Wales. They followed the usual European convention of seeking a route through the mountains using valleys and mountain passes. All these attempts failed. It was only when the explorers Blaxland, Wentworth and Lawson

    tried crossing the Blue Mountains using the ridges that they were successful.

2. Divide the big problem into a series of smaller ones and tackle them one at a time.

3. Try to understand what the real problem is, what lies behind the obstruction. Is there a political or personal agenda behind the problem? Tackle the real cause, not the revealed cause.

4. Even if a problem is not solved, extract from the situation another sort of victory. You may not have been the best team at scoring goals, baskets or points, but be the best team in terms of sportsmanship.

5. If the problem remains, view the experience as one that has taught you a lesson. Look for what can be learned from the experience.[7]

Resilience

Life is not going to provide a constant stream of undiluted fun, praise and success. Disappointment happens, discouragement happens, distress happens. Therefore, some resilience is required in our sons and daughters.

This is not to condone a callous indifference to their worries. It is to suggest that life will inevitably bring trials and tribulations. Therefore, coping strategies have to be learned. These strategies do not include petulant rage, defeatist withdrawal or escapist denial.

The foundation of resilience rests in:

- A realistic understanding of oneself.
- A realistic understanding of others.
- An ability to cope with the strengths and weaknesses in oneself.
- An ability to cope with the strengths and weaknesses in others.

The capacity to cope can be increased by a person having:

- Someone with whom they can share their deepest thoughts. More than one person is needed. There is wisdom in having someone:
  - within the family,
  - outside the family,
  - who is older,
  - who is a similar age.
- A knowledge that they are unconditionally loved by at least one other person.
- Skills at dealing with:
  - failure and success,
  - threats and fear,
  - rejection and disappointment,
  - anger and hurt.

Sometimes, our sons and daughters will feel insecure and scared. This is not always a bad thing. In Herman Melville's book *Moby-Dick*, Starbuck addresses his crew and says that he will not have a man in his company who is not afraid of a whale. Starbuck saw in the human frailty of fearfulness a positive asset. An over-confident person was a liability in a whaling boat.

However, there are other characters in literature who react very differently, such as Chicken Little, who ran around believing that the sky was falling in when all that had happened was an acorn had fallen on her head.

Some children have to cope with the most appalling burdens in life and fully deserve our help and understanding. There are others whose burdens are more imagined than real. They may still need professional help. However, at other times they may need to be told to *get over it* and *get on with it*.

Dealing with stress

Whether real or imagined, whether sensible or not, stress in our children needs to be taken seriously and medical assistance sought if the stress becomes significant or prolonged.

Within the life of a teen, there are many triggers of stress. It can be the result of bullying, rejection, parental break-up, sickness in the family, exams or the pressures of being a senior student.

Sitting atop the seniority pyramid at school can give wonderful views but it can be an uncomfortable perch. Year 12 students have to deal with exams, eighteenth birthday parties, 'friending' the 'right' people on Facebook, persuading Mum to take them out for more driving practice, dealing with the drop-dead gorgeous boy/ girlfriend who is not showing as much enthusiasm as they should, coping with zits, saying something sensible to the careers advisor, meeting all the sporting commitments, saving up for the car, feeding the cat . . . one could go on.

Stress is a reality in the lives of our sons and daughters. When dealing with this stress, a starting point is to get them to understand that feelings of stress are not unique to them. Others have survived in the past and they will probably survive in the future.

Secondly, remind them that wanting a life of unrelenting bliss with perfect relationships, perfect figures, perfect health and rivers of calorie-free chocolate is entirely understandable but a touch unrealistic. Should all our indulgent prayers be answered, we might be driven into greater misery rather than being elevated to a sublime state of constant joy.

Thirdly, suggest that some stress can be good for us. There are African desert tribes who will deliberately not camp close to water for fear it will cause their tribe to stop valuing water. Goodness can come from periods of stress. Resilience, character and wisdom can grow through stress. Out of the stress associated with disaster can come improved laws and a resolve to do better.

Having noted the above, it is not entirely accurate to suggest that if a little stress is a good thing then a lot of stress is a better thing. It is not. The adverse effects of stress should not be trivialised.

STRESS IS GOOD, BUT DISTRESS IS BAD.

Two types of stress have been identified:

- **Eustress** is short-term stress that is generally characterised by the body producing adrenalin to help it cope with an immediate emergency.
- **Distress** is long-term stress that can be chronic if it allows the body to be sapped of energy, morale to plummet and the immune system to be adversely affected.

Depression is one of the fastest-growing illnesses in society, particularly among school students. Bullying, social isolation, teasing, rejection and harassment are rife in schools as they are rife in marriages, work and society in general. There is stress out there, and our sons and daughters need to learn to cope with it. If they can't, expert medical help should be sought.

There are initiatives to take and attitudes to encourage if our sons and daughters are feeling down.

- Don't catastrophise. Although some people face non-trivial challenges, many have faced similar challenges before and survived.
- Be optimistic. See the issue as a problem that can be reduced, if not removed, by taking it a step at a time and a day at a time.
- Control negative thoughts. Identify them when they come. Stop, relax, breathe the black despair out and inhale pure, life-giving hope.
- Learn to be happy now rather than waiting to be happy when . . .

- Look after your health. Endeavour to sleep well, eat well and exercise well.
- Choose your company. Hang around those who love and like you, and those who make you smile.
- Don't engage in self-pity. Bad stuff doesn't happen only to you. Imagine telling your story to a child-slave working in a brick-pit in India.
- Go out and do something nice for someone. It can make you feel good.
- Squeeze good from the bad. Maybe you've stuffed up. Now unstuff! Learn from the event. Make amends. Say sorry. Be wiser. Move on.

Technology can also help with unhappiness. Given the way modern technologies are part and parcel of our children's lives, the capacity for this technology to be used to help those who suffer anxiety and depression is significant.

Several apps are out there that can help those with low mood and similar problems. The range of apps is increasing all the time. To this can be added a range of websites that can give advice and counselling. An example would be the ReachOut website, which has developed a number of apps, including:[8]

- **Worry Time.** This app encourages you to deal with your worries once a day rather than all the time. Using cognitive behavioural techniques, the app aims to reduce stress in a person's life.
- **Breathe.** By using calming visuals, shortness of breath and associated anxiety is reduced.

Having noted the above, if short-term unhappiness degenerates into long-term despair, expert medical hope should be sought.

Courage

Courage is the third ingredient in helping our sons and daughters to finish well. Courage is needed to start as a leader and to finish as a leader. Courage is needed to assume leadership responsibility and to shoulder the accountability. Courage is needed to cope with the vulnerability of command. Courage is needed to surrender leadership and cope with being less significant.

> *Cowards die many times before their deaths:*
> *The valiant never taste of death but once.*
>
> William Shakespeare, *Julius Caesar*, Act II Scene 2

TWO STORIES TO SHARE

EDITH CAVELL (1865-1915)

On 12 October 1915, Edith Cavell was driven to the main rifle range of Brussels by a German firing squad. Beside her was Philippe Baucq, who had worked with Nurse Cavell in organising an escape route for British soldiers and their allies out of German-occupied Belgium. Both were executed.

The killing of the British nurse sparked outrage in Britain and led to an outpouring of anger that was not far short of that felt in Britain when Germany sank the *Lusitania* at the start of World War I. For this reason, the execution of Nurse Cavell led to the enlistment of thousands of further recruits into Britain's army.

The circumstances leading to the execution of Cavell began with her inheriting a sum of money that allowed her to travel throughout Europe. Cavell worked as a governess in Brussels, the capital of Belgium. When she returned to England to train as a nurse, Cavell was glad to accept an opportunity to go back to Brussels, where she began work on turning a nursing home into a teaching hospital. Her success in this task won her great respect.

Such was Cavell's devotion that not even the invasion of Belgium by the Germans at the outbreak of World War I would see her leave. She decided to stay in Brussels and tend the wounded. Both the German and the Allied soldier were to benefit from her devotion.

Cavell nursed two British veterans, disguised as civilians, who had been wounded in the fighting around Mons. After tending their wounds, Cavell led them to an escape route that took them through Holland and back to Britain. Up to eighteen wounded Belgian, British and French soldiers would be hidden in her hospital at any one time, and hundreds were led to the escape route.

Cavell knew that one day she would be caught, because the escape operation was becoming well known. This did not deter her from her work, however, which continued until her arrest on 5 August 1915. She was sent to the prison at Saint Gilles, where she retained her composure and comforted herself by reading and sending advice to her nurses.

Thirty-four people were arrested in relation to the escape route, thirteen of them women. Several were released, but not Cavell. She admitted helping about 200 soldiers escape, arguing that she was merely assisting wounded men to go back to the frontier. Her trial was held in the Belgian Parliament Building, where she was questioned for five minutes before being sentenced to death.

Cavell did not ask for mercy. Her last message was given to her chaplain, the Reverend Stirling Gahan. It read:

Standing as I do in view of God and Eternity,
I realise that patriotism is not enough.
I must have no hatred or bitterness toward anyone.

The next morning Nurse Edith Cavell was shot.

Some years later, a statue of Cavell was erected in St Martin's Place, London, to commemorate her bravery. On the statue are inscribed the words: *Patriotism is not enough.*

Edith Cavell finished well.[9]

CATHERINE FREEMAN (1973–)

Catherine Astrid Salome Freeman, otherwise known as 'Cathy', did not have an easy start in life. The death of close relatives, the divorce of her parents, and being born an Aboriginal Australian in a country still blighted with racism, meant that her life would be difficult. However, Cathy soon learned she could run.

Her stepfather, Bruce Barlow, began training her as a track-and-field sprinter. Later, she won a scholarship to Fairholme College in Queensland and was coached by Mike Danilo. Cathy's amazing capacity as a runner led her to being selected to represent Australia in the Commonwealth Games in Auckland in 1990. Despite being the youngest competitor in the team, she won a gold medal in the 4 x 100 metres relay event.

Cathy made her first appearance at an Olympics in 1992. However, it was not until 1994 that she came to international prominence when she won the 200-metre and 400-metre sprints at the Commonwealth Games held in Canada.

It was her win at the 2000 Olympic Games in Sydney that endeared her to millions. Running in a distinctive green and gold 'sprint suit', Cathy was an imposing spectacle. She had also been an imposing spectacle as she lit a reluctant Olympic Flame at the Opening Ceremony. Such was her awesome presence, the Olympic 400-metre women's champion, Marie-José Pérec of France, was completely spooked and returned home to France before the 400-metre finals. She cited harassment from strangers.

Cathy won the 400-metre sprint in a time of 49.11 seconds. She was only the second Aboriginal Australian to win a gold medal at an Olympic Games. The first was Nova Peris-Kneebone, who won a gold medal in the women's hockey in 1996.

Cathy retired from athletics in 2003 but took up many charities and causes. She was Ambassador of the Australian Indigenous Education Foundation until 2012 and Ambassador for the 'Cottage by the Sea' charity, which specialised in providing short-term respite care for disadvantaged families. In 2007, Cathy established the Cathy Freeman Foundation.

Named as Australian of the Year in 1998, Cathy was given a Medal of the Order of Australia in 2001. Cathy Freeman is an example of someone who is finishing well.[10]

THE IMPORTANCE OF HUMILITY

Those who are successful face some very real challenges when they step down as leaders. It is not easy to finish well and to retire with due humility. Leaders must never accept the plaudits of admirers and followers without proper reserve. They must also acknowledge those who have supported them as leaders.

Success can be just as difficult to handle as failure. The trouble with success is that people expect it to continue. If it does continue, there are other dangers, including pride. Swelled-headedness needs to be avoided but so too should self-deprecation.

When being complimented, many are tempted to say: 'Oh . . . it was nothing.' If a leader has risked their reputation, and invested a huge amount of energy and countless hours on a job, it was not 'nothing'. It was something! Compliments should be accepted with a polite: 'Thank you.'

A proper understanding of one's contribution is appropriate. An inflated elaboration of one's contribution is not.

LEADING TO THE END

Leaving a formal leadership role does not mean an end to leadership opportunities. The company executive can still be an active leader after retirement. This might be providing leadership to a local golf club, body corporate, or the development of the grandchildren's character, but it is still leadership.

Even in death we can lead. Through our faith and example, through our strength and courage, others can be inspired and encouraged. If we live the prayer of Saint Francis of Assisi, we can be leaders to the end . . . and even beyond.

A PHOTO TO TAKE

THE PEACE PRAYER

Lord make me an instrument of your peace.
Where there is hatred let me sow love.
Where there is injury, pardon.
Where there is doubt, faith.
Where there is darkness, light.
Where there is sadness, joy.
Grant that I may not so much seek to be consoled as to console;
To be understood as to understand.
To be loved as to love.
For it is in giving that we receive.
It is in pardoning that we are pardoned.
It is in dying that we are born to eternal life.

Saint Francis of Assisi (adapted)

EXITING AT THE RIGHT TIME

One of the great skills of a performer is to know when to leave. Some leaders stay on too long and become an irritation to their followers. A time comes when the memories of yesterday's triumphs are not sufficient to overcome the fears of tomorrow's disasters. Quite simply, the leader has become a liability.

A STORY TO SHARE

CATHERINE THE GREAT (1729-1796)

EMPRESS OF RUSSIA

Catherine II was a powerful leader who built upon the transforming work of Peter the Great to make Russia stronger and even more progressive. However, the end of her reign was marked by a growing alienation from her people and a brutal reinforcement of a feudalistic society whereby the great majority of Russians were kept in poverty as they worked for Russia's nobility. Catherine wanted to maintain the status of the powerful ruling class.

Born a princess in the small Prussian state of Anhalt-Zerbst, Sophia Augusta Frederica changed her name to Catherine Alekseyevna when she was baptised into the Russian Orthodox faith at the age of fifteen. This initiative was motivated more by political than religious reasons, because she wanted to present herself as a serious contender as wife for her second cousin, Peter Ulrich, the heir to the throne of Russia. Winning the favour of the Russian Royal Court also required Catherine to study Russian and inform herself of the internal and external affairs of the country.

In 1745, Catherine married Peter, who now rejoiced in the title of Grand Duke. However, Peter was not so grand as his title suggested and this required Catherine to have a succession of lovers, one of whom was probably the father of her son, Paul. Catherine's inadequate husband was an inconvenience to her. Although the exact details are not known with certainty, it is well known that Peter was killed.

Now in total control of Russia, Catherine instituted an energetic program of reform and enlightenment. Education, commerce, banking and the arts felt the benefit of her policies. In the realm of foreign affairs, Catherine was also triumphant. She annexed much of Poland, the Baltic, Crimea and the Ukraine, and colonised Alaska. Russia's influence was extended into Central Europe, and Catherine became an active stateswoman, mediating between Prussia and Austria during the War of the Bavarian Succession in 1778-1779.

However, at home she had to endure a peasant uprising in 1773-1774 and this seemed to strengthen her resolve that the 'haves' of Russia would continue to 'have', and that the 'have nots' would continue to have nothing. This political blind spot was to sow the seeds of the Russian Revolution in 1917. Catherine's increasing inability to connect with the majority of her subjects began to make her a liability as a leader.

Although she was given a magnificent funeral when she died in 1796, Catherine ended her days much less admired than when she started. As Empress of Russia, she did not finish as well as she might have done.[11]

FINALLY

Some don't have to worry about how they finish because they never started! Fearing how things might end up has paralysed more than one person and prevented them from exploring what their purpose in life is. For a leader to finish, they must have started.

TAKE YOUR DREAM

Take your dream and visualise it complete.
Repeat the process until the dream begins to take form.
Gently stir in some common sense but not too much lest it lose its originality.
Add a responsible amount of research and a good-sized amount of effort.
Flavour with some trusted advice. Avoid half-baking.
Leave the mixture to face the heat of critical evaluation until the dream has risen and becomes firm.
Leave to cool until the right moment comes to serve.

SUMMARY

- We tend to be defined by how we finish rather than how we start.
- Not many leaders finish well.
- A good way to reflect on whether a son or daughter is finishing their school days well is to get them to write a reference about themselves.

- It can be challenging to finish school days well. However, there are ways to exit leaving a good impression.
- A great way to finish well is to raise up suitable successors.
- Investing time in a protégé allows one's influence to continue.
- Failure is normal in the life of a leader. Therefore, it is important to learn how to deal with failure as well as success.
- Finishing well requires persistence, resilience and courage.
- Life can present hard spots that can frustrate the reaching of a goal. How we overcome these 'Hillary Steps' can sort the leader from the non-leader.
- The hard spots can sometimes be turned into opportunities.
- The foundation of resilience rests in a realistic understanding of oneself and of others, and an ability to use the strengths in oneself and others.
- The ability to cope is assisted when one has appropriate friends and mentors, someone who loves and cares for one.
- There is a cost to leadership that should not be trivialised.
- Sometimes, professional help is needed to help cope with stress and depression.
- Some stress is good but distress is bad.
- There are attitudes and initiatives that can be taken to improve wellbeing.
- Finishing well requires an ability to deal with both failure and success.
- Knowing when to step down from a leadership position is important.

Conclusion

LEADERSHIP EXPECTATIONS

Having considered ways leadership skills might be encouraged in our sons and daughters, it is appropriate to remind ourselves that there is little that is more destructive than hounding children to fulfil leadership expectations that are totally unrealistic. Not every child is going to be in the 'A' team. Not every child is going to be the school captain. Not every child will go to university to study nuclear physics.

It is also worth remembering that one generation defines success differently from another. A parent may think leadership is about titled positions, whereas their offspring may not give a stuff about being a prefect or class captain. For them, leadership may be more about having 500 'friends' on Facebook and having 'a set of wheels' that makes others green with envy.

Leadership can also mean different things to different people. This is because leadership is influenced by needs. To the person being bullied, leadership is being strong enough to stand up to the bullies. To the insecure, leadership is having greater confidence. To the creative, leadership is releasing their creative spirit.

Although the generally accepted expression of leadership may change from one generation to another, and although the motives for wanting to lead may vary from one generation to another, everyone still needs to:

- Learn how to take command and control of themselves.
- Find what they are uniquely gifted in and be able to use this gift not only for their own benefit, but for the benefit of others.

EFFECTIVE LEADERSHIP

The thesis of this book is that although only in their teens, our sons and daughters can lead. Whether they lead well is another matter.

Effective leadership skills need to be learned in two areas: leadership of oneself and leadership of others.

Leadership of oneself

Whatever the generation and whatever the culture, society is crying out for authentic leadership. The expression of this leadership is desperately required in the leadership of self. Too many have habits, addictions and besetting diversions that have captured and controlled them. Whether it be eating or drinking inappropriately, watching pornography, online gaming or social-media addiction, there are too many who seek to lead others when they cannot even control themselves.

If this book does nothing else, it is hoped that it encourages us all to be better people – people who are in control of ourselves.

Leadership of others

Howard Gardner, in his 1983 book *Frames of Mind*, argues that each of us has a strength in some area, be it in mathematics, literacy, dance, sport and movement, interpersonal skills, music and so on. Even though our sons and daughters may not be gifted in winning wars or in solving the economic ills of their country, they may have an ability to do wondrous things with computers, or to support a deserving charity.

Engagement in activities that impact positively on others means they are leading. It may not be for long and it might be limited, but they are still leading.

THE MANDATE TO LEAD

Not everyone will be followed.

It is well for our children to know this and to recognise that their mandate to lead rests with others. A leader is not a leader unless they are being followed.

Compliance by followers may be forced, but it will not last for long. Compliance given willingly lasts longer. Leaders remain leaders for as long as their followers let them.

The bloodiest revolutions have occurred when leaders lost the respect of their people and, with it, their right to govern. The British were reminded of this in 1776 when they lost the support of a people and the possession of the continent of North America. Thomas Jefferson reminds us that the ultimate destiny of a people is determined by the people themselves. The American Declaration of Independence is worth reading. It reminds us that power is given only with the consent of the people.

The Declaration of Independence

We hold these truths to be self-evident, that all men are created equal, that they are endowed by their Creator with certain unalienable Rights, that among these are Life, Liberty and the pursuit of Happiness. That to secure these rights, Governments are instituted among Men, deriving their just powers from the consent of the governed. That whenever any Form of Government becomes destructive to these ends, it is the Right of the People to alter or to abolish it, and to institute new Government, laying its foundation on such principles and organizing its power in such form, as to them shall seem most likely to effect their Safety and Happiness.

None may presume they will always be followed. Ultimately, followership is more powerful than leadership.

FOLLOWERSHIP

Our airport bookshops suggest a growing desire to learn leadership skills. However, there is not so much appetite to learn 'followership' skills.

No-one can be a leader all the time. I may run the school, but there is a very different power balance in the home!

A good leader also needs to be a good follower. We all need to be good team players. We all need to be supportive of others.

The most effective leader is the 'servant-hearted' leader, the one who uses their gifts for the benefit of others. The term 'servant leader' is a strange one. Almost oxymoronic, it hints at an impossibility. Not so. Those leaders who have had the most impact on our society have been those who have set out to enrich the lives of others.

WHY THIS BOOK IS DIFFERENT

This book is different from many books on leadership. This is because it has not been written for the corporate high-flyer who is looking for a bit of distraction while munching on peanuts at 10000 feet. This is a book for mums and dads to share with their teenage children.

Many real-life heroes and heroines are mentioned, but the leadership challenges presented here are largely based on what the contemporary teen can reasonably be expected to achieve.

Furthermore, this is a book that acknowledges the important role that women play in leadership as well as men. The contemporary style of leadership, which uses a more consultative and communal style of decision making, is an art form women perfected centuries before any man latched on to the idea.

Another important element of *Ten Leadership Lessons You Must Teach Your Teenager* is the realistic expectations it makes of parents and their children. Airport books usually require you to have made your first million dollars by the age of twenty-one. This book suggests you start by learning to change a tyre.

Another aim of this book is to encourage conversation between parents and their children. There are photos to share, there are discussions to have, stories to tell and exercises to complete. Not all the stimulus material will be appropriate and may need to be modified to make it relevant. However, a start is provided that, hopefully, will enrich interaction between parents and their teens as well as improve their understanding of leadership.

SUMMARY

Within *Ten Leadership Lessons You Must Teach Your Teenager* it is suggested that there is:

1. **A choice to make**: We are all called to lead at certain points in our life. The question is, will we lead? If so, why? Motives for leadership can vary from the selfish to the altruistic. Our sons and daughters can choose to lead and choose to follow.
2. **A discipline to learn**: Life is not just about finding yourself – it is about creating yourself. This can take time and effort. Our sons and daughters need to understand that creating something special requires sacrifice and discipline.
3. **An example to follow**: History is awash with examples of leadership, but so too is contemporary life. Today, the definition of leadership is rather different from that of past years. Our sons and daughters need to adopt a leadership style that suits the time in which they live.

4. **A villain to defeat**: There is evil in the world that must be confronted. Institutional and individual wrongdoing needs to be identified and dealt with. Our sons and daughters need to know there is a place for moral outrage and a time for action.

5. **A calling to hear**: There is a need to be informed about what is going on in the world. This enables the adoption of causes, formation of convictions and creation of goals. Our sons and daughters should be encouraged to find out what it is they were put on this earth to achieve.

6. **A skill to have**: For leadership to be effective, it must have impact. There is an armoury of skills that can be acquired, which can result in more persuasive leadership. Our sons and daughters should become gifted in at least one skill they can use to benefit the broader community.

7. **A team to assist**: Leadership is not about being able to do things. It is about being able to get things done. This requires teamwork. Teams can be virtual or real. In either case, our sons and daughters need to learn the art of delegation and being part of a team.

8. **A strategy to adopt**: It is not good enough for a leader to have a plan – it needs to be a strategic plan. Skilled problem solving can lead to more successful leadership. Our sons and daughters need to recognise that different strategies are needed for different situations.

9. **A costume to wear**: How we act and how we look can determine how convincing we are as leaders. Bearing and behaviour are also important. Our sons and daughters have many 'costumes' to choose from. They need to make the right choice at the right time.

10. **An ending to have**: Leaders tend to be judged more on how they finished than on how they started. Our sons and daughters will require persistence, resilience and courage to finish well.

FINALLY

Each of our sons and daughters is unique and must be allowed to remain so rather than conforming to a definition of success imposed on them by others. That said, there is a compendium of leadership wisdom provided by history and validated by the present that can profitably be taught by parents.

If *Ten Leadership Lessons You Must Teach Your Teenager* has captured some of this wisdom and suggested ways in which it might be shared with our sons and daughters, it will have served its purpose.

ENDNOTES

Talking about leadership

1 Lickona, T (1993) *The Return of Character Education,* Educational Leadership, November
2 Seligman, M (1995) *The Optimistic Child*, Adelaide, Griffin
3 For more detail, go to: www.theoceancleanup.com
4 www.biography.com/people/malala-yousafzai-21362253

Lesson One: A choice to make

1 Schwartz, B (2004) *The Paradox of Choice*, New York, Perennial
2 Short, P (2004) *The History of a Nightmare*, London, John Murray
3 Benge, J and Benge, G (1998) *Gladys Aylward: The Adventure of a Lifetime*, Seattle, YWAM

Lesson two: A discipline to learn

1 www.youtube.com/watch?v=G-5S5mvayCw
2 www.perseus.tufts.edu/Herakles/labors.html; Storrie, P and Kurth, S (2007) *Hercules: The Twelve Labors, A Greek Myth*, Minneapolis, MN, Lerner Publishing (this book tells the tale of Hercules in picture format)
3 www.youtube.com/watch?v=hrSs_DiJ-ZA; www.artofmanliness. com/2012/06/28/sewing-on-a-button/
4 Syed, M (2010) *Bounce,* New York, HarperCollins
5 www.olympic.org/olympic-games
6 Gladwell, M (2011) *Outliers*, New York, Little, Brown and Co.
7 www.australianoftheyear.org.au/honour-roll/?view+fullView&recipient ID=485

Lesson three: An example to follow

1 Hart, M (1978) *The 100: A Ranking of the Most Influential Persons in History*, New York, Hart Publishing
2 Felder, D (1997) *The 100 Most Influential Women of All Time*, London, Robinson Publishing
3 Duiker, W (2001) *Ho Chi Minh: A Life*, New York, Hyperion Books
4 Shackleton, E (2002) *Shackleton: The Polar Journeys*, Edinburgh, Birlinn

5 'Jihadist teens from Australian suburbs raise questions about counter-radicalisation effectiveness', *7.30*, ABC, 11 March: www.abc.net.au/7.30/content/2015/s4195874.htm
Radicalisation of UK schoolgirls: www.huffingtonpost.co.uk/ruwayda-mustafah/isis-girls_b_6732326.html

6 For further information on Odette Hallows (Sansom) go to: Heroes of the SOE: https://www.youtube.com/watch?v=RE-IOGS94ck

Lesson four: A villain to conquer

1 https://www.themonthly.com.au/issue/2014/october/1412085600/helen-garner/mother-courage

2 Metaxas, E (2007) *Amazing Grace: William Wilberforce and the Heroic Campaign to End Slavery*, New York, HarperCollins.

3 Larson, K (2004) *Bound for the Promised Land: Harriet Tubman*, New York, Random House

4 Isaacson, W (2008) *Einstein: His Life and Universe*, New York, Simon & Schuster

5 Thatcher, M (2013) *Margaret Thatcher: The Autobiography, 1925–2013*, London, Harper Press

Lesson five: A calling to hear

1 Hawkes, T (2014) *Ten Conversations You Must Have With Your Son*, Sydney, Hachette Australia, p 72

2 Sobel, D (1995) *Longitude: The True Story of a Lone Genius Who Solved the Greatest Scientific Problem of His Time*, New York, Walker

3 Hibbert, C (2008) *Mussolini: The Rise and Fall of Il Duce*, New York, Palgrave Macmillan

4 Popham, P (2011) *The Lady and the Peacock*, London, Rider Books

5 Huntford, R (2010) *Race for the South Pole*, London, Continuum

6 Fraser, D (2002) *Dawn: One Hell of a Life*, Sydney, Hodder

7 Arana, M (2013) *Bolívar: American Liberator*, New York, Simon & Schuster

8 Castor, H (2014) *Joan of Arc: A History*, London, Faber & Faber

9 Kousoulas, D (2007) *The Life and Times of Constantine the Great*, Bethesda, Provost Books

10 www.australianoftheyear.org.au/the-awards/awards-history/young-australians/

Lesson six: A skill to have

1 www.dccomics.com/characters/wonder-woman

2 https://www.discinsights.com/william-marston#.VXnZBcd--M8

3   A short but rather graphic video story about Sadako can be found in comic book format at: www.youtube.com/watch?v=fABpssKWCoE

4   The story about Major Nesmith is taken from: Taylor, D (2002) *The Naked Leader*, Oxford, Capstone, p 132

5   Nicholl, C (2004) *Leonardo da Vinci: Flights of the Mind*, New York, Viking Penguin

6   Perry, R (2014) *Monash: The Outsider Who Won a War*, Sydney, Random House Australia

7   Gardner, H (1983) *Frames of Mind: The Theory of Multiple Intelligences*, New York, Basic Books

8   For more information, go to: www.midnightoil.com/biography

9   For more information, go to: www.bobmarley.com/

10 To see Julia Gillard's speech, go to: www.youtube.com/watch?v=SOPsxpMzYw4

11 To see Noel Pearson's speech, go to: www.youtube.com/watch?v=JsXmYHiuJ8s

12 www.history.com/topics/black-history/rosa-parks

13 For more information about John F Kennedy, go to: www.biography.com/people/john-f-kennedy-9362930

Lesson seven: A team to assist

1   www.npr.org/2011/06/04/136723316/dont-believe-facebook-you-only-have-150-friends

2   www.selfgrowth.com/articles/McRae19.html; Jamie Oliver's parenting tip for kids and the internet: http://www.kidspot.com.au/parenting/teenager/cybersafety/jamie-olivers-tech-safety-message-to-parents-makes-a-lot-of-sense

3   Goleman, D, Boyatzis, R and McKee, A (2013) *Primal Leadership*, Boston, Harvard Business School Press

4   www.biography.com/people/angela-merkel-9406424

5   www.south-pole.com/p0000089.htm

6   Morrell, M and Capparell, S (2001) *Shackleton's Way*, London, Nicholas Brearley
    Survival! The Shackleton Story: https://www.youtube.com/watch?v=sgh_77TtX5I

7   www.afb.org/asm/asmgallery.asp?FrameID=98

Lesson eight: A strategy to adopt

1   www.historyhome.co.uk/pms/wellingt.htm

2   www.aboutnelson.co.uk

3   Marina Raskova and the Soviet Women Pilots of World War II: www.ctie.
    monash.edu.au/hargrave/soviet_women_pilots.html
4   Sloan, E (2012) *Modern Military Strategy: An Introduction*, New York,
    Routledge; Kane, T and Lonsdale, D (2012) *Understanding Contemporary
    Strategy*, New York, Routledge
5   www.eyewitnesstohistory.com/lightbrigade.htm
6   www.biography.com/people/galileo-9305220
7   Top 10 Self-Made Teen Millionaires: https://www.youtube.com/
    watch?v=ITI03rkwukQ
8   www.huffingtonpost.com/2014/10/06/app-pets-video-chat_n_5939320.
    html; for other examples of teens doing well in business, see:
    www.teenbusiness.com/current-news2/

Lesson nine: A costume to wear
1   The Grand Levée of the King: partylike1660.com
2   www.touregypt.net/cleopatr.htm
3   www.realmenrealstyle.com/mens-dress-code-formal-events;
    www.youtube.com/watch?v=IPWPg0FxUUY; www.entrepreneur.com/
    article/238953; www.boston.com/jobs/topworkplaces/2009/dresstoimpress
4   www.biography.com/people/coco-chanel-9244165
5   www.freedieting.com/body_types.htm
6   www.nationaleatingdisorders.org/general-information
7   www.mythman.com/echo.html
8   www.teenadvice.about.com/library/teenquiz/17/bltattooyouquiz.htm;
    www.shoulditattoo.com
9   www.biography.com/people/muhammad-ali-9181165;
    www.muhammadali.com
10 Vanderbilt, A (1995) *Complete Book of Etiquette*, New York, Doubleday;
    Von Adlerstein, M (2002) *The Penguin Book of Etiquette*, Camberwell,
    Viking
11 Fox, R (1973) *Alexander the Great*, London, Allen Lane
12 www.biography.com/people/confucius-9254926;
13 Agrippina the Younger Facts: biography.yourdictionary.com/agrippina-
    the-younger

Lesson ten: An ending to have
1   Innes, J (2012) *The CV Book*, London, Pearson Education
2   Alexander the Great: http://www.sparknotes.com/biography/alexander/
    section2.rhtml
3   Donald, D (1996) *Lincoln*, New York, Touchstone
4   Sampson, A (2011) *Mandela: The Authorised Biography*, London, HarperCollins

5   Gilbert, M (1991) *Churchill: A Life*, London, Pimlico

6   Johnston, A (2013) *Sir Edmund Hillary: An Extraordinary Life*, Rosedale, Penguin Group New Zealand

7   Roy, S (2005) *Managing Stress*, Slough, New Dawn Press Group

8   www.au.reachout.com

9   Souhami, D (2010) *Edith Cavell*, London, Quercus

10 To see Cathy Freeman win the 400 metres in the 2000 Olympics, go to: www.youtube.com/watch?v=xNmuyxlZ9Kk
    Freeman, C (2007) *Born to Run*, Camberwell, Puffin Books

11 Massie, R (2011) *Catherine the Great: Portrait of a Woman*, New York, Random House

REFERENCES

Adair, J (2006) *Leadership and Motivation*, London, Kogan Page Ltd.

Adair, J (2007) *Develop Your Leadership Skills,* London, Kogan Page Ltd.

Addison, J and Mann, J (2016) *Real Leadership*, New York, McGraw-Hill.

Aesop (1954) *Fables of Aesop*, translated by SA Hanford, New York, Penguin Books.

Alvesson, M and Willmott, H (1996) *Making Sense of Management*, California, Sage.

Archer, C (2014) *Everybody Paddles*, New York, BookBady.

Aristotle, 'Nichomachean ethics' (Hippocrates P. Apostle and Lloyd P. Gerson, Trans.), in *Aristotle: Selected Works* (1991).

Ashton, K (2015) *How to Fly a Horse,* New York, Doubleday.

Bardwick, J (1988) *In Praise of Good Business,* New York, John Wiley & Sons.

Barker, C and Coy, R (2005) *Understanding Influence for Leaders at All Levels*, Australian Institute of Management, Sydney, McGraw-Hill.

Barthelemy, B (1997) *The Sky is Not the Limit*, Baton Rouge, St Lucie Press.

Bass, B (1985) *Leadership and Performance Beyond Expectations*, New York, Free Press.

Bass, B (1989) *Bass and Stogdill's Handbook of Leadership: A Survey of Theory and Research*, New York, Free Press.

Bauman, Z (2004) *Wasted Lives,* Cambridge, Polity Press.

Baylis, N (2005) *Learning from Wonderful Lives,* Cambridge, Wellbeing Press.

Beatty, J (1998) *The World According to Drucker*, London, Orion.

Bellah, R, Madsen, R, Sullivan, W, Swindler, A and Tipton, S (1996) *Habits of the Heart* (rev. ed.), Berkeley, University of California Press.

Bellman, G (1992) *Getting Things Done When You Are Not in Charge*, San Francisco, Berrett-Koehler.

Benfari, I (1991) *Understanding Your Management Style*, Sydney, Simon & Schuster.

Bennett, W J (1993) *The Book of Virtues: A Treasury of Great Moral Stories*, New York, Simon & Schuster.

Bennis, W (1997) *Managing People is Like Herding Cats*, Provo, UT, Executive Excellence.

Bennis, W and Nanus, B (1985) *Leaders: The Strategies for Taking Charge*, New York, HarperCollins.

Blanchard, K and Johnson, S (1982) *The One Minute Manager*, New York, William Morrow and Co.

Blanchard, K and O'Connor, M (1995) *Managing by Values*, Los Angeles, Blanchard Training and Development Inc.

Blanchard, K and Waghorn, T (1997) *Mission Possible*, New York, McGraw-Hill.

Blanchard, K, Carlos, J and Randolph, A (1996) *Empowerment Takes More Than a Minute*, San Francisco, Berrett-Koehler.

Block, P (1993) *Stewardship: Choosing Service over Self-Interest*, San Francisco, Berrett-Koehler.

Bloodworth, D and Ching Ping (1976) *The Chinese Machiavelli*, Farrar, New York, Straus and Giroux.

Bolman, T and Deal, L (1995) *Leading with Soul: An Uncommon Journey of Spirit*, San Francisco, Jossey-Bass.

Bradberry, T and Greaves, J (2009) *Emotional Intelligence 2.0*, San Diego, CA, TalentSmart.

Brown, B (2015) *Rising Strong*, New York, Spiegel & Grau.

Brzezinski, M (2011) *Knowing Your Value: Women, Money and Getting What You're Worth*, New York, Weinstein Books.

Burns, J (1978) *Leadership*, New York, Harper & Row.

Butler, G and Hope, T (1996) *Managing Your Mind*, New York, Oxford University Press.

Byers, A (2007) *Jeff Bezos*, New York, The Rosen Publishing Group.

Carlson, R (1998) *Don't Sweat the Small Stuff at Work: Simple Ways to Minimise Stress and Conflict While Bringing Out the Best in Yourself and Others*, New York, Hyperion.

Carnegie, D (1956) *How to Develop Self-Confidence and Influence People by Public Speaking*, New York, Pocket Books.

Cassidy, J (2003) *Dot Con*, New York, Perennial Press.

Catmull, E (2014) *Creativity Inc.*, New York, Random House.

Chaleff, I (1995) *The Courageous Follower: Standing Up to and for Our Leaders*, San Francisco, Berrett-Koehler.

Champy, J (1995) *Reengineering Management*, New York, Harper & Row.

Chinen, A (1993) *Beyond the Hero: Classic Stories of Men in Search of Soul*, New York, Putnam.

Chinen, A (1996) *Waking the World: Classic Tales of Women and the Heroic Feminine*, Los Angeles, Tarcher.

Christensen, C (2011) *The Innovator's Dilemma*, New York, Harper Business.

Clark, L (2006) *Female Entrepreneurs*, Sydney, New Holland.

Clements, A (2008) *Aung San Suu Kyi*, New York, Ebury.

Cloud, H (2006) *Integrity*, New York, HarperCollins.

Cohen, A and Bradford, D (1991) *Influence Without Authority*, New York, John Wiley & Sons.

Cohen, W (2000) *The New Art of the Leader*, Paramus, NJ, Prentice Hall.

Collins, J (2001) *Good to Great*, New York, Harper Business.

Covey, S (1990) *The Seven Habits of Highly Effective People*, New York, Simon & Schuster.

Covey, S (2006) *The Speed of Trust*, New York, Simon & Schuster.

Covey, S (2008) *The Leader in Me*, New York, Simon & Schuster.

Cranston, N and Ehrich, L (2007) *What is This Thing Called Leadership?*, Brisbane, Australian Academic Press.

Dalai Lama (2008) *The Leader's Way*, London, Nicholas Brealey Publishing.

de Guillaume, A (2002) *How to Rule the World*, Sydney, Allen & Unwin.

De Pree, M (1998) *Leadership is an Art*, New York, Doubleday.

De Vries, M (2001) *The Leadership Mystique*, London, Pearson Education.

Dewey, J (1981) 'The Pattern of Inquiry,' in John J McDermott (ed.). *The Philosophy of John Dewey*, Chicago, University of Chicago Press, p. 223-239.

Dourado, P and Blackburn, P (2005) *Seven Secrets of Inspired Leaders*, Oxford, Capstone.

Downtown, J (1973) *Rebel Leadership: Commitment and Charisma in the Revolutionary Process*, New York, Free Press.

Drucker, P (1955) *The Practice of Management*, London, Pan Books.

Du Brin, A (2000) *The Complete Idiot's Guide to Leadership*, Indianapolis, Alpha Books.

Emmett, R (2000) *The Procrastinator's Handbook*, New York, Walker and Company.

Erikson, E (1968) *Indentity, Youth and Crisis*, New York, WW Norton.

Estes, C (1992) *Women Who Run with the Wolves*, London, Rider.

Farson, R (1996) *Management of the Absurd: Paradoxes in Leadership*, New York, Simon & Schuster.

Felder, D (1996) *The 100 Greatest Women of All Time*, Special Edition for Past Times, Oxford, London, Constable & Robinson.

Fenton, R and Waltz, A (2010) *Go for No*, Orlando, FL, Courage Crafters.

Ferling, J (2000) *Setting the World Ablaze*, New York, Oxford University Press.

Fernandes, C (2005) *Reluctant Saviour*, Sydney, Scribe.

Fertman, C and Long, J (1990) "All students are leaders", *School Counsellor*, 37, 5, pp. 391-396.

Folley, M (1998) *People in History: A Young Person's Introduction*, London, Mitchell Beazley International Ltd.

Fortune [Eds] (2006) *Secrets of Greatness*, New York, Time Inc.

Frankel, L (2014) *Nice Girls Don't Get the Corner Office*, New York, Hachette.

Fry, R (2002) *Your First Interview*, Wayne, NJ, Career Press.

Fullan, M (2005) *Leadership and Sustainability*, Thousand Oaks, CA, Corwin.

Gardner, J (1990) *On Leadership*, New York, The Free Press.

Garfield, C (1986) Secrets of Super Achievers, *Reader's Digest*, June, p. 91.

Garratt, B (1996) *The Fish Rots from the Head*, London, HarperCollins.

Gates, B (1995) *The Road Ahead*, New York, Viking.

Giuliani, R (2002) *Leadership*, London, Little Brown and Company.

Gladwell, M (2007) *Blink*, New York, Little Brown and Company.

Glei, J [ed] (2013) *Manage Your Day-to-Day*, Las Vegas, NV, Amazon.

Godard, A and Lenhardt, V (1999) *Transformation*, New York, Palgrave.

Goleman, D (1996) *Emotional intelligence*, London, Bloomsbury.

Goleman, D Boyatzis, R and McKee, A (2002) *Primal Leadership: Realising the Power of Emotional Intelligence*, Boston, Harvard Business School Publishing.

Grant, A and Sandberg, S (2016) *Originals: How Non-Conformists Move the World*, New York, Viking.

Greene, R (2001) *The 48 Laws of Power*, Sydney, Hodder Headline Australia.

Greenleaf, R (1977) *Servant Leadership: A Journey into the Nature of Legitimate Power and Greatness*, New York, Paulist Press.

Greenleaf, R (1991) *The Servant as Leader*, Atlanta, The Robert K Greenleaf Centre.

Gregerman, A (2000) *Lessons from the Sandbox: Using the 13 Gifts of Childhood to Rediscover the Keys to Business Success*, Chicago, Contemporary Books.

Grint, K [Ed] (1997) *Leadership*, Oxford, Oxford Management Readers.

Handy, C (1985) *Understanding Organisations*, (2nd ed.), London, Penguin.

Handy, C (1994) *The Empty Raincoat*, London, Hutchinson.

Handy, C (1995) *Beyond Certainty*, London, Random House.

Hanson, N (2005) *The Unknown Soldier*, London, Doubleday.

Harrison, B (2006) *Tabloid Love*, New York, Da Capo Press.

Hawkes, T (2001) *Boy Oh Boy*, Sydney, Pearson Education Australia.

Hawkes, T (2004) What is Leadership? *Independence-The Journal of the Association of Heads of Independent Schools of Australia*, 29, 2, pp. 27-33.

Heath, C and Heath D (2011) *Switch*, New York, Crown Publishing Group.

Heifetz, R (1994) *Leadership Without Easy Answers*, Cambridge, The Bellnap Press of Harvard University Press.

Hicks, G (2003) *Leader Shock*, New York, McGraw-Hill.

Hodgkinson, C (1991) *Educational Leadership: The Moral Art*, New York, State University of New York Press.

Hollander, E (1964) *Leaders, Groups and Influence*, New York, Oxford University Press.

Hollander, E and Offerman, L (1997) *KLSP: The Balance of Leadership and Followship*, Baltimore Academy of Leadership Press.

Hollander, E and Offermann, L (1990) 'Power and leadership in organisations: Relationships in Transition', *American Psychologist*, 45, pp 179-189.

Holmes, A and Wilson, D (2004) *Pains in the Office,* Oxford, Capstone.

Honor Books (2001) *God's Little Lessons for Leaders*, Tulsa, OK, Honor Books.

Horn, A (1997) *Gifts of Leadership*, Toronto, Stoddart.

Howel, J and Avolio, B (1992) 'The ethics of charismatic leadership: Submission or liberation?' *Academy of Management Executive*, pp. 43-54.

Hughes, R Ginnett, R and Curphy, G (1993) *Leadership: Enhancing the Lessons of Experience*, Boston, Irwin.

Humes, J (1994) *The Wit and Wisdom of Winston Churchill*, New York, Harper Perennial.

Iacocca, L (2007) *Where Have All the Leaders Gone?* New York, Scribner.

Imparto, N and Harari, O (1995) *Jumping the Curve*, San Francisco, Jossey-Bass.

Isaacson, W (2011) *Steve Jobs*, New York, Simon & Schuster.

Jackall, R (1988) *Moral Mazes: The World of Corporate Managers*, New York, Oxford University Press.

Jackson, I and Nelson, J (2004) *Profits with Principles,* New York, Doubleday.

Jacobs, W (1992) *World Government: Great Lives*, New York, Charles Scribner's Sons.

Johnson, C (1997) 'Are we losing potential leaders at an early age?', *A Leadership Journal: Women in Leadership*, 2,1, pp. 125–132.

Johnson, P (2008) *Heroes,* London, Weidenfeld & Nicolson.

Jones, L (1995) *Jesus CEO*, New York, Hyperion.

Kaagan, S (1999) *Leadership Games*, Thousand Oaks, CA, Sage.

Kahneman, D (2011) *Thinking, Fast and Slow,* New York, Farrer Straus and Giroux.

Katzenbach, J and Smith, D (1986) *The Wisdom of Teams*, Boston, Harvard Business Review Press.

Kehoe, D and Godden, S (2003) *You Lead, They'll Follow*, Sydney, McGraw-Hill.

Kelley, R (1992) *The Power of Followership: How to Create Leaders People Want to Follow and Followers Who Lead Themselves*, New York, Doubleday.

Kelley, R (1995) *The Leader's Companion: Insight on Leadership Through the Ages*, New York, The Free Press.

Kohlberg, L (1981) *The Philosophy of Moral Development*, New York, HarperCollins.

Komives, S, Lucas, N and McMahan, T (1998) *Exploring Leadership for College Students Who Want to Make a Difference*, San Francisco, Jossey-Bass.

Kosko, B (1994) *Fuzzy Thinking: The New Science of Fuzzy Logic*, London, Flamingo.

Kotter, J (1996) *Leading Change*, Boston, Harvard Business School Press.

Kouzes, J and Posner, B (1987) *The Leadership Challenge*, San Francisco, Jossey-Bass.

Landes, D (2006) *Dynasties*, New York, Viking.

Landsberg, M (2000) *The Tools of Leadership,* London, HarperCollins.

Landsberg, M (2003) *The Tao of Coaching,* London, Profile Books.

Lee, R and King, S (2001) *Discovering the Leader in You: A Guide to Realising Your Personal Leadership Potential*, San Francisco, Jossey-Bass.

Leob, M and Kindel, S (1999) *Leadership for Dummies*, New York, JOG Books.

Levicki, C (2002) *Developing Leadership Genius*, Maidenhead, McGraw-Hill.

Lindsay, P (2006) *Cosgrove,* Sydney, Random House.

Livesey, A (1987) *Great Commanders and Their Battles*, London, Greenwich Editions.

Long, J Wald, H and Graf, O (1996) Student Leadership, *Keystone Leader* 29, 1, pp. 21-24.

Ludwig, E (1928) *Bismarck: The Story of a Fighter,* translated by Eden and Cedar Paul, Boston, Little Brown and Company.

MacArthur, B [Ed.] (1992) *The Penguin Book of Twentieth Century Speeches,* London, Harmondsworth, Penguin.

MacDonald, G (1985) *Ordering Your Private World*, Nashville, Oliver-Nelson.

Mangham, I (1986) *Power and Performance in Organisations*, Oxford, Basil Blackwell.

Mant, A (1994) *Leaders We Deserve*, Oxford, Basil Blackwell.

Mant, A (1997) *Intelligent Leadership*, Sydney, Allen & Unwin.

Manz, C and Sims, H (1989) *Super-Leadership: Leading Others to Lead Themselves*, New York, Berkley Books.

Manz, C and Sims, H (1993) *Business Without Bosses*, New York, Wiley and Sons.

Margerison, C (2002) *Team Leadership*, London, Thomson.

Marquet, L and Covey, S (2012) *Turn the Ship Around*, New York, Penguin.

Maslow, A (1954) *Motivation and Personality*, New York, Harper & Row.

Mathews, J (1988) *Escalante: The Best Teacher in America*, New York, Henry Holt.

Matusak, L (1996) *Finding Your Voice: Learning to Lead ... Anywhere You Want to Make a Difference*, San Francisco, Jossey-Bass.

Maxwell, J (1998) *The 21 Irrefutable Laws of Leadership: Follow Them and People Will Follow You*, Nashville, TN, Thomas Nelson.

Maxwell, J (1999) *The 21 Indispensible Qualities of a Leader*, Nashville, TN, Thomas Nelson.

McGraw, P (1999) *Life Strategies*, New York, Hyperion.

McLynn, F (2007) *Heroes & Villians*, London, Random House.

Meisler, S (2007) *Kofi Annan*, Hoboken, NJ, John Wiley & Sons.

Millan, B (1983) *Monstrous Regiment: Women Rulers in Men's World*, Berks, UK, Kensal Press.

Miller, W (2000) *The Mystery of Courage*, New York, Harvard University Press.

Minto, B (2005) *The Pyramid Principle,* London, Prentice Hall.

Mintzberg, H (1996) *The Strategy Process*, New York, Prentice-Hall.

Moore, T (1992) *Care of the Soul*, New York, HarperCollins.

Morgan, P (2007) *Don't You Know Who I Am?*, London, Ebury Press.

Morrell, M and Capparell, S (2001) *Shackleton's Way*, London, Nicholas Brealey.

Morris, D (1995) *Behind the Oval Office*, New York, Random House.

Mrazek, J (1968) *The Art of Winning Wars*, New York, Walker and Company.

Nair, K (1994) *A Higher Standard of Leadership: Lessons From the Life of Gandhi*, San Francisco, Berrett-Koehler.

Naisbitt, J and Aburdene, P (1990) *Megatrends 2000*, New York, Morrow and Co.

Niebuhr, H (1963) *The Responsible Self: An Essay in Christian Moral Philosophy*, New York, HarperCollins.

Oliver, R (2001) *Inspirational Leadership*, London, Spiro Press.

O'Neil, J (1995) *The Paradox of Success: When Winning at Work Means Losing at Life*, New York, McGraw-Hill.

O'Toole, J (1999) *Leadership A to Z: A Guide for the Appropriately Ambitious*, San Francisco, Jossey-Bass.

Owen, J (2005) *How to Lead,* Harlow, UK, Prentice Hall.

Owen, J (2006) *The Leadership Skills Handbook,* London, Kogan Page.

Parker, J [Ed] (2007) *Historica's Women*, Sydney, Millenium House.

Patterson, K, Grenny, J, McMillan, R and Switzler, A (2012) *Crucial Conversations,* New York, McGraw-Hill.

Peale, NV (1956) *The Power of Positive Thinking*, New York, Fawcett Crest.

Pegg, M (1989) *Positive Leadership*, Oxford, Alden Press.

Peters, T (1987) *Thriving on Chaos: Handbook for a Management Revolution*, New York, Knopf.

Peters, T (2005) *Leadership*, New York, DK Publishing.

Peters, T and Waterman, R (1982) *In Search of Excellence: Lessons from America's Best Run Companies*, New York, Harper & Row.

Piaget, J (1932) *The Moral Judgement of the Child*, London, Routledge and Kegan Paul.

Pilger, J (1986) *Heroes*, London, Jonathan Cape.

Post, J (1986) 'Narcissism and the charismatic leader-follower relationship', *Political Psychology*, 7, pp. 675-688.

Rae, S and Wong, K (1996) *Beyond Integrity: A Judea-Christian Approach to Business Ethics,* Grand Rapids, MI, Zondervan.

Reader's Digest (1966) *Great Lives, Great Deeds,* Adelaide, Griffin Press.

Rickets, C (2003) *Leadership,* Delmar, NY, Thomson Learning.

Rickets, C (2003) *Leadership, Personal Development and Career Success,* Delmar, NY, Thomson Learning.

Robertson, J (2005) *Coaching Leadership,* Wellington, The New Zealand Council for Educational Research.

Robertson, R (2014) *Leading on the Edge,* Brisbane, John Wiley & Sons.

Roels, S (1997) *Organisation Man, Organisation Woman: Calling, Leadership and Culture,* Nashville, TN, Abingdon.

Rohmann, C (2000) *A World of Ideas: The Dictionary of Important Ideas and Thinkers,* London, Arrow Books.

Rost, J (1991) *Leadership for the Twenty-First Century,* New York, Praeger.

Ryan, J (2005) *Inclusive Leadership,* San Francisco, Jossey-Bass.

Sandberg, S (2013) *Lean in: Women, Work and the Will to Lead,* New York, Alfred A Knopf.

Sarros, J and Butchatsky, 0 (1996) *Leadership,* Sydney, HarperCollins.

Sashkin, M and Sashkin, M (2003) *Leadership That Matters,* San Francisco, Berret-Koehler Publishers.

Schlender, B and Tetzeli, R (2015) *Becoming Steve Jobs,* London, Hodder & Stoughton.

Schwarzkopf, N and Peter, P (1992) *It Doesn't Take a Her,* New York, Bantam Books.

Scott, S (2002) *Fierce Conversations,* New York, Berkley.

Sculley, J (1987) *Odyssey: Pepsi to Apple – a Journey of Adventure, Idea and the Future,* New York, Harper & Row.

Senge, P (1990) *The Fifth Discipline: The Art and Practice of the Learning Organisation,* New York, Doubleday.

Sergiovanni, T (1992) *Moral Leadership: Getting to the Heart of School Improvement,* San Francisco, Jossey-Bass.

Shaw, G (1952) *Man and Superman,* Baltimore, Penguin.

Shula, D and Blanchard, K (1995) *Everyone's a Coach,* New York, Harper Business and Zondervan.

Sinek, S (2009) *Start with Why,* New York, Penguin.

Siu, R (1979) *The Craft of Power,* New York, John Wiley & Sons.

Smith-Davies Publishing (2006) *Women Who Changed the World,* Sydney, Murdoch Books.

Solomon, R (1992) *Ethics and Excellence: Cooperation and Integrity in Business,* New York, Oxford University Press.

Spillane, J (2006) *Distributed Leadership,* San Francisco, Jossey-Bass.

Starratt, R (2004) *Ethical Leadership*, San Francisco, Jossey-Bass.

Stogdill, R (1974) *Handbook of Leadership: A Survey of the Literature*, New York, The Free Press.

Sun Tzu (2003) *The Art of War*, Philadelphia, PA, Running Press Miniature Editions.

Suzuki, D (2003) *The David Suzuki Reader*, Vancouver, Greystone Books.

Taylor, D (2002) *The Naked Leader*, Oxford, Capstone.

Thomas, B (1968) *Abraham Lincoln: A Biography*, New York, New York Modern Library.

Toffler, A (1980) *The Third Wave*, New York, William Morrow and Company.

Trump, D (2009) *Think Like a Champion*, New York, Vanguard Press.

van Linden and Fertman, C (1998) *Youth Leadership*, San Francisco, Jossey-Bass.

Vogelstein, F (2013) *Dogfight*, New York, Sarah Crichton Books.

von Adlerstein, M (2002) *The Penguin Book of Etiquette: The Complete Australian Guide to Modern Manners*, Camberwell, Viking.

Vroom, V (1964) *Work and Motivation*, New York, John Wiley & Sons.

Weisbord, M (1987) *Productive Workplaces: Organising and Managing for Dignity, Meaning and Community*, San Francisco, Jossey-Bass.

Wheatley, M (1992) *Leadership and the New Science: Learning About Organisations from an Orderly Universe*, San Francisco, Berrett-Koehler.

Willink, J and Babin, L (2015) *Extreme Ownership*, New York, Macmillan.

Wolff, M (2008) *The Man Who Owns the News*, Sydney, Random House.

Wooden, J and Tobin, J (1988) *They Call Me Coach*, Chicago, Contemporary Books.

Yuki, G (1994) *Leadership in Organisations*, Englewood Cliffs, NJ, Prentice Hall.

Zacharatos, A Barling, J and Kelloway, E (2000) 'Development and effects of transformational leadership in adolescents', *The Leadership Quarterly*, 11, 2, pp. 222–226.

Zenger, J and Folkman, J (2002) *The Extraordinary Leader*, New York, McGraw-Hill.

Zenger, J, Musselwhite E, Hurson, K and Perrin, C (1994) *Leading Teams*, Homewood, IL, Zenger Miller.

ACKNOWLEDGEMENTS

I wish to pay tribute to my colleagues in the teaching profession. I have watched them, learned from them and been inspired by them. Their example has given me a significant amount of the material for this book.

A further source of help has been the four books that make up the *Learning Leadership* series. This leadership course for students of secondary-school age was trialled by the staff and students of The King's School, Parramatta, in Sydney. Their advice and helpful suggestions have not only infused the *Learning Leadership* series with wisdom but informed my thinking in *Ten Leadership Lessons You Must Teach Your Teenager.*

The editing and production of and publicity for *Ten Leadership Lessons You Must Teach Your Teenager* were faithfully and effectively undertaken by Sophie Hamley, Claire de Medici Jones, Tom Bailey-Smith, Chris Kunz, Nathan Grice and Jordan Weaver-Keeney. The care shown in the exercise of this task was greatly appreciated.

Much support was also given by my Executive Assistant, Michelle White, whose help with proofing and layout was invaluable.

Finally, I thank my wife, Jane, for her forbearance, love and support during the hours spent writing this book. She has modelled many of the leadership qualities described within.

Tim Hawkes

INDEX

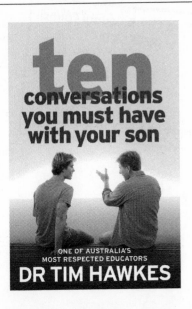

ten
conversations
you must have
with your son

ONE OF AUSTRALIA'S
MOST RESPECTED EDUCATORS
DR TIM HAWKES

EMPOWERING PARENTS TO MENTOR AND PREPARE THEIR SONS FOR LIFE

Every parent of a teenage boy knows there are certain essential conversations they must have with their son. But too often they put them off – or don't have them at all – because they simply don't know where to begin. Internationally recognised in the field of raising and educating boys, Dr Tim Hawkes provides practical, accessible and invaluable advice about how to get these discussions started.

Helping parents to negotiate their way through what can be difficult territory, Dr Hawkes explores the *why, what* and *how* of ten key topics: *love, identity, values, leadership, achievement, sex, money, health, living together* and *resilience*. For each topic, Dr Hawkes offers ideas about how parents can share their own experiences, values and knowledge with their sons.

This book will help you prepare your son for adulthood.

hachette
AUSTRALIA

If you would like to find out more about Hachette Australia,
our authors, upcoming events and new releases you can visit
our website, Facebook or follow us on Twitter:

www.hachette.com.au
www.facebook.com/HachetteAustralia
www.twitter.com/HachetteAus